Michael Ash
London Ont
Nov '91

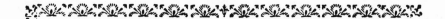

Devils and Angels
Textual Editing and Literary Theory

Devils and
Angels

Textual Editing and Literary Theory

EDITED BY PHILIP COHEN

University Press of Virginia
Charlottesville and London

THE UNIVERSITY PRESS OF VIRGINIA
Copyright © 1991 by the Rector and Visitors
of the University of Virginia
First published 1991

Library of Congress Cataloging-in-Publication Data

Devils and angels : textual editing and literary theory / edited by
Philip Cohen.
p.   cm.
Includes bibliographical references and index.
ISBN 0-8139-1315-2
1. Editing.   2. Criticism, Textual.   I. Cohen, Philip G.
PN162.D48   1991
808'.02—dc20   90-22580
CIP

Printed in the United States of America

Contents

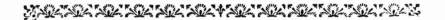

Acknowledgments

Like authors, an editor of a collection of essays has some debts to acknowledge. John McGuigan, my editor at the University Press of Virginia, has provided encouragement and advice at every stage of this undertaking, and I thank him. At the Press, Gerald Trett schooled me in preparing the manuscript for publication; while here in Arlington, Tom Iwanski helped compile the index. At different times, James L. W. West III, Peter Shillingsburg, and Noel Polk have also offered suggestions that proved to be invaluable. Finally, I would like to dedicate this book with much love to my parents Jacob and Gloria, to my wife Gretchen, and to my daughter Caitlin.

PHILIP COHEN

Introduction

PHILIP COHEN

HE RIFT BETWEEN TEXTUAL CRITICISM, which studies the genesis and transmission of texts, and literary theory, which examines the means by which textual meaning is produced and validated, has too often seemed a given in critical discourse. This rift is unfortunate because literary theory and textual criticism have much to teach each other. Both are profoundly theoretical enterprises, concerning themselves with the same first questions that precede serious criticism. Nevertheless, literary theorists and textual critics often fail to interact with one another and even occasionally view each other with disdain. Convinced of its own diversity of opinion, each group eyes the other warily as a monolith of antagonism and hardened opinion. A symposium on textual criticism and contemporary literary theory I attended several years ago provides an example. Many of the theorists there viewed all editors as rigid adherents to the school of Greg, Bowers, and Tanselle and excoriated editorial pretensions to scientific objectivity and neutrality, rhetoric that many editors have quietly abandoned over the last decade. One theorist even used the Hinman collator as a symbol of the dangerous scientific and technological mentality of the West that has ravaged the world. For their part, many of the editors remained convinced that the theorists were willfully oblivious to the theoretical implications of textual evidence and editorial work and to the origins of the texts about which they theorized.

While such rhetoric and polemic are unhelpful at best, this schism within literary studies probably originated in the New Criticism's tendency in practice to ignore the biographical, historical, and bibliographical circumstances of composition and transmission surrounding a literary work of art. Over forty years ago, New Critics Wimsatt and Beardsley argued in "The Intentional Fallacy" that authorial intention is neither available nor desirable as a standard for evaluating literary works. In his *Anatomy of Criticism,* Northrop Frye argued as well from an early structuralist perspective against the recuperability or utility of authorial intention in literary studies (17–18). Although traditional editors have often criticized the New Critics' focus on the aesthetic autonomy of literary works, it was, curiously enough, the New Criticism's emphasis on close readings of single texts that made the massive editorial projects of the 1960s and the 1970s possible. Perhaps even more curiously, traditional editors have frequently relied upon standard New Critical aesthetic criteria such as irony, ambiguity, and complexity in emending copytext.

Traditional editors and contemporary literary theorists have drawn even farther apart because the former's common theoretical ground and intellectual tradition, which has enabled them to concentrate on methodological issues, has been problematized by much recent literary theory. While textual scholars in the Anglo-American tradition have stressed the recuperability of authorial intention and its relevance to interpretation and evaluation as well as to editorial work, theorists have followed the continental tendency to banish the author and his intention from any serious discussion of literature. Thus while much contemporary literary theory bolsters the New Critical attack on authorial intention, it does so from perspectives based on post-Saussurean linguistics, which often repudiate the New Critical doctrine of semantic autonomy.

Indeed, some structuralists and poststructuralists have launched a systematic and formidable assault on the traditional relation between authorial intention and meaning-production and validation by arguing that an author's intention cannot be recovered from the self-reflexive net of language. Derrida's metaphysics of absence and the subsequent decentering of the text, for example, provide formidable counters to the belief that authorial intention can be recovered and employed to establish a text. Moses may once have brought the Word inscribed on tablets of stone down the slopes of Sinai from God to the Israelites, but even those days seem eternally lost to us now because the act was recorded in writing.

Authorial intention has also been deemed irrelevant by those poststructuralist theorists whose social and intertextual view of language and literature leads them to view the act of literary creation as a communal process involving the elaboration and modification of social discursive formations. Even when the author is alone in his garret composing odes that will never see print, he thus functions as a fully socialized Foucauldian figure rather than an autonomous Coleridgean poet. Thus twentieth-century critics with different theoretical orientations have frequently seconded Morse Peckham's contention that "the notion of 'reconstructing the author's intention' is theoretically ridiculous. (1) It is doubtful if an 'intention' in the sense it is used ever existed. (2) Even if it did, its existence was 'subjective' or 'psychological' and is now historical, and thus doubly inaccessible. (3) An author's statement of intention is subject to modification in action, like everyone else's, and thus can be relied upon if it is demonstrated that the results correspond to the intention" (403).

Despite such provocative challenges from the camp of theory, most scholarly Anglo-American editors still work within the dominant editorial tradition instituted by W. W. Greg and elaborated first by Fredson Bowers and then by G. Thomas Tanselle. This tradition consists of eclectically constructing a single ideal text that approximates what an author finally intended to appear before his audience. Perhaps eclectic has triumphed because over the years Bowers and Tanselle have articulated and defended a method as well as a theory of editing, and editing, more than any other discipline, requires such a method. Most editors have also been reluctant to challenge the notion that an author has the right to control the presentation and content of his work. Moreover, Greg and Bowers's conception of divided authority as regards accidentals and substantives and their procedures for eclectic editing were adopted by the Center for Editions of American Authors (1963–1976) and the Center for Scholarly Editions (1976–). An observer of the contemporary critical scene quickly notes the central contradiction here: many theorists deny the recuperability of authorial intention and its usefulness in discussing and evaluating texts that have been constituted by referring to that same intention.

Unfortunately, a number of Anglo-American editors have too easily divorced the procedures of text-establishment from the theoretical issues in which such an activity is irretrievably enmeshed. If different theories of language and literature will generate different editorial procedures for selecting, emending, and presenting copytext, then editorial assumptions must be articulated and defended lest complacency ensue. It does no good to protest that establishing the text of that metaphysical abstraction called a literary work and interpreting its meanings are two different propositions, for literary judgment and interpretation are inseparable from the editor's task.[1] Even with a complete array of bibliographical materials from rough draft manuscript to page proofs at his disposal, an eclectic editor must often formulate from his sense of the work as a whole an author's intended meaning and then rely upon that formulation in particular textual situations to determine which words the author intended to appear before his public. Such activity presupposes a theory of language and reading that is not always made explicit and defended. Instead editors frequently validate their judgments by relying upon the evidence of analytical bibliography and upon general statements about the necessity of familiarity with the author's canon as well as with the text being edited, with biographical and historical knowledge. More importantly, the traditional notion that a literary work is best represented by a single critical authorial text and that such a text is the only object worthy of scholarly investigation assumes a theoretical consensus about the nature and aims of literary studies that no longer exists.

For their part, theorists have doubtless too quickly buried the much larger issues of text-constitution and textual instability along with the author and his intention. Some of the competing varieties of literary theory have frequently shared a desire for universal or absolute explanations of how literary texts are created and interpreted rather than pragmatic explanations that contextualize literary activity by situating it firmly within a set of social and historical constraints. Pursuing foundational or antifoundational explanations of literary phenomena without knowing about or attempting to account for the varying material circumstances of the production of texts—their composition, revision, dissemination, and transmission—seems a sort of willful blindness.

The importance of these concerns is illustrated by any number of textual histories, which editors gleefully like to throw at the feet of theorists. Henry Binder's edition of Stephen Crane's *The Red Badge of Courage,* for example, restored most of the excisions Crane made in his novel just before publication.[2] In much of the material excised, Henry Fleming's interior monologues ironically revealed an immature egotism that remains with him throughout all his Civil War exploits. In "*The Red Badge of Courage* Nobody Knows," Binder argues from circumstantial bibliographical, biographical, and interpretative evidence that Ripley Hitchcock, Crane's editor at Appleton, pressured him into making the excisions in order to render the novel less ironic and unconventional. These excisions also "reduced the psychological complexity of Henry Fleming . . . and left the text incoherent at several places, in particular the final chapter" (Binder 9). The extreme critical disagreements over the significance of Fleming's experiences, Binder contends, are the product of critical reliance on a maimed text that embodies a conflict between Crane's aesthetic intentions and Hitchcock's genteel expurgations. Whether a critic observes irony or ambiguity in Crane's tale of the Civil War may depend on which text of the novel he has on his bookshelf, on whether he has an individualized or a socialized view of textual and perhaps literary authority. Yet contemporary theorists and critics have generally proved reluctant to investigate the theoretical implications of the genesis and transmission of literary texts. The lessons of such a textual situation, however, cut both ways: that is, it reminds us that editors too have often failed to recognize that their work is not neutral, that editors working under different assumptions about what a literary work is will produce different texts of a specific work.

To put the problem more simply, theorists and editors alike have traditionally neglected to grapple with the ontological implications of the fact that a literary work more often than not exists in a variety of textual states. *What*, for example, is *The Sound and the Fury* and how may it be said to exist? Cape and Smith first published the novel in 1929 without the Compson Appendix Faulkner wrote sixteen years later in 1945 for inclusion in Malcolm Cowley's Viking *Portable Faulkner* (1946). This genealogy then appeared, at Faulkner's insistence, at the beginning of the 1946 Modern Library dual edition of *The Sound and the Fury* and *As I Lay Dying*. In 1963, the Appendix appeared at the back of the 1963 Vintage paperback edition. In 1984 Noel Polk omitted the piece from his corrected text of the novel. Not only was Faulkner primarily concerned with reviving his moribund reputation when he wrote the Appendix, Polk argues, but the piece itself is a new and discrete work, to be viewed separately from *The Sound and the Fury* (Polk 17–8). Placing the Appendix at the front of the novel certainly compromises the novel's "deliberately controlled revelation and concealment of the Compson family history, and its carefully contrived ambiguities" (Polk 19) and thus creates a different work. The Appendix, I would add, also creates a variety of problems for readers of the novel because it contains changes in the "facts" of the story and reinterprets and reassesses the book's characters and themes. Moreover, the broad historical scope of the Appendix has also often caused readers to situate the novel in a historical framework and to foreground the decline of the southern aristocracy, a reading that seems less primary in the 1929 edition.

Plausible as these arguments may sound, the theoretical question remains: Is the work we know as *The Sound and the Fury* best represented by an eclectic critical text, by one or several or all of the historical texts, or by some form of genetic text? Even asking such a question makes one realize that assembling or choosing the text itself, let alone its interpretation, is no mere question of methodology despite wishful efforts to reduce it to such. Textual criticism is a theoretical activity. Moreover, since different editorial approaches are based on different theoretical assumptions that are probably not susceptible to logical or empirical proof, no single method of text-constitution will satisfy all of the different factions in this our contentious age.

We are thus at a crucial impasse that perhaps may turn out to be a crucial beginning. Literary works and their interpretation depend, to a great extent, upon which text or combination of texts one reads, just as a different historical score might produce a different Ninth Symphony than the one we currently hear. Yet for a number of editors and theorists business still proceeds as usual: that is, separately. Some recent editorial proposals, however, have evinced an increasingly theoretical self-consciousness and have begun challenging the dominant Anglo-American tradition. The theoretical and practical editorial work of Hershel Parker, Jerome J. McGann, Peter Shillingsburg, and Hans Walter Gabler, for example, suggests that a paradigm shift in textual criticism may be underway. In restricting or rejecting authorial intention as a means of discriminating among authorial versions, in questioning the validity of eclectic critical editing, and in emphasizing the instability of the textual manifestations of literary works, some of these proposals correlate with certain developments in literary theory.

Literary theorists have yet to respond to the implications of this growing body of stimulating editorial work. Yet such provocative attempts to think about the theoretical consequences of editorial work in new ways are essential in order to end the mutual isolation of literary theory and textual criticism. At a time when the subject and scope and theoretical

assumptions of literary studies are being redefined, both textualists and
theorists are exploring such relevant questions as What is a text and how is
it constituted? What is a literary work of art? When is the literary work
finished? How do we determine authorial intention and textual authority?
Editorial discussion of such fundamental aspects of textual ontology
might benefit from literary theory's examination of the same issues. Similarly, theorists might benefit from testing their elegant theories against the
wealth of empirical data about the composition, revision, publication, and
reception of literary works that textualists possess. Such an exchange
might help some editors become more self-conscious about the theoretical implications of their principles and procedures for establishing scholarly texts and editions. Contemporary theorists who have decentered the
text and exploded the notion of unitary meaning would no longer be able
to regard the constitution of a text as mere drudgery for a few eccentric
pedants and an army of graduate students. Instead they would have to
realize that the acts undertaken by bibliographers and textual critics are
the most theoretical of all, that literary texts and works themselves are, to a
degree not heretofore recognized, constructed out of different historical
documents and reflect the ideological assumptions of different interpretative communities.

The essays in this volume address different aspects of the relationship
between editorial theory and literary theory: while seeking to advance the
dialogue between these two camps, they theorize about editorial practice
and textual ontology. Some of the contributors attempt to rethink in their
essays the assumptions and procedures of Anglo-American editorial
scholarship. Jerome J. McGann's "Literary Pragmatics and the Editorial
Horizon" contends that a theory of texts, an understanding of literature
and textual studies, consists of "a set of practices that will be elaborated in
specific social and institutional settings." In "The Autonomous Author,
the Sociology of Texts, and the Polemics of Textual Criticism," Peter
Shillingsburg discusses several problems in contemporary textual criticism: the disputes over the validity of critical editions as historical constructs and over what is the correct or best way to edit and the controversy
over whether the product of editing should present the work of art as
finished product or as a developing process. Paul Eggert takes up the third
problem as well in "Textual Product or Textual Process: Procedures and
Assumptions of Critical Editing." In "The Manifestation and Accommodation of Theory in Textual Editing," D. C. Greetham examines the

ways in which the theories of psychoanalytic thinkers from Freud to Kristeva would transform our textual assumptions as a means of illustrating the relationship between textual and literary theories and their concrete manifestation in the formal features of actual editions. In "Notes on Emerging Paradigms in Editorial Theory," David H. Jackson and I review some recent editorial proposals as a means of discussing the relationship between textual ontology and editorial procedure and illustrating how these proposals suggest correlations with contemporary literary theory's interpretative assumptions and ontological conceptions of literary works. James McLaverty concerns himself in "Issues of Identity and Utterance: An Intentionalist Response to 'Textual Instability'" with how the editorial process should deal with literary works that exist in several versions. In "Unsought Encounters," Hans Walter Gabler contributes a critical review of some recent Anglo-American editorial discussions from the perspective of German editorial theory and practice and contends that our editorial debate stands to profit from European reflections on the nature of textuality and on accompanying conceptions and designs of the editorial apparatus. Finally, Joseph Grigely's "The Textual Event" uses semiotics, deconstruction, and philosophy to undermine textual criticism's claim to recover a text and to propose a radical interdisciplinary theory of texts as events and material texts as outcomes.

An additional feature of this volume is the participation of three respondents who comment on the various essays: T. Howard-Hill, Steven Mailloux, and William E. Cain. I should also note that this volume is not a collection of practical criticism or of pedagogical essays. Although the contributors frequently make use of practical examples, their goal is rather to help stimulate an interchange between editors and theorists on a group of common topics that are hotly contested in literary studies today.

In an essay entitled "The Monks and the Giants: Textual and Bibliographical Studies and the Interpretation of Literary Works," Jerome McGann has wittily written of "the angels of hermeneutics" who "have long feared to tread in the fields of textual/bibliographical studies, which are widely regarded, in fact, as a world well lost. Reciprocally, the bibliographers, editors, and textual critics have largely agreed to the bad eminence they have achieved, whence they may hurl defiance at the heavens of the interpreters" (181). The schism between textual criticism and contemporary literary theory has enormous consequences because works depend on texts, and establishing texts depends not on mechanical procedures but on theories of literatures and interpretation. Healing the breach between these two disciplines by no means depends on an unqualified substitution of structuralist and deconstructionist truisms for traditional intentionalist ones. If the "angels of hermeneutics" would descend from the heavens and if the textualists would leave their "darkness visible" and address each other's concerns on some earthly middle ground, all of us engaged in literary studies would benefit. The purpose of this volume is to help editors and theorists see that heaven and hell may not be all that far apart.

Notes

1. For an excellent discussion of this relationship, see Tanselle's "Textual Study and Literary Judgment."
2. Binder's text first appeared in the first edition of the *Norton Anthology of American Literature* (1979), then in a separate Norton edition (1982), and finally in an Avon paperback edition (1983).

Works Cited

Binder, Henry. "The *Red Badge of Courage* Nobody Knows." *Studies in the Novel* 10 (Spring 1978): 9–47.
Crane, Stephen. *The Red Badge of Courage.* Ed. Henry Binder. New York: Avon, 1983.
Faulkner, William. *The Sound and the Fury: The Corrected Edition.* Ed. Noel Polk. New York: Random House, 1984.
Frye, Northrop. *Anatomy of Criticism: Four Essays.* Princeton: Princeton UP, 1957.
Gabler, Hans Walter. "The Synchrony and Diachrony of Texts: Practice and Theory of the Critical Edition of James Joyce's *Ulysses.*" *Text* 1 (1981): 305–26.
———, Wolfhard Steppe, Claus Melchior, eds. *Ulysses: A Critical and Synoptic Edition.* By James Joyce. 3 vols. New York: Garland, 1984.
McGann, Jerome J. *A Critique of Modern Textual Criticism.* Chicago: U of Chicago P, 1983.
———. "The Monks and the Giants: Textual and Bibliographical Studies and the Interpretation of Literary Works." In *Textual Criticism and Literary Interpretation.* Ed. McGann. Chicago: U of Chicago P, 1985. 180–99.
Parker, Hershel. *Flawed Texts and Verbal Icons: Literary Authority in American Fiction.* Evanston: Northwestern UP, 1984.
Peckham, Morse. "Notes on Freehafer and the CEAA." *Studies in the Novel* 7 (1975): 402–4.
Polk, Noel. *An Editorial Handbook to William Faulkner's "The Sound and the Fury."* New York: Garland, 1985.

Shillingsburg, Peter. *Scholarly Editing in the Computer Age*. Athens: U of Georgia
P, 1986.
Tanselle, G. Thomas. "Textual Studies and Literary Judgment." *Publications of the
Bibliographical Society of America* 65 (1971): 109–22.
Wimsatt, W. K., Jr. and Monroe C. Beardsley. "The Intentional Fallacy." *Sewanee
Review* 54 (July–September 1946): 468–88.

Devils and Angels
Textual Editing and Literary Theory

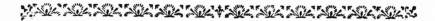

I

Literary Pragmatics and the Editorial Horizon

JEROME J. MCGANN

T THE SOCIETY FOR TEXTUAL SCHOLARSHIP (STS) in 1989 I gave a paper, "What Is Critical Editing?," and was asked the following question in the subsequent discussion: If you were editing Byron's poetry now, what would you do?

This pragmatic (and deceptively simple) question raised complex problems in literary theory, critical method, and—finally—textual hermeneutics. At the time I could hardly respond adequately to the question and its implications. I would like to explore these matters more thoroughly here. To do so, I shall have to rehearse the context of the question.

When I began editing Byron in 1971, I had no special editorial expertise. I had not sought the job, was surprised when I was asked, and I accepted without knowing what would be involved in such a task. This state of original innocence is important to realize because it forced me to set aside two years for studying textual and editorial theory and method. That course of study, moreover, was undertaken from a distinctly Anglo-American perspective, which effectively meant that I kept seeing my subject within the horizon of what has come to be called the Greg-Bowers (or "eclectic") theory of editing.

Armed by these studies, I began the project of the edition: searching out the documentary materials for the texts and preparing these materials for Byron's early works (i.e., the poems written through 1815). Serious problems began to emerge very quickly, for I had decided that I would test my methodology by editing *The Giaour* first. This seemed a good thing to do because *The Giaour* involved such a large and complex body of documentary materials. As it turned out, work on *The Giaour* threw the entire project into a condition of crisis. It became clear to me that my framework of editorial theory—in effect, the theory of the eclectic edition—was not adequate to the problems presented by *The Giaour*. As I sought to solve these problems, I began a new series of investigations into textual and editorial theory—this was in 1976–78. These inquiries concentrated on a historical investigation of textual studies in general, with a particular concentration on classical, biblical, and medieval textual studies from the late eighteenth century to the present. My object was to try to understand the larger context in which the eclectic theory of editing had developed.

As a consequence, I finally began to understand what I was doing in my edition—what was possible to be done, what was not possible to be done, and why these possibilities and impossibilities existed. As the edition went forward, I no longer struggled against the limitations imposed by the Oxford English Texts series format, and I accepted the fact that, for better and for worse, I had (undeliberately) undertaken to do a *certain kind of edition,* a critical edition squarely in the Greg-Bowers line of eclectic editing. I also accepted the fact, though far less easily, that in 1977 I was too far gone in the edition to take full advantage of computerized word processing as an editing tool. Once again my ignorance had closed down certain possibilities; and when I later (1984) learned about hypertexts and their powers, I had to swallow further regrets arising from my backward history.

What does it mean to say that an edition of Byron begun in 1987 would look very different from the one I began in 1971? Obviously it is to say that during those seventeen years I acquired a certain critical and theoretical understanding of texts and textual studies. But it is also to say that the practical and material demands of editing cut back across my previous views about theory and critical reflection in general.

Between 1971 and 1987 one overriding fact grew upon me as I worked to produce the edition of Byron: that texts are produced and reproduced under specific social and institutional conditions, and hence that every text, including those that may appear to be purely private, is a social text. This view entails a corollary understanding, that a "text" is not a "material thing" but a material event or set of events, a point in time (or a moment in space) where certain communicative interchanges are being practiced. This view of the matter—this *theoria*, or way of seeing—holds true as much for the texts we inherit and study as it does for the texts we will execute ourselves.

When texts are interpreted, the readings frequently ("characteristically" is the word we should use for the period between 1940 and 1980) avoid reflecting on the material conditions of the works being "read" and the readings being executed. Those material and institutional conditions, however, are impossible to set aside entirely if one is editing a text; and if one intends to execute a scholarly edition of a work, the social conditions of textual production become manifest and even imperative. Consequently, one comes to see that texts always stand within an editorial horizon (the horizon of their production and reproduction).

That editorial horizon entails serious consequences for the practice of literary theory *as such*—a practice (or set of practices) that came to dominate literary studies through the 1970s. Briefly, the editorial horizon forces one to reimagine the theory of texts—and, ultimately, theory of literature—as a specific set of social operations. To the extent that recent theoretical work in literary studies has left its social dimensions unexplicated, to that extent a reasonable "resistance to theory" will be raised.[1]

But as the editorial horizon forces one to confront literary studies as a specific set of social and institutional practices, the reemergence of a socio-historically oriented "literary pragmatics" (as it has come to be called) turns back upon editorial and bibliographical studies.[2] In twentieth-century Anglo-American studies (culminating in the scholarship of Fredson Bowers), work in these areas had become as technical, specialized, and ahistorical as the formal and thematic hermeneutics that ran a parallel course in interpretative studies.

The editorial horizon—*in the context of the 1970s and 80s*[3]—thus came to turn back on itself and on textual studies in general by its passage through a critical encounter with literary theory. The consequence was paradoxical in the extreme, for modern textual studies—which were founded two centuries ago in the deepest kind of socio-historical self-consciousness—now appeared to itself as a scene of narrow empiricist and even positivist practices, with habits of reflexiveness maintained merely at the technical level, as specialized goals. The sudden and even catastrophic revolution in Shakespearean textual studies in the 1970s and 80s is both the sign and the consequence of what had been happening (and not happening) in textual studies for the previous sixty years.[4]

In this context, textual studies today have begun to move in many new directions. The editorial horizon can now be seen, not merely as the locus of certain established technical procedures, but as the very emblem of what is meant by the *praxis* of literature, and the imperative to *praxis*. If, therefore, one tries to acquire a comprehensive understanding of literature and textual studies—a "Theory of Texts"—one is forced in the direction of literary pragmatics. Theory of Texts comprehends, comprises, a set of practices that will be elaborated in specific social and institutional settings.

For the remainder of this paper I want to concentrate on this idea that the Theory of Texts is ultimately a set of institutional (textual) practices. To elaborate the idea, I will offer three case histories. Two of these represent operations I have been actively involved with, and the third—which I shall consider first—is a hypothetical case.

The hypothetical case involves a question very like the one I began with: if one were to edit Dante Gabriel Rossetti today, what would one do?

In a moment I will be plunging into a body of detailed and even technical matters, but before doing so I must call attention to the fact that the initiating question conceals a number of other important problems and questions. For example, why ask this question of D. G. Rossetti at all, a poet who is seen by the academy as a marginal figure? One might respond by saying that Rossetti's works have not been edited since his brother William Michael undertook that task immediately after his death over one hundred years ago.[5] This would be a perfectly good response, especially—as we shall see—in light of what we now know about the state of Rossetti's texts.

But of course the same response could be given for William Morris's poetry, or Swinburne's, or any number of other writers. Why choose Rossetti in particular—or, perhaps even more to the point, why did *I* choose Rossetti?

That form of the question is pertinent because it forces into view the ethical and cultural interests that are at stake in a proposal to edit Rossetti. The fact that Rossetti's work has been neglected is obviously relevant, but more relevant would be an explanation of Rossetti's immediate cultural importance. Why do (I think) we need Rossetti now?[6]

Furthermore, the question asks "what would one *do*," as if the editorial procedure were open to various options. This is in fact the case. Minimally one might ask whether a critical edition is being proposed, and whether the edition is being imagined as a complete edition or a selection—and why. The pursuit of these questions underlying the initial question would eventually force detailed explanations of such matters. In my particular case, it would (or should) reveal that an edition of D. G. Rossetti looms in my mind as important for two related reasons. The first I shall not deal with in this paper: that Rossetti's work (and the world which it both reflects and interrogates) has much to say to people in (or in the orbit of) an imperial culture like that of late twentieth-century America. Second, Rossetti's works present an editor with a great opportunity: to make an edition of his writings a vehicle for displaying a significant range of issues and problems in textual criticism.

An edition of Rossetti, in short, can be imagined and carried out as a theoretical act of special importance at this critical moment in the history of textual studies. To reflect upon the possibility of such an edition is to see that making an edition—making this edition in particular—is not a preinterpretative operation. By the same token, reading Rossetti (or any other author) in a particular editorial format means that one has already been set within a definite hermeneutical horizon.

In taking up the problem of editing Rossetti, I will concentrate on his most important work, *The House of Life.* But I must first consider briefly some of the more general problems I have been alluding to.

Should the edition be a *Complete Works,* poetry and prose alike; or should it be *Complete Poetical Works,* perhaps with a selection of the prose? Should either of these include the translations, which represent such an extensive body of material? These are important questions, obviously, for it would make quite a difference if, for example, a press were to issue today a *Complete Works of Dante Gabriel Rossetti* rather than some sort of selection. Were I free to make a decision about such a matter, I would without question say that a *Complete Works* was needed—not merely for technical and textual reasons (e.g., the standard available editions are inadequate textually) but for larger cultural reasons as well.

But the fact is that I would not be able to make such a decision on my own—any publisher would demand a voice in the matter. This fact brings up another important issue: who would publish such an edition? The options here are seriously limited, for various reasons. Furthermore, given the special problems of Rossetti's texts and my theoretical goals, the choice of Oxford University Press (which would otherwise be a natural one) might in the end prove too problematic.[7]

But let us pass beyond that initial set of problems and suppose them solved in one way or another; and let us suppose as well that the next practical problem, how to gather the necessary materials, has also been solved.[8] We then face the question of how to present the material that *is* to be included, and in particular how to present the work known as *The House of Life*. To answer that question, we have to confront a prior question: What *is The House of Life?*[9]

It seems an easy enough question, at least if we judge by the texts that have come down to us as the standard ones used either by scholars in their specialized work or by teachers in the classroom. But the question is no more transparent to itself than is that master question of which it is merely a special case: What is a text?[10]

According to the standard classroom texts (e.g., Baum's, Lang's, and the texts presented in anthologies of Victorian poetry, and so forth), *HL* is a sonnet sequence of 103 units—a basic group of 101 sonnets, so numbered; an introductory sonnet called "The Sonnet"; and the notorious sonnet known as 6a (originally titled "Nuptial Sleep") that was published in the 1870 version of the work by Rossetti but was subsequently withdrawn by Rossetti when he was preparing the 1881 edition of his *Poems,* where he published a 102 sonnet version of *HL*. Rossetti died in 1886 without reprinting the sonnet.

In that year his brother William Michael published his two-volume edition of his brother's *Works,* but sonnet 6a was not part of the *HL* sequence. This edition went through several reprintings, but William Michael Rossetti kept 6a out of the work until 1904, when he reinserted it. In 1911 he augmented his edition of his brother's works and explained why he kept the sonnet back in his 1886 edition, and why he finally put it back in 1904:

> My own comment on this sonnet, in the original preface to the "Collected Works" from which I ommitted [*sic*] it, ran as follows: "'Nuptial Sleep' appeared in the volume of 'Poems' 1870 but was objected to by Mr. Buchanan, and I suppose by some other censors, as being indelicate; and my brother excluded it from 'The House of Life' in his third volume [i.e., 1881]. I consider that there is nothing in the sonnet which need imperatively banish it from his Collected Works. But his own decision commands mine:

and besides it could not now be re-introduced into 'The House of Life,' which he moulded into a complete whole without it, and would be misplaced if isolated by itself—a point as to which his opinion is very plainly set forth in his prose paper, 'The Stealthy School of Criticism.'" As I now hold that "Nuptial Sleep" ought to be "banished" no longer, I have inserted the item in its original sequence; I number it *6a*, leaving the numeration otherwise unaltered. (Rossetti, 1911, 653)

Although William Michael raises two strong arguments against printing sonnet 6a, when he tells us that he has changed his mind about the sonnet he does not address either of those arguments. He simply replaces its, as if the arguments he had originally given carried no weight at all and did not have to be addressed.

No one now would print *HL* without 6a, I think, though it is important to see that in thus printing the sonnet editors are not following "the author's (final) intentions." They *are* "establishing the / a text" of *HL,* but the editorial work is completely involved in a hermeneutical operation. This is, I hasten to add, not unusual—indeed, it is what all editors do. The illusion is the idea that editors "establish" the texts that critics then go on to "interpret." All editing is an act of interpretation, and this instance from Rossetti is merely a dramatic illustration of that fact.

The appearance of 6a in 1904 was not, however, the first time the banished sonnet was printed with *HL* after Dante Gabriel Rossetti's death. It already had one posthumous appearance, in 1894, when a pirated edition of *HL* was issued by the Boston publishers Copeland and Day. In fact, this 1894 piracy has not only the full 103 sonnet sequence of *HL,* it also prints as part of the work called *The House of Life* eleven additional songs. Copeland and Day announce this as the *HL* "now for the first time given in its full text"—which text includes the eleven songs plus sonnet 6a.[11]

And the situation is still more complex. For the 1870 text printed by Rossetti—while it had those eleven songs—was a sonnet sequence of only 50 (rather than 102 or 103) sonnets. It was titled *Sonnets and Songs Toward a Work to be called "The House of Life."* That is an important title because it shows that Rossetti (at any rate) regarded his work in 1870 as a project, or a poem in process. It is a title that might well lead one to decide—as William Michael Rossetti temporarily decided in 1886—that the 1881 text is the final one, since that text was titled, simply and with apparent conclusiveness, *The House of Life.*

The 1870 text itself was preceded by a whole series of other, earlier printed texts—most immediately by the series of so-called "trial books" Rossetti had privately printed in 1869–70 which he used as working manuscripts or working proofs through which he could test out different possible versions of his work. Before that—in March 1869—he printed in *The Fortnightly Review* a sequence of 16 sonnets under the title "Of Love Life and Death." All 16 would eventually find a place in the work we know as *HL*. Finally, individual sonnets and sonnet-groups that eventually found their way into *HL* had been printed and published at various times and places before 1870.[12]

Each of these versions mentioned so far are printed texts, though of course each traces itself back to different manuscripts. Let me summarize the situation briefly (I here leave aside the matter of sonnets published separately, and not as part of an imagination of the *HL* project):

—March 1869: 16 sonnets published in *The Fortnightly Review*

—spring 1870: 50 sonnets plus 11 songs

—1881: 102 sonnets

—1894: 103 sonnets plus 11 songs

—1904 (and thereafter): 103 sonnets

This is a complex situation, but there are two other texts of the *HL* sequence (one is a distinct version, the other is not) that are important. The first of these seems relatively inconsequential except to bibliographers: I mean the 1873 Tauchnitz edition of Rossetti's works produced for a European audience. This book reproduces, with minor local alterations, the work Rossetti had already printed at various times in England. In this edition *HL* is the 1870 version and includes sonnet 6a.

The other text is more startling, and clearly alters the whole textual situation in a drastic way. In the summer of 1871 Rossetti copied out a version of *HL* that comprised 25 sonnets plus 5 songs. None of these songs or sonnets were included in the 1869–70 printings because, in fact, they had all been written after the publication of the 1870 *Poems,* and most had been written that summer of 1871, when Rossetti was living at Kelmscott with Jane Morris. William was away at the time on a trip to Iceland. This 1871 manuscript version of *HL* is a text of *HL* that Rossetti presented to Jane Morris sometime in the late 1870s—a series of sonnets that dramatizes love as a cycle of satisfactions.[13] All of the other versions are more or less dominated by nightmare visions.

Two other matters are perhaps relevant to note here. About 20 percent of this material was written before Rossetti had any notion of the project that would come to be called *HL*. In 1869 he reached back, sometimes as much as fourteen years, to choose work that had originally been written in entirely different contexts; and he would continue to do this throughout the 1870s. As for sonnet 6a, Rossetti removed this as a consequence of the attack made upon his work, and upon this sonnet in particular, by Robert Buchanan in his 1871 essay "The Fleshly School of Poetry," published under the pseudonym of Thomas Maitland.

The question therefore is: If one were to edit this material, how would it be presented?

There are I think three basic choices that could be made if one were imagining a book-formatted critical edition: (A) One could try to analyze the material in order to arrive at an ideal version—an eclectic text that would work from a basic copytext into which would be incorporated certain materials from texts other than the copytext. Classically, this might work by choosing the 1881 text as copytext (or perhaps the ultimate corrected proofs for 1881) and, through a process of collation, introduce into 1881 any changes deemed necessary—e.g., most dramatically, sonnet 6a. Basically this is what was done by William Michael Rossetti in 1904 and 1911, and later by Baum and Lang, so that this is the text most readers now work from. (B) One could distinguish a series of versions and offer diplomatic texts of each one, adding (perhaps) a set of collations where necessary. This would yield at least four distinct "Houses of Life":
—the 16 sonnet version of 1869
—the 50 sonnet and 11 song version of 1870
—the 25 sonnet and 5 song version of 1871
—the 102 sonnet version of 1881
In this case sonnet 6a would not belong in any version but the one that appeared in 1870. Collations would be complex only for the 1870 and the 1881 texts.

One might also present a fifth version, i.e., the 103 sonnet version constructed for Rossetti's work after his death by his brother and subsequent editors. In this version some accommodations would have to be made for the various "songs," which might be included in an appendix.

(C) The third option is to treat the entire corpus of material as an evolving compositional or historical project and attempt to construct a text which would represent that textual evolution. This would be to produce one of two kinds of evolutionary texts. One would be a "genetic text," in the manner of various editions currently being pursued in Europe—in which case the text would ignore the published texts (and perhaps the trial books as well) and strive to produce a continuous compositional text—a portrait of the authorial process of creation.

A modified version of this procedure can be observed, for example, in Hans Gabler's edition of *Ulysses*. That model's variations from the usual "genetic" edition point toward the second type of evolutionary text one might try to produce: not a "continuous manuscript text" (as Gabler has called it) but a "continuous production text," where the effort is to display the work's evolution from its earliest to its latest productive phases in the author's lifetime. This last procedure would be difficult to manage, however, because Rossetti's *HL* evolved radially even as it was also evolving "continuously." One sees this radial development most clearly in the way Rossetti temporarily decides to include, or to remove, the sequence of associated songs; one sees it as well in the twenty-five-sonnet five-song version he gave to Jane Morris (a clear radial version); and one sees it finally in the existence of the 1873 Tauchnitz edition of Rossetti's works. This edition was produced under Rossetti's supervision, and it includes the 1870 version of *HL*.

I must pause for a moment to consider the Tauchnitz edition a bit further. In one sense the edition is clearly a radial development of Rossetti's work in *HL,* and thus is kin to the Jane Morris manuscript text and to the texts that play with the inclusion of the song material. The Tauchnitz edition is a variant of the 1870 version in which sonnet 6a does not figure as a problematical passage because the Tauchnitz edition is produced for a different—that is to say, for a non-English—audience. Furthermore, this 1873 edition shows that Rossetti regarded 1870 as a relatively integral work, something that could be reprinted with only minor local changes in the text. In fact, the 1870 edition was reprinted five times up to 1872. The 1881 edition evolves from the 1870 text and even supersedes it in a sense; but 1881 does not obliterate the integrity of the 1870 edition, any more than it does the integrity of the other versions of the work.

In this situation, were I editing *HL* I would certainly choose either option B or the continuous production text of option C. But that practical editorial matter is not my principal concern at this moment. I am rather concerned with clarifying how each of the editorial options impinges on the interpretation of the work.

This can be done by invoking the distinctions comprehended by the terms *text, poem,* and *work.* Each term frames the literary product in a different way. The *text* is the literary product conceived as a purely lexical event; the *poem* is the locus of a specific process of production (or repro-duction) and consumption; and the *work* comprehends the global set of all the texts and poems that have emerged in the literary production and reproduction processes.[14] Looking at Rossetti's *HL* in these terms, we can see how a choice of editorial procedure will amount to a profound hermeneutic definition of Rossetti's work.

If one edited along the lines of option A, for example, one would be foregrounding *HL* as a poem and as a text—as well as privileging one particular version of *HL* as poem. This interpretative emphasis would follow from the edition's desire to pursue *HL* as a single authoritative production. If one were to choose option B one would be foregrounding the poem and the work, because such an edition presents *HL* to us in a series of discrete versions that are related to each other through discon-tinuous (and not exclusively authorial) filiations. If one chose option C one would privilege the text and the work because a major part of the production process is foregrounded in the editorial process. One could also say that option C would frame Rossetti's materials for stylistic, intertextual, and socio-historical readings. Option B, on the other hand, would set *HL* for structural, formal, and socio-historical inquiries. Option A—which is the option that dominated editing during the period of New Critical hermeneutics—organizes the material along lines that call out stylistic and formal investigations.

Let us suppose that I chose option B—i.e., that I chose to edit so that four, or perhaps five, different versions were presented as independent units. To do this immediately sets a privilege upon *HL* as a set of integral poetic units, each of which could be "read" on its own in the manner of any New Critical, structural, or even deconstructive reading (for all are formalistically grounded operations). But because each of the versions would stand in the edition in a set of differential relations with the others, the reader would also be urged to investigate those sets of relations. Many sorts of reading could be generated from such a situation, but it is certain that socio-historical factors would enter into the investigations—for the simple reason that the edition has brought strongly to our attention issues of textual production, as well as other social and contextual matters that bear upon the very existence of multiple versions.

So we conclude that producing editions is one of the ways we produce literary meanings; and we see once again that this aspect of literary production is as complex as all the others and involves a ramified set of interconnected individuals and institutions. We are reminded, finally, that every part of the productive process is meaning-constitutive—so that we are compelled, if we want to understand a literary work, to examine it in all its multiple aspects. The words that lie immediately before a reader on some page provide one with the merest glimpse of that complex world we call a literary work and the meanings it produces. We all start from some localized place of reading, but no one who reads seriously will ever end up there—or if you do return, you will see that place very differently, perhaps begin to see it truly only then for the first time.

Or consider the following story, which is not a hypothetical case but a brief narrative of my involvement in a current editorial project.

Several years ago Oxford University Press asked me to edit *The New Oxford Book of Romantic Poetry*. I thought about it briefly and declined. Shortly afterwards Roger Lonsdale published his splendid *New Oxford Book of Eighteenth Century Verse*. This work had so completely reimagined the Oxford anthology along historicist lines that it made me see what might be done for the poetry of the Romantic period. I therefore reversed my original decision about doing the edition.

To edit an anthology is to set forth a constellation of related (and relative) literary judgments in historical terms. Even to decide on the chronological limits of a "Romantic" anthology is to pass certain judgments. In the present case the "Romantic anthology will comprise the years 1785–1832, for reasons that I shall indicate shortly.

The problem of chronology is, in this case, only a special aspect of a more general problem that students of the Romantic period often lose sight of: that the poetry of the period is by no means monologically "Romantic." This truth even appears in the historiography of the previous *Oxford Book of Romantic Verse* edited by H. S. Milford. When this anthology was first published in 1928, Milford titled it the *The Oxford Book of Regency Verse*. It was given its new title when it went into a second printing, in 1935.[15]

The discrepancy between the words *Romantic* and *Regency* calls attention to far more than a chronological differential. It reminds us that the poetry of the period need not be imagined only in terms of the work of the six so-called great romantics. Other frames of reference were once operative and remain significant. It makes a great difference, for example, if one takes Burn's *Poems, Chiefly in the Scottish Dialect* (1786) as a point of departure for the period rather than Blake's *Songs* (1789–93) or Wordsworth's and Coleridge's *Lyrical Ballads* (1798).[16]

The work of Burns calls attention to a pair of related but perhaps even more serious problems in our literary and cultural histories. The first of these concerns the years 1790–1800, a period of great literary significance and even greater literary volatility. Our poetry anthologies give little sense of the kind of writing that dominated this important cultural scene. To take only one problem: Romantic ideology, which privileges conventions of "sincerity" over conventions of "premeditation," has all but obliterated our received sense of the satiric traditions that were being worked between 1790–1832. The satiric tradition in the years 1790–1832 is strong and continuous, and includes people like William Hone, Moore, James and Horace Smith, John Hookham Frere, William Mackworth Praed, Peacock, Hood, and William Frederick Deacon. In this context the period of the 1790s is especially important because it is the period when those traditions were being laid down, most significantly in the poetical wars that raged over issues connected with the French Revolution.

Of course we remember—if we remember at all—the brilliant reactionary satire of *The Poetry of the Anti-Jacobin*. But do we remember that the precursors of that work were William Gifford's *The Baviad* (1791) and *The Maeviad* (1795). I recall them here, however, not because they are especially interesting as poetry. His two satires, "famous in [their] time," are scholastic machines turning out pure products of pedantic wit (if that phrase be not a contradiction in itself). *The Baviad* and *The Maeviad* ought to be holding our attention today not on their own behalf but on behalf of their satiric objects: I mean the (at that time notorious) school of writers known as the Della Cruscans.

The Della Cruscans did not write satire—on the contrary, they wrote sentimental and erotic poetry. More, they achieved great celebrity and influence by transforming the public pages of various magazines, like *The European Magazine, The World,* and *The Oracle* into a kind of love-theatre of poetry where (for example) Robert Merry, writing as "Della Crusca," would engage in poetic love dialogues with (for example) Mrs. Anna Cowley (writing as "Anna Matilda"). The romantic love poetry of Byron, Shelley, and Keats constitutes a massive act of invisible appropriation of the erotic tradition these writers set in motion. As poetical children of

Laurence Sterne, the Della Cruscans and their early imitators drove conservative figures like Gifford and J. T. Mathias to their satiric denunciations.[17] The *Poetry of the Anti-Jacobin* is part of that reactive tradition, just as Richard Polwhele's *The Unsex'd Females* (1798) is part of the reaction.

I mention the latter in this connection because it is a poem that lays out most explicitly the case of the reactionaries' grievances. To Polwhele, English poetry in the 1790s had been invaded by women who write on subjects they should not be writing about, least of all in public. The Della Cruscan movement is partly to blame for the infamous transportation of their Italian coterie verse (e.g., *The Florence Miscellany*, 1785) from Florence to London. But the evil represented by Della Cruscan poetry is greatly exacerbated by having entered England at the worst of times—just as the jacobinical ideas of the revolution were gaining interest and support.

Only in this context will one be able to appreciate the importance of the poetry of 1790s writers like Helen Maria Williams or (slightly later) Charlotte Dacre. Indeed, only in this context will one be able to understand the intimate relation that holds between those two (apparently so divergent) strains in the poetry of Thomas Moore: on one hand his political work (supporting Irish independence, and attacking English imperialism), and on the other his sentimental-erotic love poetry.

Or imagine an anthology that emphasized the importance of the translations of Sir William Jones. The appearance of the *Asiatic Miscellany* in 1787, which Jones coedited and which contained several of his most influential translations, was an important event in literary history as well as in anthropology. Romantic anthologies now do not recognize the impact those translations made, not merely in the development of orientalism, but as part of the new ethnological approach to literature and cultural production. It was the Romantic period that set in motion a drive for translations and imitations that were imagining themselves along anthropological lines. This is very different from the approaches toward poetical translation that antedate the coming of Macpherson and Chatterton.

These examples mean to say, simply, that a reimagination of the poetry of the Romantic period might well begin with a reimagination of the poetry of the 1790s in England. To reshape the poetry of the 1790s is to have begun a more comprehensive rereading of the work of the entire period that stretches to 1830. Such a reimagination, however, requires as well an understanding of the significance of the Della Cruscan movement, of Burns's 1786 volume, and the orientalist writing initiated by the translations of Sir William Jones.

In that larger context, moreover, we have to confront yet another "dark age"—by which I mean the poetry that appeared between the death of Byron (1824) and the publication of Tennyson's *Poems* (December 1832). So far as poetry is concerned these are the years literary historians have seen as standing between two worlds, one dying and the other apparently not ready to be born. Literary history has found them embarrassing years, a period dominated by scribbling women and their supposedly vapid literary outlets, those infamous "Annuals" like *Friendship's Offering* and *Forget-Me Not* that began to appear on the scene in 1823. The Tennyson and Browning of our received histories could not come soon enough to put those years out of memory.

And it is *in fact* true that the 1820s were dominated by women's poetry, were dominated by two writers in particular: Felicia Hemans, the most published poet of the nineteenth-century (more published even than Byron), and Laetitia Elizabeth Landon, a late romantic writer now all but forgotten. Landon's work (she published under the initials L.E.L.) went through numerous editions and clearly had a major impact on the writing of Tennyson in particular—although literary history seems to have all but completely forgotten that fact. In her meteoric career she articulated, for the first time in a comprehensive way, an English and female version of the sorrows of Werther. Her tragic and mysterious death in 1838 became a commemorative date of enormous significance for English women poets for the rest of the century.

It seems clear to me that we no longer know how to read a poet like Landon, and that we have lost all connection with the Sternian legacy inherited and transformed by the Della Cruscans. More than that, our readings of the so-called great romantics continue to be pursued under such historical ignorance as to blind us to much of what is happening even in that work we seem so familiar with. Marlon Ross's recently published *The Contours of Masculine Desire* (1990) represents an important new intervention into this situation—a reading of the "major" romantics in the context of those networks of desire which their poetry skirts, re-presses, and transforms.

The New Oxford Book of Verse of the Romantic Period will be attempting some similar, as well as some other, revisionary moves through its editorial policies and procedures. These departures are to be signaled in the title of the book itself, which is not decided as yet but which—in *any* case—will not be able to follow the standard formula "of Victorian Poetry," "of Eighteenth-Century Poetry," "of *Romantic* Poetry."[18]

In general, the anthology will try to represent more comprehensive and accurate "contours" for the poetical work being done between 1785–1832. The aim is to open the field of such writing beyond the limits that have been so carefully erected during the past 150 years. Those limits have been defined through certain overlapping but closely related "romantic ideologies," the two most significant of which have been those descending to us through Wordsworth and through Byron. There are, of course, other romantic ideologies—Blake's, for example, is a late but quite a distinctive development. One of these is the line I associate with certain women writers, though Sterne is probably its immediate point of departure.

By no means all the women who wrote between 1785 and 1832 fell into any of these romantic lines, however. Felicia Hemans, for example, plainly and directly draws upon both of those very different legacies of Wordsworth and Byron, but her own work could scarcely be more different from either of those men. Unlike them, the arena of Hemans' work—the site of its preoccupations as well as its contradictions—is fundamentally domestic.

We want to remember this because it calls our attention, once again, to the fact that the period 1785–1832 is marked by many more differentials than the rubric *Romantic poetry*—however variously that term is understood—will be able to comprehend. This new edition will try to honor those differentials. To do so asks for the display of a large population of writers, many of whom were not principally—or even professionally—"poets." The broadening of the poetic franchise seems to me an imperative scholarly task, particularly at this time when certain narrow and even imperial concepts of writing and culture are once again seeking to define the limits of what is best and culturally possible. The edition, in short, will be trying to reimagine the field of writing in 1785–1832, and through that reimagination to continue a further reimagination of the later history of writing in English.

The foregoing are two specific tasks that illustrate how editorial horizons establish the field in which hermeneutical questions are raised and addressed. In this respect, these examples point toward more general issues in pedagogy, and the need to reintegrate textual and bibliographical studies into the literary curriculum.

That need brings me to my closing example: curricular procedures in graduate literary studies today.

The social text, the praxis of theory, and the editorial horizon of inter- pretation: each of these (interrelated) ideas can and should be argued in essays like the one I am writing now, but they require a clear and relatively simple curricular methodology if they are to establish for themselves something more than a passing interest. Here is a sketch of the program I have been following, with some success, for the past ten years in my graduate seminars.

The class is divided into study units with two or three students responsible for each unit. The study units will involve reading some body of textual material and the presentation of that material to the class in the form of questions or topics for discussion. These questions and discus- sion topics are not normally predefined. However, what *are* predefined are a pair of analytical tasks the students have to carry out on the material in the study unit. Specifically, the students responsible have to provide the class with a detailed analytical description of (A) the history of the texts that are to be taken up in class, and (B) the history of the reception of those texts.

Obviously neither strand of this double helix could, under the con- straints of a graduate seminar, be presented exhaustively. This limitation, however, offers as many opportunities as it does problems. Under such conditions, the student has to address these tasks of socio-historical recon- struction in very self-conscious and deliberate ways—choosing a particu- lar focus on some part of the historical materials and deliberately letting the rest go.

The function of these research and classroom protocols is, of course, to force the student to confront the editorial horizon(s) of the various works they are studying. The procedures ask the student to realize, in very particular and concrete ways, how and why one must speak of texts as "social." The exercises are "elementary" in the sense that they do not, in themselves, put the student in touch with the largest and most important socio-historical and ideological issues engaged by literary work. Nev- ertheless, if the exercises are "elementary," they are also "fundamental." All our forms of "Higher Criticism" depend upon the meticulous examina- tion and analysis of these "elementary" materials. Without such work, a criticism that aspires to an engagement with the social text risks mistaking fantasy and ideology for imagination and understanding.

I close by mentioning one further classroom protocol for my graduate seminars. Besides the seminar reports (mentioned above) and the final critical paper (which is usually an expansion of the material initially developed in one or another of the reports), the students are held responsible for a collective project. This project is specifically editorial. The class may be asked to edit a particular text (e.g., Blake's *The French Revolution*) or book (Byron's *Poems* [1816]), or to produce an outline or proposal for an edition (e.g., an edition of Wordsworth's five-book *Prelude* or of Pound's first thirty Cantos). In these cases the editorial horizon has to be confronted within a set of perspectives that are very different from those developed in the individual class reports.

One interpretive consequence of this task is to bring immediate acts of scholarship within the critical and hermeneutic field of inquiry. Texts and their editions are produced for particular purposes by particular people and institutions, and they may be used (and reused) in multiple ways, many of which run counter to uses otherwise or elsewhere imagined. To edit a text is to be situated in a historical relation to the text's transmissions, but it is also to be placed in an immediate relation to specific cultural and conceptual goals. Nor are these simply the goals and purposes of the editor-as-technical-functionary. While that imagination of the editorial horizon remains common among editors and hermeneuts alike, it is deeply mistaken—not a "blinded" imagination but a deluded one.[19] Carrying forward an actual editorial project, in a context where bibliography and interpretation are continually being forced to confront each other, leaves the student less room for mistaking those purposes and goals.

Notes

1. The allusion here is to Paul De Man's *The Resistance to Theory*.
2. Perhaps the best introduction to literary pragmatics would be in the papers given at the 1988 Abo Symposium on Literary Pragmatics. The papers will shortly be published in a book edited by Roger D. Sell.
3. That is to say, in the period when Anglo-American literary studies were experiencing a strong and widespread turn to theoretical studies in general.

4. A good introduction to the revolution in Shakespearean textual studies is Taylor and Warren's *The Division of the Kingdoms: Shakespeare's Two Versions of King Lear.*

5. William Michael Rossetti's first edition of the poems appeared in 1886. He reprinted it several times, augmenting it in 1904 and again, more comprehensively, in 1911.

6. I sketch an answer to this question in "Dante Gabriel Rossetti, or the Truth Betrayed," in *Towards a Literature of Knowledge,* esp. 79–85.

7. "Natural" because of my long association with the press and because of their interest in producing critical editions of English authors.

8. This is no small supposition in itself, as one may see very clearly in the case of imagining a possible edition of Ezra Pound; or even in the case of the current editions from Garland of the Younger Romantics. The editing of Byron, in the Garland series, is subject to certain constraints and limitations because of restrictions on the use of original manuscript materials.

9. I refer to this work henceforth with the abbreviation *HL.*

10. In this discussion one might reasonably take my question "What is a text?" to be a sociological and historical question *rather than* a philosophical and ontological one. In the context of a materialist pragmatics, however, the distinction between sociological/historical questions and philosophical/ontological ones is itself understood as a socio-historical distinction. The distinction is therefore highly problematic, and—in my view—can only be made in the full consciousness that it is not an ontological distinction. It is (or can be) a "philosophical" distinction if "philosophy" is understood as the history of certain social practices and if it is pursued within the consciousness of that horizon of practices.

11. I have not seen this edition, but it is noted and discussed in Fredeman 299n. What Copeland and Day allude to in their promotion of their edition is the fact that *HL* at one time—in particular, in 1870—had been printed by Rossetti in a form that had included these eleven songs. Like 6a, however, these songs were removed by Rossetti when he printed the 102 sonnet *HL* in 1881. When Copeland and Day restore the songs, they represent their act as giving the work in its "full text" for "the first time."

This is no misrepresentation, though it is also not "the truth." Copeland and Day are simply mistaken about what constitutes (or what might constitute) the "full text" of *HL.*

12. For a schedule of these printings see Fredeman, esp. 336–41.

13. This MS version was printed in 1954 in an (unsatisfactory) edition. See Wahl, 3–33.

14. For a further treatment of these distinctions see McGann, *Social Values and Poetic Acts,* n. 28, 260–61.

15. This book was reprinted in 1971 under yet another title, *The Oxford Book of English Verse of the Romantic Period, 1798–1837.* These changing titles exhibit the chief problem I am discussing here. Milford was keenly aware of the problem, as the following remark from his 1928 preface shows: "The title [of this book] is

unsatisfactory. It is, however, convenient, intelligible, and easily remembered; and if the poets—except the satirists—and the Regency had little to do with one another, yet the head of the State during most of the period was the Prince Regent, and the book may be fairly named from the top of its chronological arch" (viii).

16. Note that the first of these books is printed in Scotland (i.e., outside of England), the second is privately printed, and the last appears through the regular trade (Longman), first with a Bristol imprint (1798), and second with a London (1800). These elementary bibliographical matters are highly significant for the meaning of each of these works, both in themselves and in the context of literary history as well.

17. See Mathias's *The Pursuits of Literature*, the first part of which appeared in 1794.

18. At this writing two titles are favored: the one just given, and *The New Oxford Book of Verse: The Romantic Age, 1785-1832*.

19. The distinction here means to recall the influential DeManian diad "blindness and insight." For a more detailed critique of De Man's dialectical concept see McGann, *Social Values and Poetic Acts*, 1–5, 101–11.

Works Cited

Baum, Paull F., ed. *The House of Life: A Sonnet Sequence by Dante Gabriel Rossetti.* Cambridge: Harvard UP, 1928.

Blake, William. *Songs of Innocence and of Experience: Shewing the Two Contrary States of the Human Soul.* The Author and Printer William Blake. 1789, 1794. Facsimile edition with an Introduction and Commentary by Sir Geoffrey Keynes. New York: Orion P, 1967.

Burns, Robert. *Poems, Chiefly in the Scottish Dialect.* Kilmarnock, 1786.

De Man, Paul. *The Resistance to Theory.* Minneapolis: U of Minnesota P, 1986.

Fredeman, William E. "Rossetti's 'In Memoriam': An Elegiac Reading of *The House of Life.*" *Bulletin of the John Rylands Library* 47 (March 1965): 298–341.

Gabler, Hans Walter. *Ulysses: A Critical and Synoptic Edition.* 3 vols. New York: Garland, 1984.

Lang, Cecil Y., ed. *The Pre-Raphaelites and Their Circle.* Boston: Houghton Mifflin, 1968.

Levine, Alice, and Jerome J. McGann, eds. *The Manuscripts of the Younger Romantics: Byron.* 4 vols. New York: Garland, 1986–88.

Lonsdale, Roger, ed. *The New Oxford Book of Eighteenth Century Verse.* Oxford: Oxford UP, 1984.

Maitland, Thomas [Robert Buchanan]. "The Fleshly School of Poetry: Mr. D. G. Rossetti." *Contemporary Review* 18 (October 1871): 334–50.

Mathias, T. J. *The Pursuits of Literature: A Satirical Poem in Dialogue, Part the First.* London: T. Becket, 1794.

McGann, Jerome J. *Social Values and Poetic Acts*. Cambridge: Harvard UP, 1988.
———. *Towards a Literature of Knowledge*. Oxford: Oxford UP, and Chicago: U of Chicago P. 1989.
Milford, H. S., ed. *The Oxford Book of Regency Verse*. Oxford: Oxford UP, 1928 [reprinted with new titles in 1935 and 1971].
Ross, Marlon. *The Contours of Masculine Desire*. New York: Oxford UP, 1989.
Rossetti. *The Collected Works of Dante Gabriel Rossetti*. Ed. with Preface and Notes by William Michael Rossetti. 2 Vols. London: Ellis, 1886.
———. *The Works of Dante Gabriel Rossetti*. Ed. with Preface and Notes by William Michael Rossetti. London: Ellis, 1911.
———. *Poems by Dante Gabriel Rossetti*. Copyright Edition. With a Memoir of the Author by Franz Hueffer. Lepizig: Tauchnitz, 1873.
Wahl, John Robert, ed. *The Kelmscott Love Sonnets of Dante Gabriel Rossetti*. Cape Town: A. A. Balkema, 1954.
[Wordsworth, William, and Samuel Taylor Coleridge]. *Lyrical Ballads, with a Few Other Poems*. Bristol: Longman, 1798.

2

The Autonomous Author, the Sociology of Texts, and the Polemics of Textual Criticism

PETER SHILLINGSBURG

E STAND AT THE CROSSROADS of textual theory and literary theory, the first concentrating on the way texts come into being, the other concentrating on the way texts are used. The textual, editorial tradition has been devoted to getting things right, while more and more the literary critical tradition tells us there is nothing to get right. We have been milling around at this crossroads for at least ten years now taking up and dropping one solution after the other in hopes of getting under way again. There was a time when textual criticism was universally understood to be the art of establishing what the author wrote and literary criticism was universally understood to be the art of understanding what the author meant. Both of those goals have been demonstrated to be beyond definitive reach. Other goals have presented themselves as equally interesting and perhaps more attainable.

The central concern of both textual critics and literary critics is meaning. The central focus or locus of that concern is the text. The problematic nature of *meaning* agitates literary critics and theorists; the problematic nature of *texts* agitates textual critics and theorists. Both should agitate us all. Literary critics need to understand more about unstable texts; textual critics need to understand more about unstable meaning. To many literary theorists, the textual critic is embroiled in a fruitless and irrelevant endeavor to establish history as if historical meaning were ascertainable and significant. To the textual critic, the literary critic often seems hopelessly naive, for though he has interesting things to say about interpretation, often he is careless about the text. Who knows, says the textual critic, what different conclusions the literary critic might have reached had he started with a better-edited text and had he understood more about its genesis and production.

When textual criticism was defined as the art of detecting errors and removing them from texts, the implicit goal was to produce purified or corrected texts. Several problems have arisen regarding this view of things. First, there is the challenge to the validity of critical editions as historical constructs. Second, a variety of competing orientations toward the text have developed, leading to disputes over what is the correct or best way to edit. And third, a fundamental question has been raised about the nature of the end product of editing: Should it present the work of art as a finished product or as a developing process? I will take up these three items in order, though I shall concentrate most of my attention on the last.

First, then, is the challenge to critical editions emanating from poststructural insights. It is objected that the validity of scholarly reconstructions of authorial intentions or the social and cultural milieus of past events resulting in the publication of a work of art cannot be verified. Editors may have brought this challenge upon themselves years ago by suggesting they were producing definitive editions or at least editions that would never have to be done again. In its simplest form the objectors argue that historical explanations cannot be verified against the reality of what was because the reality of what *was* can only be known as a mental construct. Attempts to reconstruct author's intentions or ideal texts or any kind of critical edition are, therefore, basically dishonest in what they claim to do. The whole concept of an established text is thus challenged for lack of certainty about its relation to objective reality.[1]

Often this challenge goes hand in hand with the recommendation that since the past is irrecoverable and all views of it are ideologically based and limited, therefore the ideological nature of our activities should be acknowledged and itself made into the focus of our endeavors. Since there cannot be objective, nonideologically-based uses of texts, let us accept that condition. For this purpose, the author is dead and the scholarly edition is not useful, except perhaps to reinforce a canon of literature. Most editors would reject these views, but one might like to know on what grounds—other than self-preservation.

Two responses can be made on an equally simple level. First, the present is no less a mental construct than the past and the utilitarian or pragmatic approach that is recommended is just as "illegitimate" as historical constructs. Both activities are equally hampered by uncertainty and a lack of verifiability; both are equally ideological. But there is something quite unsatisfactory about restoring to the purely utilitarian or pragmatic approach, for there is no corrective within it; any use of the text might be equal in value to any other.

The second answer is that a test other than verification can be employed. One such test is coherence. Coherence requires that within a postulated context or set of parameters, all the evidence that can be adduced as relevant to that context must be coherently accounted for. In general terms, we can apply this idea to the concept of historical explanation or reconstruction as the attempt to account coherently for every piece of known or knowable evidence relating to the origination of a text. Such a context can be placed in contrast to other competing contexts with their own coherent explanations such as that posed by the poststructural critics. This process has several consequences.

First, it does not attempt to say anything about the past or the present as objective realities. It knows it cannot do that; its test of "truth" is coherence, not verification. Secondly, it does not refute one explanation in favor of the other, but instead recognizes that interpretation of meaning and significance depends on the context of the discourse. Third, we can begin to understand the achievement of the famous editors of the recent past as careful attempts to produce editions reflecting coherent explanations of contexts that were defined differently from the way they now tend to be defined. That is, an editor such as Fredson Bowers, editing works by Nathaniel Hawthorne in such a way as to recreate the author's final intentions, was fulfilling the dictates of a context defined in relation to the author. Later editors coming on the scene need not say, "Poor Mr. Bowers, he was hopelessly committed to an objective view of reality and thought he could reconstruct the past. We know better now." No. Bowers knew there was no verification. That's why he called what he did *critical* editing. But he did define rather narrowly the context within which a coherent explanation of text must be conducted.

When Jerome McGann proposes that the relevant context for understanding what texts of literary works are must be enlarged to include the production process as part of the social context within which artistic creations become novels and poems, he is merely changing the concept of authority for texts. Insofar as McGann vests the production process with absolute authority over the text, he decenters the author and offers a polemical alternative to Bowers's author-centric view. At other times, when McGann speaks of including or adding the production process to the mix of influences already in use, including authorial intention, then he not only enlarges the context relevant to our notion of text but offers that enlarged context as a competing authority for determining what the text should be.

The second question I want to take up is whether there is a correct or better way to edit. I would pose this question as three questions. The first is, What are the currently competing options claiming to be the better way? The second is, What do these ways of editing imply about the nature of scholarly editions and their proper uses? And the third is, Are there any alternatives to this view of the nature of scholarly editions and their uses?

In *Scholarly Editing in the Computer Age* I suggested that there are four basically different competing orientations toward texts that lead to opposing editorial principles: the documentary, the authorial, the social, and the aesthetic (18–30). Proponents of each of these orientations vest textual authority in a different entity and proceed to edit in such a way as to fulfill the dictates of that authority. It is a tendency of editors and critics milling at the crossroads to wish for an answer to the problems of interpretation and editing that can be followed by rule. When we ask questions like: To whom does the work of art belong? or By what enabling authority or authorities did it come into being and continue to exist? we think we are trying to see what the work of art is by seeing what gave it existence so that we will know what is the right way to edit. But there are different answers to these questions and, therefore, ways to edit. One answer is that the work belongs to the author, the creator, and reviser. Another is that it belongs to the publisher, the financier, producer, and editor. A third is that it belongs to the reader, the recreator, and exploiter. A fourth is that it belongs to itself, a free-floating text inviolate once it has entered time. Recently, particularly in the writings of D. F. McKenzie and Jerome McGann, a theory has emerged claiming that works of art are a product of an unwritten but naturally recognizable social contract in which authors, editors, printers, publishers, booksellers, book buyers, and readers are all caught up in varying degrees of willingness. In this view of things the text does not belong to anyone; in fact, it is possible to see that the people belong to the text. Specifically, they belong to the socialized text—a text that came into being through collaborative social effort, which has socialized the common readers of that text.[2]

Each of these answers is in a way true; but none can be used to provide a comprehensive principle of textual criticism. Various attempts have been made to provide such a principle, and from time to time one or another of them prevails. If the text belongs to the author, let us edit the author's final intentions. If it belongs to the enabling production crews, let us not edit the resulting documents or else carry on the process of regularizing the text begun by the production crews. If it belongs to the reader, any reprint will do. If it belongs to itself, then a photofacsimile is as close as one can get to a good edition. The newest ruling view, of literary texts as products of a social contract, holds that scholarly editions should trace and respect the development and transmogrification of the text by the succession of entities that have appropriated the work for publication. These competing views cannot be melded into one as long as the underlying assumption about the goal of scholarly editions remains the establishment of a single finished-product text.

That brings us to the second part of the second question: What does any proposal for a better way to present the work of art as a single, finished end-product imply about the nature of scholarly editing? First, it makes the editor a mediator and restorer. He or she stands between the work and the reader, clearing away problems and ambiguities that the reader would find misleading or distracting. The editor is collaborator with the author, doing better what the originating production crew did poorly. As mediator and restorer, the editor must be trusted by the reader who is supposed to be grateful for a finished product. Established scholarly editions and the CEAA/CSE seal of approval tend to foster the view that textual critics are purifiers of texts, not interpreters, and that literary critics do not need to bother with what the textual critics have already settled—the established text is good for use in literary criticism.[3]

In the 1980s another view of the nature of scholarly editions has arisen that offers an alternative to the polemics of competing, better ways to edit. It is the view that scholarly editions organize and present works of art primarily as *process* not primarily as *product.* I suggest that this view rises above, rather than adds to, the polemics I've indicated. A comprehensive textual criticism must understand and respond to the truths of those varying orientations by identifying each of them as a context for a potential form which the work can have as the linear, or reading, text of the edition. According to this view there is no single correct way to edit texts, and scholarly editors are not the discoverers and guardians of correct texts. Evidence does not cry out for a certain treatment, for the same evidence cries out in different ways to different editors according to the particular critical theories uppermost in their minds and according to the context they have chosen to privilege as the determiner of "meaning." A textual critic establishing the all-purpose reading text is rather like a literary critic establishing the standard interpretation. Most of us would scoff at such a literary critic, but how many of us have learned to scoff at such a textual critic?

We have arrived then at the third of my original questions: Should (3) scholarly editions present works of art as product or process? I have already indicated what I think, but I want to put a specific case to demonstrate why I think as I do. In pursuing this issue, I will try to show the connection between the interpretation of texts and the establishment of texts in order to demonstrate further the impossibility of editing correctly in a satisfactory way.

Implicit in my answer to the challenge from literary critical theory was the idea that coherent explanations could be attempted within defined contexts. We know in everyday practice that the meanings of verbal utterances are guided heavily if not actually established by contexts. The principle of interpretation to which I refer is well known to everyone whether or not they allow it to influence their editorial practice. Take Thackeray's *The History of Henry Esmond*, for example. Thackeray, the author, writing in 1851–52, had a mid-nineteenth-century audience consisting of book reviewers, circulating library readers, his mother, his publishers, his friends, and his ex–lady love Jane Brookfield. These people can be seen as having been addressed by the novel. But Thackeray says not one word in *Henry Esmond*, for his narrator, the aged Esmond, and the memoir's editors and commentators, Esmond's wife and daughter, do all the writing. The writing is understood to take place in the second and third decades of the eighteenth century and to record events said to have occurred between 1670 and 1720. Esmond's memoirs are addressed to his grandsons, but his audience clearly includes his wife, who is thought by most critics to resemble Jane Brookfield. The speakers in the novel, in passages of dialogue, also produce their utterances in contexts that help identify their meanings. We can ask what the character meant, what

Esmond meant by reporting the character's speech, and what Thackeray meant by having Esmond report it. We can ask what the passage might have meant to a Victorian totally ignorant of the author and what it might have meant to Jane Brookfield. And of course, we can produce our own responses to these meanings by contrasting them with our own sense of acceptable beliefs and behaviors. Thus we contextualize the text in various specific ways as a means of producing what we think are appropriate understandings of the text.

I have only touched the tip of an iceberg of contexts within which the novel's words can be set and understood. Each context illuminates the text in a different way. We know this and act upon that knowledge almost without reflection—we are that good at using and understanding language. And when a scholar/critic points out to us an aspect of context we had not considered, we gratefully add it to the mix of factors that influence our understanding of the text. The study of genre, the author's other works, biography, cultural history, the history of ideas, all these are understood to extend our awareness of the contexts within which texts create and convey meaning. Even the physical embodiments of texts, the books themselves as paper, ink, and bindings, influence interpretations.[4]

Most readers of classic texts have been encouraged to ignore physical texts. We read Tennyson's *In Memoriam* in a cut version in the *Norton Anthology* and think we can understand the work. There is a willing suspension of disbelief about the repackaging in which we confront the linguistic text, and we pretend nothing is lost. If the artifact embodying the text is part of its meaning, then an important aspect of meaningful context has been lost in the *re*contextualization that any reprinting involves. Consequently, emended, abridged, and reshaped texts are inadequate for access to the work of art in its original context. That same argument carried forward nullifies newly edited scholarly editions, also, unless one thinks of them merely as new contextualizations of the work.

Now, if we assume that the text of a work is stable, that is, if we work with a text that we think has been *established*, we use the principle of contexts to produce "readings of the text" for contemplation. But if we recognize that the text itself is not stable, we tend to use the principle of contexts to produce a "reading of the text" that will help establish what the text is by leading us to the right critical choices amongst variants. If that strikes you as circular, it is. If it leads you to be suspicious of the resulting text, it should. But the situation is worse than that. It does not matter that no variant survives at a given point in the text; each word and piece of punctuation is potentially an erroneous witness to the context you have identified and are using to interpret the text. That might seem good to the editor, for that is what makes emendation of errors possible. Editors tend to think that some errors, like typographical errors and scribal errors, are "demonstrable," and they emend them. But they might be too quick to believe an error to be demonstrable because they are not sufficiently aware of the influence of the contextualization they are using to determine the meaning that identifies the textual anomaly as a demonstrable error.

To illustrate the potential and the pitfalls of this approach as a key to editorial procedures, I would like to focus attention on Thackeray's *The History of Henry Esmond,* which for these purposes we will have to examine in the original edition, published in London by Smith, Elder and Co., in 1852 in three volumes. In what follows I speak as an editor of *Henry Esmond,* but I mean to imply that, in order for the editor to know what is being edited and why it is being edited, he or she must first be a reader, must know how to read, and must know what effects editing has on reading. Consequently everything I say about the editor is true also of any careful reader. The questions underlying this discussion are: What do the reader and editor owe to the concept of a social contract for the work? What place has the author's creative individuality which we assume meant to communicate his or her own intentionality to the implied or actual readers? And how does an understanding of what the text means influence editorial policy?

To do a contextual reading right we would have to do it all. In order to see *Henry Esmond* in its original context, we must draw together the historical details of authorship as a profession, and of printing and publishing as a complex of economic traditions and interests in a continuous struggle with innovation—both technical and moral—and with attitudes toward gender, family, and moral conventions, particularly as they reflected the audiences for lending libraries. While trying not to forget that authors attempt to create something original that will fulfill their own purposes (including the purpose of making money), we would have to examine bibliography, printing history, papermaking, taxes on books and newspapers, copyright law, labor relations, trade guilds relating to printing publishing and bookselling, marketing associations, professional so-

cieties, the apprentice system, lending libraries, the three-deckers in relationship to parts publication and magazine serials, the growth of the
literate public, the development of authorship as a profession, and the
developing division of labor into literary agents, publishers, printers,
wholesalers, and booksellers. Each of these matters should be thought of
as a force field influencing what the work became, limiting what the work
could say, shaping the work and thereby influencing reactions to and
understandings of the final product.

Now obviously I cannot detail all of that here, but it has been done and
its salient details can be summarized here.[5] *The History of Henry Esmond* is
Thackeray's only book to appear originally as a three-decker. It was
published by a firm whose head, George Smith, was an executive member
of the Booksellers Association. It was Thackeray's second book with
Smith, Elder, and Co.—his first major book with them—and it represented the first major step in an attempt by George Smith to make
Thackeray one of "his" authors—an object he accomplished thoroughly
and completely in 1859. Smith "descended" into publishing from the
banking business by way of substantial reference works and scientific
publications. His literature list, his fiction, was respectable; yet he was
bold and aggressive. He published Charlotte Brontë's *Jane Eyre,* and later
went on to acquire as his authors Anthony Trollope and George Eliot.
Henry Esmond, therefore, by virtue of its publishing house, belongs to a
tradition of book production controlled by establishment wealth and
power. To be published by Smith implied certain standards of literary and
moral content that Thackeray had never been clearly subject to before,
though he was clearly subject in a general way to the Mrs. Grundy
censorship affecting all Victorian publications above pulp street literature
(James). Thackeray "rose" to the Smith, Elder house from his major
publisher, Bradbury and Evans, who in turn had "risen" into publishing
from bookselling, newspaper publishing, and publishing that low comic
magazine *Punch* and other comic and sporting publications. They were
journalists belonging to a decidedly antiestablishment point of view, and
in the 1840s Thackeray was one of their chief writers. Thackeray himself
had been a gentleman of independent means, raised to no profession and
partially educated at Cambridge where his love for cards apparently ex-
ceeded his desire or need for academic distinction. Though he famously
lost a considerable amount in gambling, he lost his fortune in a bank
failure in India (Ray, *Adversity* 162). His sojourn in bohemia as an art

student in Paris and his period as a writing hack in London were social and financial descents from which the economic success of books like *Vanity Fair* and *Pendennis* were raising him. Those works and the bulk of his writings in the 1840s (*The Book of Snobs, Novels by Eminent Hands, Barry Lyndon, Catherine, The Yellowplush Papers, The Reminiscences of Major Gahagan*) all reflect the satirical, antisnob, antiestablishment attitudes of *Punch* and *Fraser's Magazine,* the main outlets for his writings.

Henry Esmond was to be different. Its author was a man financially and socially restored to the level of his upbringing. He was a popular writer and successful public lecturer, having delivered his urbane lectures on the eighteenth-century English humorists to receptive and aristocratic audiences in London, Edinburgh, Oxford, Cambridge and the larger industrial cities. *Henry Esmond* was to be his "calling card" and proof that he could write a thoroughly good, artistically complete, and serious work of art. By and large, this novel has been seen, both by his contemporaries and by generations of literary critics up to our own day, as a peak in Thackeray's rising career as a writer and artist.

The book belongs to "the establishment" in other ways, too. The three-decker was, in mid-Victorian England, a thoroughly "establishment" commodity, an expensive book made possible and necessary by circulating libraries whose large guaranteed prepublication purchases made three-decker production a book publisher's staple. It was nearly impossible for a book publisher to lose money on a three-decker that had been adopted by Mudie's library, but the discounts Mudie demanded and the price regulations that kept most ordinary customers from purchasing their own copies instead of subscribing to Mudie's made it equally difficult for a publisher to make very much money on a three-decker. The price maintenance system for three-deckers worked to the benefit of publishers and the circulating libraries from the mid-1840s to the mid-1890s by providing stability. No one was making a killing, but it could be counted on. This stability depended not only on control of prices but also on certain simple controls over the content and size of the books. These constraints imposed by Mudie's are now relatively easy to document; their primary focus was on the length of the book and the moral character of the plot and characterizations. An author and publisher who could work within the library constraints and win selection could count on a sound though not spectacular financial return.

But the respectability of the publisher and the demands of the libraries were not the only determining or constraining forces observable. *Esmond* is a historical novel created within a tradition of historical fiction that Thackeray might be said to have modified but not to have invented. Among these constraints was the demand for historical plausibility and the historical research which that demand entailed. Plausibility was judged by the depth and breadth and accuracy of the historical detail surrounding the fictional characters and events, although it was not necessary to maintain historical perspective in moral and intellectual concerns or issues, Sir Walter Scott having made the historical novel both respectable and relevant to current moral and political concerns. But the freedom offered by historical fiction within the establishment contours of the three-decker published by Smith, Elder in 1852 was a narrow freedom indeed.

N. N. Feltes, in considering *Esmond* in its marketplace context, notes that the Booksellers Association and the circulating libraries were fighting a losing battle against an encroaching democratizing, proletarian invasion of the world of books and literature represented by cheap books, serializations in shilling parts, and shilling magazines. The battle was to save the "commodity" which three-deckers epitomized and thereby save the economic control and stability the booksellers enjoyed primarily through the three-decker. Feltes sees the three-decker as symbolic of the upper class resistance to progressing economic forces and finds in the three-decker morality and traditional structures a corollary conservatism and reactionary spirit. He finds in *Henry Esmond,* a historical novel redolent with nostalgia for a past age, the same conservatism and establishment resistance to mass values, mass mores, and mass tastes. He finds in the novel's literary reputation a confirmation of its conservative tastes and socio-economic politics. In the social history of the last half of the nineteenth century, on the other hand, Feltes sees the slow but irresistible subversion of the commodity *book* by the new cheap democratizing commodity *text*. The triumph of this movement is the demise of the three-decker novel in the 1890s. For Feltes, therefore, *Henry Esmond* represents a reactionary, establishment work. As such it represents a change or an anomaly in Thackeray's role, which for *Vanity Fair* and the early journalism was that of satirist of the establishment. Feltes posits the explanation that within the constraints of the three-decker, Thackeray was forced or determined by cultural forces greater than himself and that an examination of these cultural contexts proves that the language and the culture speak the author, that the autonomous author is a figment of the Romantic imagination; "reality" is the reality of social determinism.

If we were to stop here, the weight of the social contract might seem irresistible; the social theory of texts would convincingly vest authority for both the linguistic text and the meaning of the work in the social context. And our editorial solution for *Henry Esmond* would be to select the first edition as copytext, emend nothing, and present the novel as a commodity book with large margins, heavy paper, and expensive packaging, thus perpetuating its role as representative of the establishment, standing as an anomaly in Thackeray's literary corpus. But the author, his text, and his meaning need not disappear behind this sociological arrangement of historical details. It is a significant shortcoming in Feltes's work that he does not apply his critical apparatus to a reading of the text.

Careful rereading suggests a conclusion opposite to the one Feltes reaches. He skates over the elements in the book that do not confirm his social-deterministic theory of book production. The flaw of his approach is the rigidity with which his view of the social-contract theory of texts controls and limits his reading of the work. It does so apparently by paralyzing his belief in authorial intentionality. Social determinism apparently obviates autonomy for Feltes. Although all that Feltes points out about the cultural milieu surrounding the book is true, it is hardly as comprehensive or constraining a view as he would have us believe. Though the book was hailed by many of its original readers (particularly its better-educated and better-heeled readers) as a critical triumph, and though it currently and for many years has been held in high regard even by readers who do not generally admire Thackeray's works, it was and is a profoundly troubling book to many others.

Many of its first readers and reviewers were shaken and angered by the ending, in which Esmond marries the woman he has long treated as his mother. That Thackeray intended this ending from the beginning is perfectly clear on rereading with close attention to Rachel's character—she knew her heart's true relation to Henry well before her husband died and years before naive Esmond himself recognized it. We see it in her nearly hysterical reaction to the news that Henry has exposed himself to smallpox by visiting Nancy Sievewright, the blacksmith's daughter, although a superficial reading allows one to think that she is reacting merely as a social snob and doting mother (bk. 1, ch. 8). We see it in her behavior to Henry on his third visit home from college when young Frank reveals that she has been fussing over Henry's room for days, having worked a new counterpane for his bed and put fresh-cut roses in his window in anticipation of his arrival, though she pretends not to know whether the housekeeper has prepared his room (bk. 1, ch. 11). We see it in her reaction to the news that "Henry" has been killed in a carriage accident, though the Henry involved turned out to be Mohun, not Esmond (bk. 1, ch. 13). We see it in the nearly psychopathic rejection scene in prison after Lord Castlewood has been killed in a duel (bk. 2, ch. 1). And we see it in the news that she has sneaked off to Southampton to watch from hiding as Esmond returns from the continental wars (bk. 2, ch. 7). Rachel clearly believes that God has punished her for her disaffection from her husband and for her secret affection for Henry by allowing her husband's death. She tells Esmond years later when they meet again that God has forgiven her sin: "But I would love you still—yes, there is no sin in such a love as mine now; and my dear lord in heaven may see my heart; and knows the tears that have washed my sin away" (bk. 2, ch. 6). Rachel's secret love was even more disturbing to the Victorian consciousness than the apparent though not real incest at the end of the book, for it portrays a good woman—the heroine angel in the house—in the grip of a powerful and lifelong illicit passion she must and does suppress with visible effort. Morally the book's psychological realism, though delicately handled, is profoundly subversive to the establishment. It is a measure of Thackeray's aristry that he portrayed these telling scenes in ways susceptible to more conventional interpretations, though to read them conventionally is to believe Thackeray has overwritten them.[6]

But the book is subversive in an even more important way, for Esmond's ostensibly weak character, his apparent vacillation and inability to cast himself passionately and unreservedly behind any cause, whether it be religious, political, economic, or amorous—though goodness knows he tries—arguably stems not from a psychological weakness but from a fundamental philosophical uncertainty and rejection of dogma that is always dangerous to establishments. The elderly narrator of the book, recounting his youthfully naive enthusiasms for Father Holt's Catholicism, Rachel's Anglicanism, the Dowager Castlewood's Jacobinism, Beatrix's twisted concepts of heroism and honor, repeatedly shows Esmond discovering himself in an assumed and uncomfortable role-playing. He spends his life trying to fulfill other people's expectations for himself and repeatedly discovering the goals not worth winning. He ends ashamed of himself as a soldier witnessing his fellows attack nuns, ashamed of Father Holt's tawdry lies and deceptions, ashamed of Frank Esmond's sacrifice of his independence to his Clotilde, ashamed of Beatrix's headhunting selfishness as courtesan, and ultimately ashamed of his own complicity in these other shames in which he has participated as a role player rather than *in propria persona*.

Esmond's superiority over other characters seems to be measured in his recognition of his self-delusions as well as those of his fellow actors. But that superiority cripples his success within the establishment. Esmond's way of thinking and suiting action to thought is antiestablishment. That is why Beatrix has no use for him. He is ultimately anti-imperialist and antiroyalist, and he rejects the optimism of the intellectual rationality for which his age, the eighteenth century, is known.

The question about Thackeray's "intentions" with regard to *Henry Esmond* and its ostensibly antiestablishment meanings can be pursued a bit further in two directions.

The first is the biographical background and in particular the events in the year immediately preceding the novel's composition concerning Thackeray's love life (Ray, *Wisdom*, and *Letters*). By 1851 Thackeray's wife had been confined under special care for insanity for seven years. In the three years preceding the writing of *Henry Esmond* his love for Jane Brookfield, the wife of his best friend, the Reverend William Brookfield, had become as heated as a platonic relationship can become. Thackeray was clearly in love, though he was fully aware of the impossibility of the situation. He imagined that Jane suffered repression and lack of appreciation by her husband, which might have been greater in Thackeray's mind than in reality. Whatever the case, in September 1851, William Brookfield, who had tolerated Thackeray's attentions in his home with increasing wariness, put his foot down, banning the novelist from the society of his home and wife. It is not hard to trace Thackeray's melancholy in the Henry Esmond–Rachel Castlewood relations in the book he was then commencing.

Though he had not written any part of the book, he signed the contract in June 1851. It was a story he claimed was boiling up within him as early as January, though his work on his lectures on eighteenth-century English humorists came first. That the rupture with the Brookfields affected the story there can be no doubt. Thackeray complained to Smith as late as December that he could not get on with the book under the effects of a disease that time alone could mend. In the book itself we can see a romanticized version of what could have been: Lord Castlewood's insensitivity to his wife can be read as William Brookfield's insensitivity to Jane writ large; Rachel's deep love for Esmond, suppressed and denied, but tortured and irrepressible, can be interpreted as Thackeray's portrait of what he saw or wished to see in Jane Brookfield's relation to himself. Thackeray seems much more interested, to judge also from his letters, in assuaging his own sorrow than in upholding establishment social mores. And in the character of Henry Esmond, Thackeray was able to make Rachel (cum Jane Brookfield) suffer the jealous pangs of seeing her unattainable love object throw himself at the feet of another—Beatrix, who was Rachel's daughter. Nor is it hard to see Thackeray beating his own breast and exploring the ecstasies of rejection while describing the perpetual and nearly irrepressible but unrequited love of Esmond for Beatrix. The psychological realism of a complicated and confusing network of love and jealousy involving mothers and sons and other forbidden attractions is carefully handled, for in Victorian fiction serious and troubling life passages could be explored only in code.

And finally, the rhetorical context of the novel casts doubt on Feltes's thesis. Its full title announces it is a memoir: *The History of Henry Esmond, Esq., A Colonel in the Service of Her Majesty Q. Anne. Written by Himself.* It has the rhetorical characteristics of an extended dramatic monologue, addressed by Esmond to his grandsons. Thackeray, the author, as I noted earlier, says not one word in the whole book; even the introduction is written by Esmond's daughter. As with any first-person narration, the potential for irony and for misapprehending irony is great. Traditionally, critics have read Esmond's narrative as the preachments of the author's alter ego. Esmond's opening comments, on the nature of history, strike readers as honest, commonsensical, and Thackerayan. "Why shall History go on kneeling to the end of Time? I am for having her rise up off her knees, and take a natural posture: not to be for ever performing cringes and congees like a Court-chamberlain, and shuffling backwards out of doors in the presence of the sovereign. In a word," Esmond writes engagingly, "I would have History familiar rather than heroic." Esmond seems to reflect Thackeray's own attitude also by placing himself and his neighbors on the stage of history and comparing them with the figures normally found there: "I have seen too much of success in life to take off my hat and huzza to it, as it passes in its gilt coach: and would do my little part with my neighbors on foot that they should not gape with too much wonder, nor applaud too loudly. Is it the Lord Mayor going in state to mince-pies and the Mansion House? Is it poor Jack of Newgate's procession, with the sheriff and javelin-men, conducting him on this last journey to Tyburn? I look into my heart and think I am as good as my Lord Mayor, and know I am as bad as Tyburn Jack."

Moreover, Esmond has a Thackerayan distrust of absolutes—that is, of other people's absolutes; he does not trust the judgment of priests, military leaders, political leaders, or kings. His love and his loyalty are always tinged with sardonic self-detachment. As one critic has noted, "Like *Vanity Fair, Henry Esmond* is a sustained argument against the reality of moral absolutes. Esmond himself does much of the arguing, for he is proficient at identifying illusory values and beliefs. His sophisticated skepticism, however, is itself founded on a dedication to one surviving absolute: truth" (Scarry 3). This personal truth of Esmond's is the foundation of his appeal to the reader in his autobiography. And, as with most monologuists, Henry constantly appeals to us to share in his personal recognition and judgment of the self-deception of others. Furthermore, he seldom asks us to take himself very seriously, and he appears to be disingenuous when he does. Many readers follow these clues, equating Esmond and Thackeray, as wise critics of society.

Feltes would probably not rejoice over this coup d'état within the camp of the dying establishment, for the book does not subvert the establishment on behalf of the rising proletariat. Instead, the subversion emanates from the principles of a small intellectual elite, the freethinkers of England's Victorian intellectual class. Thackeray's philosophy is revealed in his letters and private papers as a deep and fundamental individual skepticism about dogmatism and special causes. It got him into trouble with his mother over the religious education of his daughters and with many proponents of causes in need of money or moral support who approached him for aid. Thackeray was generous to a fault with the needy, but he opposed a guild for literature and evangelical schools and causes. He did not trust institutionalized schemes. *Henry Esmond* is subversive of the establishment it represents, but not on behalf of emerging socio-economic ideologies. Even the fact that both Thackeray and his publisher made a good bit of money from the book, which was an unusually good seller despite its price, does not indicate that its themes or its production were determined or dominated by either a vested production tradition or an emerging public taste.

If this is an "establishment" book, it has a strikingly antiestablishment text—it is a wolf in sheep's clothing. With this interpretation we cannot accept a social-contract solution to the editorial problem. Now, it happens that in 1852 the publisher George Smith did not own his own printing house, so he sent Thackeray's manuscript to Bradbury and Evans to be typeset and printed. We might find comfort in the fact that the compositors of Thackeray's "proletarian serial novels" also typeset his "establishment commodity book," but the principle of authorial autonomy that our interpretation tends to support leads us to question the whole production process. That is to say, belief in the possibility of authorial autonomy, even of a limited sort, requires that we reject any blanket rules for editing.

In rejecting N. N. Feltes's conclusions about the meaning of *Henry Esmond* in three volumes, and in rejecting the conclusion that a social contract requires special respect, from an editorial view, I am not saying that the three-volume format and the production process are unimportant. Quite the contrary. The book couldn't be a wolf in sheep's clothing without the sheep's clothing, and such a wolf means far different things from regular wolves or regular sheep. The novel is quite definitely a collaboration or at least a joint venture between the author and the social institutions of book production and marketing. And that identifies serious editorial problems.

When we look closely at the novel, we see an extensive network of evidence suggesting an intentional subversion of the narrator by the author. Thackeray seems not to trust Esmond's foundation rock of personal truth. Elaine Scarry, in a 1975 article that has gone almost totally unremarked by Thackeray critics, compiled an extensive list of errors in the book. These she invariably attributes to Esmond, claiming that Thackeray put them there on purpose. Scarry was not the first to notice that Esmond occasionally contradicts himself or forgets what he has said earlier in the narrative, but she is the first to attribute these errors to Esmond instead of to Thackeray or to the publishers. John Sutherland's Penguin edition annotations, for example, point out scores of historical and plotting errors, but Sutherland encourages us to ignore them as understandable though regrettable characteristics of Thackeray's fiction.

It would take too much space to detail the errors Scarry has identified; there is an astonishing array of them, including an undermining of the rhetorical force of Esmond's own protestations—as when, having renounced the doctrine of divine right of kings and declared himself a republican, he nevertheless couches his adoration for Beatrix in the language of subjugation to royalty—and other more direct contradictions—

as when he declares that an event so impressed him that memory would never fail him, whereupon he recounts the event in such a way as to contradict or distort his own earlier account of it. If we believe Scarry is right to say that Esmond, "who has taken truth for his motto" is ironically undercut by Thackeray, "who has taken the absence of truth for his theme," then we must choose an editorial solution different from those we have contemplated yet.

The point of all that is this: the contexts we identify as relevant to the text we read determine our interpretation, and the interpretation we adopt determines the text we establish or edit. If we adopt Feltes's interpretation, we choose the first edition as copytext and make our reading text ape the result of the social contract that originally produced it. Our emendations policy will be documentary and conservative. If, however, we adopt John Sutherland's interpretation, we will select the 1858 Cheap Edition because it was the most corrected in Thackeray's lifetime and emend the text to conform as closely as we can to our notion of Thackeray's intentions by correcting as many errors as possible and writing notes for all the rest to explain them away or de-emphasize any damage they might do to our enjoyment of Thackeray's tour de force historical pastiche. But if we adopt Elaine Scarry's interpretation we shall choose the manuscript as copytext and emend the text so that it effectively undermines the narrator's credibility, thus emphasizing Thackeray's rejection even of Esmond's attachment to personal truth.

If our goal as editors is to produce the text as a finished product, emended according to a "better way" of editing, then we must take a stand on answers to the following questions: To what extent was the author aware of and in control of the book's potential ironies? Did Thackeray intend to undermine Esmond's trust in personal truth or did he share Esmond's view? Did Thackeray deliberately undercut Esmond's credibility by introducing obvious errors and memory lapses into Esmond's memoirs, or are the errors those of the novelist, Thackeray? To what extent did the production crew understand the author's intention and enhance or inhibit it? These questions are to be answered by critical inquiry and judgment, not by ascertaining discoverable facts. This situation illustrates well what is critical about editing. But it also illustrates the way any single-text edition of the book is capable of distorting it and hiding its possible meanings by privileging one context over others as the determiner of meaning. It does not take genius to see that an editorial approach to *Henry Esmond* that sets about correcting errors might well be thwarting the author's intentional and meaningful introduction of those errors. On the other hand, *not* to correct the errors also might thwart authorial intention. Only persons who regard their personal solutions to these imponderables as universally acceptable would say that editing can be done by *anyone* correctly.

The economic, biographical, and rhetorical contexts in the cultural envelope within which *Henry Esmond* became a three-decker historical novel all influenced what that book became; but it is a monstrous over-simplification to conclude that the book was determined. Our concept of the editorial task is not helped by the glittering generalities that suggest "the language speaks the artist" or "the social complex employs authors to produce books" or "the author is dead." These conclusions are half-truths. Likewise, it does not help us to understand the business of editing if we conclude that the author is autonomous, the sole authority over text. That view tends to cast the scholarly editor in the role of rescuer and restorer. But the illustration I have just detailed demonstrates that it is impossible to say with certainty what Thackeray is to be rescued from or what needs to be restored.

If we insist on a polemical view of editing (and we do if we insist on *establishing a single text*), we must ignore the lessons of my illustration, edit by one or another oversimplified view of the task, and hope literary critics accept the result—they probably will, being on the whole a pretty defenseless lot. But if we can adopt a comprehensive textual criticism, we will develop an aim for editing that embraces comprehensively the materials and their problems. The complexities of *Henry Esmond* do not simply show that editing is a difficult task that must be done somehow. Instead it shows that editing the novel correctly is an impossible task. I think I have demonstrated the richness rather than the corruption of the materials. A comprehensive textual criticism will not simplify the editorial task by positing a polemical view of the work. It will, instead, do its best to organize and foreground richness.

Textual editors have discovered many interesting things about com-position and book production that affect literary criticism. Why then do they hide their discoveries by foregrounding a single text? I believe we have the makings of a mission to our profession here. We have been caught out trying to promote the purity of texts, but we have discovered richness, not purity. We have discovered fundamental instability and indeterminate progression, not simple corruption. We have uncovered materials that should make the results of literary criticism both more difficult and more satisfying. Literary criticism at its best is an attempt to understand what texts are, how texts work, what texts have meant and can mean, and to understand these things within the contexts of language, history, values, politics, and the conflicting interests of the past and present. A significant aspect of the context of texts is the composition and production of the physical documents that record them. That has been the traditional focus of textual criticism. Now we must understand that focus to be an affair of literary criticism within the larger cultural envelope, not just as a bibliographical investigation undertaken in isolation. Textual criticism is interpretation. Interpretation is most satisfying when it takes into account all that can be thought of as relevant to its concerns.

My survey of the complexities of Thackeray's text suggests that the author's communication to the reader is not only individual and free but constrained and directed by external forces. That is not a contradiction or tragedy but a fact. Nothing understandable can be said or thought without the contextual frame of language and society and genre and custom and economic realities. But all establishments and power structures have within them the capacity to be satirized, subverted, criticized, and amended—that is to say, the author is free within the limits allowed by the medium. The power of some texts is that their subsurfaces purposefully subvert their surface meanings. The reader and editor have a dual responsibility to authorial intention and to the social contract; both are operative. It follows that a critical theory that ignores either is a lopsided theory; and it also follows that an editorial theory that edits away the evidence of either is equally lopsided.

The concept of editions that emphasize the importance of process and avoid extravagant claims for the correctness of the product is gaining ground but not without resistance—resistance stemming from *editors* who are reluctant to give up power over the texts, from *critics* who want a stable text, and from *publishers* who, market driven, wish to save expense. Editions such as Hans Gabler's of *Ulysses*, Michael Warren's of *King Lear*, and my Thackeray edition are attempts in different ways to emphasize alternative texts, or multiple texts, or indeterminate texts, but all these editions are controversial. Resistance to them in preference for editions with supposedly unproblematic, stabilized texts account for the polemics of textual theory. Any single solution requires commitment to one of several mutually exclusive orientations toward texts. A comprehensive view of textual criticism would promote, I think, editorial solutions that foreground multiple, unstable texts about which much is known but upon which little dogmatic confidence can be placed. The idea of rich editions rather than correct editions may be ideological, too, but not on the same level with the various alternate "correct" methodologies currently in vogue amongst scholarly editors pursuing what I think are misguided efforts to give literary critics "unproblematical texts" about whose composition and production they can remain blissfully ignorant.

Notes

1. This challenge is not recent in origin, nor has it gone undiscussed in editorial theory. See Peckham; Tanselle; and Shillingsburg, *Scholarly Editing,* particularly chs. 2 and 3.

2. I have discussed this concept at length in Shillingsburg, "An Inquiry."

3. The CSE itself does not claim to approve "correct" texts, but the effect its emblem of approval has on the less well informed is to promote confidence in the authenticity and reliability of the text. In fact, all the emblem really signifies is that the text is responsibly edited along lines indicated in the editor's editorial principles. ("Responsibly edited" means that all the relevant research material was considered by the editor and that the text and apparatus are, within reason, accurate typographically.) Another editor following the same principles or the same editor following different principles would likely produce a different but equally approvable edition.

4. McKenzie and McGann developed this idea, which owes much to the influence of ideas current in the so-called New Historicism.

5. The basis for this summary can be found in the following works: my *Pegasus in Harness: Thackeray and His Publishers* (forthcoming) traces Thackeray's works, including *Henry Esmond,* through production and refers to the economic, social and mercantile relations of the books. See also Feltes, whose chapter on *Esmond* (18–35) depends very heavily on Sutherland's *Victorian Novelists* (101–16). Harden's edition of *Henry Esmond* (391–546) reveals a great deal about the composition and revision of the novel. Altick's *The English Common Reader* is a well-known standard. Patten's *Dickens and His Publishers* was ground breaking in its analysis of Victorian publishing procedures and conditions. So is Griest's *Mudie's Circulating Library.* Nowell-Smith's *English Copy-right Law in the Age of Queen Victoria* dispels many myths that could mislead students of the social contract. And West's manuscript in progress explores the development of literary agents and cross-currents in book production and author/publisher relations between England and America.

6. Tillotson provides a particularly good assessment of Thackeray's "philosophy" and the way it influenced how he wrote (152–86).

Works Cited

Altick, Richard. *The English Common Reader*. Columbus: Ohio State UP, 1957.

Feltes, N. N. *Modes of Production of Victorian Novels*. Chicago: U of Chicago P, 1986.

Griest, Guinevere L. *Mudie's Circulating Library*. Bloomington: Indiana UP, 1970.

James, Louis. *Fiction for the Working Man*. Harmondsworth: Penguin, 1974.

McGann, Jerome. *A Critique of Modern Textual Criticism*. Chicago: U of Chicago P, 1983.

McKenzie, D. F. *The Sociology of Texts*. London: British Library, 1987.

Nowell-Smith, Simon. *English Copy-right Law in the Age of Queen Victoria*. Oxford: Oxford UP, 1968.

Patten, Robert L. *Dickens and His Publishers*. Oxford: Clarendon P, 1978.

Peckham, Morse. "Reflections on the Foundations of Textual Criticism." *Proof* 1 (1971): 122–55.

Ray, Gordon. *Thackeray: The Uses of Adversity*. New York: McGraw Hill, 1955.

——. *Thackeray: The Age of Wisdom*. New York: McGraw-Hill, 1958.

——, ed. *The Letters and Private Papers of William Makepeace Thackeray*. Cambridge: Harvard UP, 1945

Scarry, Elaine. "*Henry Esmond:* The Rookery at Castlewood." *Literary Monographs Volume 7: Thackeray, Hawthorne and Melville, and Dreiser*. Ed. Eric Rothsheim and Joseph A. Wittreich, Jr. Madison: U of Wisconsin P, 1975.

Shillingsburg, Peter. "An Inquiry into the Social Status of Texts and Modes of Textual Criticism," *Studies in Bibliography* 42 (1989): 55–78.

——. *Pegasus in Harness: Thackeray and His Publishers*. Ms forthcoming.

——. *Scholarly Editing in the Computer Age*. Athens: U of Georgia P, 1986.

Sutherland, John. *Victorian Novelists and Publishers*. Athens: U of Chicago P, 1976.

Thackeray, William Makepeace. *The History of Henry Esmond*. 3 vols. London: Smith, Elder, 1852.

——. *The History of Henry Esmond*. Cheap Edition. London: Smith, Elder 1858.

——. *The History of Henry Esmond*. Ed. Edgar Harden. New York: Garland, 1989.

——. *The History of Henry Esmond*. Ed. John Sutherland. Harmondsworth: Penguin, 1970.

Tanselle, G. Thomas. "The Concept of the Author's Final Intentions." *Studies in Bibliography* 29 (1976): 167–211.

Tillotson, Geoffrey. *A View of Victorian Literature*. Oxford: Clarendon P, 1978.

West, James L. W. Ms in progress, "Friction between the Cultures: Book Publishing in England and America since 1840."

3

Variety in Editing and Reading: A Response to McGann and Shillingsburg

T.H. HOWARD-HILL

> *That's your ignorance,*
> *And therefore shall that idiot still conduct you*
> *That knows no way but one, nor ever seeks it.*
> *If there be twenty ways to some poor village,*
> *'Tis strange that virtue should be put to one.*
> Middleton, *A Game at Chess*

HE TWO ESSAYS TO WHICH I have to respond are the products of wide knowledge and deep experience in editing and literary studies, and so they must be treated. However, the essays are also merely local manifestations of their authors' long-standing and persistent engagement with the editorial process: what we have are the public signs of a continuous private involvement with a complex set of interrelated issues. The essays are as much provisional as they are definitive and need to be situated within the context of their authors' other writings. This is too great a task to undertake here, as is a thorough discussion of the broader issues they mention. Furthermore, for these reasons and because I was asked to "respond" to the essays rather than to criticize them (in the adverse sense), I shall limit myself to remarks on some matters that seem to deserve notice.

E. J. Kenny gives a traditional and broadly acceptable definition when he writes that textual criticism is "the technique of restoring texts as nearly as possible to their original form" (676). The first step in this process is to find out what textual materials exist and to collect information bearing on their relationships (*recensio*), the second is to decide whereabouts original (i.e., not corrupted) text exists (*examinatio*), and the third is to correct the text closest to the original (*emendatio*). I rehearse these simplicities because those who read the essays by McGann and Shillingsburg as attentively as they demand will not find it easy to remember that editing is basically as straightforward as 1, 2, 3. (Here, like the two authors on occasions, I use *textual criticism* and *editing* synonymously). The cases with which they illustrate the interrelatedness of textual and literary criticism were chosen, no doubt, to illustrate the exceptional complexities with which a modern editor must deal.

It is doubtful that editors of classical texts encounter such problems very often. Kenny states that the concern of the textual critic "is with the reconstruction of what no longer exists" (676), i.e., a text purged of the corruptions invariably attendant on transmission. On the other hand, a modern work may survive in a variety of bibliographical forms (e.g., manuscripts, typescripts, trial printings, periodical and book printings) that supply extensive information about its genesis and evolution. The editor's concern then is not so much to remove transmissional corruptions (though he must do that too) as to decide what form or forms of the work he should transmit in his edition. For instance, McGann summarizes the bibliotextual situation of Rossetti's *The House of Life* and gives no information about the extent to which successive printings may have corrupted the text. His principal concern is to decide "how would it be presented?"— "it" being the seven versions written or published between 1869 and 1904, with another radial tradition based on the 1870 version that was begun with the Tauchnitz edition of 1873. The alternative methods of presenting this material in a critical edition that he considers are all reasonable options in the present development of editorial practice. It is interesting, however, that McGann represents the choice amongst *A* ("an ideal version"), *B* (diplomatic texts of each of a series of versions) and *C* ("one of two kinds of evolutionary texts") as "a practical editorial matter" that "impinges on the interpretation of the work." This of course is true: literary criticism depends on the kinds of information supplied by the editions from which it originates. However, McGann appears to maintain, editorial choice here is not governed by literary considerations, still less literary theory or the kinds of readings that conceivably might be generated by different editorial presentations of *The House of Life* but is simply a matter of editorial convenience. This observation might take advantage of McGann's wish to take up the effect rather than the basis of the editor's choosing *A* or *B* or *C*, but in any event he is correct: the presentation of textual material is very much a practical editorial matter.

However, that statement and the subsequent discussion of *HL* as "text," "poem," and "work" reveal the distinction that should be made between textual criticism and editing, one that is often overlooked even by writers as well-informed as McGann and Shillingsburg. The difference between them consists of the varying preponderance of literary criticism and also in certain practical matters particular to each activity. A reader who recalls the description of textual criticism given earlier and notes its substantial irrelevance to these two papers will recognize at once that textual criticism and editing are *not* synonymous, even if we adopt a definition of editing that most blurs the distinction. Kenny again reminds us that traditionally textual criticism is "designed to lay the foundations for the so-called higher criticism, which deals with questions of authenticity and attribution, of interpretation, and of literary and historical evaluation" (676). These are all matters conventionally treated of in editions although not exclusively there. (And not all textual criticism is published in the form of editions). When McGann examines which of the versions of *HL* to represent in an edition he is "doing" higher criticism: presumably he has already found the witnesses, determined their originality, and purged their errors. No one validly, I believe, when establishing a text, examines readings or offers conjectural emendations with their likely critical reception as the foremost consideration, but the utility of an edition to readers is an important concern for an editor, as McGann's paper illustrates. The *choice* of which authorized or original texts are to be printed in full in an edition is determined primarily by literary concerns; the *method* of presentation is a practical editorial choice.

Why is this so particularly in the case of Rossetti's *HL*? Because McGann has identified the different combinations of sonnets as versions: from the different textual apparitions of *HL* he has located certain recurrent patterns of similarity and difference and situated those patterns in literary history, assigning each of them as a distinctive literary value. The basis for the distinction between a variant state of text and a version of a work is appraisal of the meanings of the verbal differences and the value that is put on them in relation to other forms or states of the work. An editor may choose to print "the entire texts of all authoritative versions of works when the entire texts are essentially variant" (Pebworth and Sullivan 44) or to subordinate the record of revisions by including it in a textual collation to a single authoritative text. There are other ways of dealing with authorized variations, amongst which an editor will choose for practical convenience depending on the amount of the variation and the extent to which it encumbers the collation. Whatever disposition of text and record of variations an editor chooses, the essential function of textual criticism to identify original or authorized text and subsequent authorized or unauthorized variations will have been served: the textual facts are not altered by the form in which they are presented to a reader. However, it may be objected, the experience of a reader who is obliged to reconstruct an authorial version of a work from the collational record given with a different version of the work is likely to be very different from that of a reader who is given access to reading texts of the different versions. (That the experience of both readers will differ from their experience of the *original* published forms of the versions, if they could find them, merely emphasizes my point.) The editorial disposition of texts responds to literary judgment because the editor anticipates the effect of one or the other arrangement of text on a reader: the textual facts of a bibliographical situation do not change with the rearrangement of editorial text and apparatus, but the value of the edition for literary criticism may be altered significantly, as McGann shows.

McGann observes in *A Critique of Modern Textual Criticism* that "editors and even textual theorists of modern literatures have shown almost no interest in the general history of their discipline" (10). We should recall then that the problem of revision has been long recognized in the classic literature of modern textual criticism, e.g., Greg's "Rationale" (386–87) and in editorial practice. Familiar to most readers are modern editions of versions of Langland's *Piers Plowman,* Sidney's *Arcadia,* Jonson's *Everyman in His Humour,* Wordsworth's *The Prelude,* to mention a few obvious examples. Greg himself edited Jonson's *Masque of Gipsies,* a work "performed in three different versions and preserved in five independent texts" (v), and as early as 1935 he wrote that "it may be legitimate to aim at a text suited to particular circumstances or a special occasion, or to seek after what an author actually wrote, or what he intended to write, or what we think he ought to have written" (Howard-Hill 272–73). McGann's recital of the complexity of the editorial history of *HL,* interesting as it is and as challenging to editorial judgment as it may be, does not introduce fresh issues.

Furthermore, his claim that certain kinds of editorial dispositions of textual materials facilitate different kinds of readings falls short of asserting that editions determine the kinds of readings. Historically that claim would be very difficult to support when we consider the variety of readings in recent years that have derived from the same edition of a work. Editions may help or hinder distinctive readings, but it is literary theory that determines the kind of reading that ensues. As for the alternative question—the extent to which literary theories may govern the kinds of arrangements of textual information an editor presents to readers— McGann gives no clear statement other than an appeal to an overarching "theory of texts" that seems to subsume theories of composition, editing, and literary criticism. However, it is not so fully articulated that discussion of it is possible. The proposition that literary theories might generate distinctive editions as well as readings is fascinating to contemplate: I hope it has been considered in the essays in this volume that I have not read. (Thomson's attempt in 1963 to demonstrate a relationship between Marxism and textual criticism [5]—exactly conceived—was perfunctory and unconvincing. Scholarly editing seems to offer a larger field for the interplay of competing ideologies since editing and textual criticism are based on an ideological assumption about the value of inscriptions.)

McGann is well known as the advocate of a view of editing characterized by the editor's responsibility to provide readers with meaning-constitutive information about the "social conditions of textual production." Shillingsburg on the other hand is associated less with advocacy of a certain kind of editing than the dispassionate (but not value-free) exposition and analysis of the different theories of modern editing. His own conception of the editorial function (or editorial functions) emerges gradually from the first part of his essay. If the reader's experience was like mine, the reader would have approved or raised objections to different statements about editing only to find that Shillingsburg disproved the statements and anticipated the objections himself. His treatment is so comprehensive that there does not seem to be room for anything else. For instance, he disposes of the notions that the text "belongs to the author," or "the enabling production crews," or to the reader, or to itself, or to the social process(es). The conclusion—that "these competing views cannot be melded into one as long as the underlying assumption about the goal of scholarly editions remains the establishment of a single finished-product text"—contemplates the further possibility, that the text belongs to everyone, but there is no future in that proposition.

It is surprising, however, that a critic as astute as Shillingsburg is did not consider the remaining possibility, namely, that the text belongs to the *editor*. As the purger of corruptions and restorer of sense, his function, like the author's, is creative; editorial conventions and the institutions within which editions are published produce texts that are significantly different overall from any that have existed previously. The editor reaches into the maelstrom of literary production and takes, molds and (re)produces *his* version of the author, works and all. Whose authority or responsibility can conceivably be greater than his, for his edition? His work is to be judged then on its fidelity to the principles the editor has professed in the introduction and the usual criteria of consistency, accuracy, and so on. It is a reasonable objection that this view displaces the concept of the "best edition" from the realm of theoretical discourse and critical examination and locates it in editorial practice and, of course, it is no help to an editor in deciding principles on which he should edit an author's works. But the concept of the "best edition" itself opens up a whole raft of indeterminable issues. Objections to locating the editor at the center of his own universe are not weighty in the context of modern arguments on behalf of diversity and plurality of editions, which Shillingsburg refers to.

Shillingsburg resolves "the polemics of competing, better ways to edit" by appealing to "the view that scholarly editions organize and present works of art primarily as *process* not primarily as *product*." This and his subsequent statement that "the same evidence cries out in different ways to different editors . . . according to the context they have chosen to privilege as the determiner of 'meaning'" obscures the special context in which these statements are acceptable. Even today, the greater part of printed works, even works of literary merit, survive in so few textual forms that it is simply not possible to edit them so as to provide any evidence of the composition process that brought them into being. For most printed works there is simply not enough surviving production information to provide textual critics with the choice of privileging different contexts. Furthermore, although texts are unstable (as Greg [259] observed before McGann, Shillingsburg, and I were born), they are not continuously unstable (even within a print run). An unstable text, or a text which, like Rossetti's *The House of Life,* was composed intermittently, presents itself to the reader in a series of stabilized products. The editor's initial relationship as textual critic to any one or all of these products remains as it has always been, that of a purifier of texts. Whatever attitude an editor may take to a work—the definition or recognition of which may be the product of evaluation of different textual forms—he cannot avoid the necessity to edit particular texts.

Shillingsburg's problematizing survey of alternative editorial attitudes brings him to a case in point, Thackeray's *The History of Henry Esmond*. That example will allow him "to show the connection between the interpretation of texts and the establishment of texts in order to demonstrate further the impossibility of editing correctly in a satisfactory way." The startling pessimism of that conclusion is continued into the discussion of the relation of "the principle of contexts" and emendation. The circularity he observes has been widely noticed (Thomson [44] provides an instance). His remarks are plausible and are appropriate to his argument, yet it is difficult to conceive in what editorial context they could be true. To take the most testing case: even if an editor had to choose between two authorial variants without the benefit of directional information, it is hard to conceive that a single variant would be so potent that it would definitively alter the interpretative context and yet could not be distinguished critically from its alternative. Also, emendation in such circumstances is a recursive process—though not infinitely recursive—and editorial emendations are not unalterable subsequently. Editors cannot allow lack of verifiability and uncertainty to undermine their capacity for judgment.

In asserting the necessity for editors to "know how to read" and to know "what effects editing has on reading," Shillingsburg identifies as the focus of his examination of *Henry Esmond* the higher functions of editing rather than of textual criticism in which, if literary criticism is evoked at all, it is restricted to a smaller domain. In fact, the priority he gives to Feltes's Marxist analysis of the production of *Henry Esmond* and McGann's social theory of texts eventually precludes the possibility of textual criticism: he would "select the first edition as copytext [but "selection" was *pre*determined by the edition's status as a "commodity book"], emend nothing, and present the novel as a commodity book with large margins, heavy paper, and expensive packaging." I assume that Shillingsburg is not serious in suggesting this kind of facsimile book production as a substitute for scholarly editing, but the question is moot: he does not accept Feltes's view of the novel. Instead, he concludes that there is no acceptable evidence that the novel's "themes or its production were determined or dominated by either a vested production tradition or an emerging public taste." *Henry Esmond* "belonged to" the author.

I have no grounds on which to disagree with Shillingsburg's analysis of the novel, particularly his conclusion that Esmond's professions of truthful speech are "ironically undercut" by Thackeray. However, I do have some trouble in understanding why "the interpretation we adopt determines the text we establish or edit." This seems more a matter of ideological choice than of necessity. On the general question, there seems to be a significant difference between the practices of an editor who says to the reader in effect: "This is how the available evidence suggests to me *Henry Esmond* should read; now get on and read it as you wish" and an editor who says, "This is how I have read *Henry Esmond* and I have edited it to show how right I was; prove my reading wrong." And it does not seem that the second editorial procedure is consistent with Shillingsburg's later aim "to organize and foreground richness" since it must inevitably restrict rather than enlarge the variety of interpretative readings. It may be that an editor who has deep understanding of the meanings of the text (work) would be more harmful than an editor who considered himself more a midwife than a parent.

In particular, I cannot understand why "our emendations policy will be documentary and conservative" if Feltes's view of the work is accepted, when Shillingsburg has previously dismissed the possibility of emendation. The rest of the paragraph is mysterious. Shillingsburg gives no examples of the emendations he conceives are possible; apparently they are the "scores of historical and plotting errors" identified in John Sutherland's Penguin edition. The 1858 Cheap Edition can be selected as copytext "because it was the most corrected in Thackeray's lifetime" (20), but that is a strange choice unless Thackeray himself had perfected his text. (There is no indication that versions are involved.) Elaine Scarry's interpretation of the author's ironic subversion of his narrator suggests the manuscript as copytext, but no reason is given. (Does it contain more subversive errors than the editions?) The choice of copytext is to be made, apparently, exclusively on critical grounds; because interpretation is paramount, there is no necessity for textual analysis.

Then the alternative copytexts are to be emended, the 1858 edition by correcting Thackeray's historical and plotting errors for him "as possible" (given such license what is *im*possible?) and the manuscript "so that it effectively undermines the narrator's credibility." In short, the editor will introduce more historical and plotting errors into the text. The possibility is rather horrific. However, no modern school or view of editing that I am familiar with would sanction editorial emendation of an author's factual or plotting errors, least of all when authentic alternatives are lacking. Shades of Bentley! The manuscript as well as the 1858 edition is protected by intentionality. If Shakespeare was really wrong to believe that Bohemia had a sea coast, an editor has no obligation to protect him from his ignorance. Consequently, the dilemma that Shillingsburg impales himself upon—to correct or not correct the errors as thwarting "authorial intervention" [*conj.* "intention"]—is illusory.

The conclusion of the essay—stridently polemical as it is—should not deter the reader from recognizing Shillingsburg's advocacy of a *special* kind of edition. Nevertheless, "editorial solutions that foreground multiple, unstable texts" seem to come close to the "all-purpose reading text" that he derided earlier since he defines them as rich texts that open up possibilities for literary criticism ignored (he claims) by editions that foreground a single text. Shillingsburg rightly emphasizes the mutual exclusivity of the competing theories of editing and bravely attempts to reconcile them under the double aegis of authorial intention and the social contract. However, his insistence that a scholarly editor is not a "rescuer and restorer" of texts and that editors "have been caught out trying to promote the purity of texts" leaves the matter of emendation in doubt. Of course misprints like "soiled" for "coiled" fish provoke and support critical interpretations of works, but if merely accidental collocations of words will satisfy the needs of literary critics, then editing is essentially unnecessary. Literary theories that emphasize the ambiguity, multivalency, and plurisignificativeness of textual utterances recommend a form of edition in which these textual properties are appropriately acknowledged. An edition that foregrounds "richness" is one such edition. Nevertheless, it seems that it would be important for critics who value these textual properties to know the source and (probably) the authority of the specific utterances on which critical attention is to be focused. Only the kind of textual criticism that results in the "establishment" of a text can furnish this information. It may be polemically advantageous for advocates of new forms of editing to denigrate and dismiss the fundamental functions of textual criticism, but ultimately it is irrational.

Most discussions of editorial theory, like the present essays on the relation of editing and literary theory, assume freedom to traffic in ideas. This is right but it is not enough. Editing aims at a product, even if the product is the representation of a process. It is, as McGann says, a collaborative and greatly institutionalized activity. McGann's discussion of his *Byron* illustrates the influence of production institutions on the edition that was published. Nevertheless, the extent that publishing institutions confine editorial practice—and thence to a debilitating extent render theoretical discussions nugatory—seems to me to be insufficiently recognized in these papers and in general.

An editor can be seen as an agent, self-appointed and underremunerated perhaps, but nevertheless one who "does something" for an author (or a body of works). Whereas composition usually but not invariably implies publication, the root meaning of editing (*edit,* from Lat. *editus,* p. participle of *edire,* to put forth, publish) identifies the editor's *essential* function as someone who introduces or reintroduces works into the public domain. An editor's task is not accomplished until his edition is published. However, generally speaking, an editor cannot even embark on an edition until he has acquired the sponsorship of a publisher. Publishers determine editorial choices tacitly by the assumption (made on both sides) that a new edition will conform to the convention and principles of editions previously issued by the publishing house, or explicitly when the edition is to conform to the requirements of a series or is subjected to contractual arrangements as to length and other matters. Hardly a modern edition is published outside series (e.g., Malone Society Reprints, Revels Plays, Oxford English Texts), for which editorial conventions are prescribed. I observe rather than complain that usually editors are not going to be able to publish multiple versions of established works or to adopt complex or novel arrangements of textual material without judicious consideration of economic and market forces. Hans Gabler's 1984 *Ulysses* may indeed be a laudable manifestation of an editorial theory that gives due weight to interpretative needs but I doubt whether the 1984 genetic text—of which Shillingsburg approves—would have reached print without the possibility of separately marketing the 1986 "single finished-product text"—of which Shillingsburg disapproves. I make these comments feelingly because I have the materials for an edition of a seventeenth-century play that survives in three versions (one the earliest example of English dramatic foul papers): the likelihood that a genetic (or any other) kind of edition of this play and the author's other dramatic works would be published is very small.

If the means of production exerts the dominant influence on published editions then, also, the possibility that editions could demonstrate the application of literary theories in any marked manner must be accounted remote. If I am correct, the marketplace, rather than demonstrating resistance to theory, shows resistance to *praxis*.

Reading McGann's and Shillingsburg's essays within the context of the last forty years' discussion of textual and critical theories, I am struck by the contrastive ironies that emerge from the conflict of ideologies. McKenzie led the advance of Bibliography into the domain of Literary Criticism and conquered it under the banner of Text. On the contrary, Shillingsburg now erects literary criticism as master of editing and allows editors no independence. Earlier, Fredson Bowers lectured literary critics on their indifference to the status of the texts they read, and their ignorance of the conditions that produced them. Now Shillingsburg (like McGann) reproves editors for their "misguided efforts to give literary critics 'unproblematical texts' about whose composition and production they can remain blissfully ignorant." So revolve the whirligigs of time.

Time was when literary criticism was "done" by men of culture and taste. The institutionalization of literary studies in universities and the concomitant professionalization of literary criticism led inevitably to the formulation of theories of composition, reading, and literary criticism in order to support and direct *praxis*. Textual criticism also was mainly untheorized before the middle of the nineteenth century and was institutionalized alongside literary criticism. These developments had interesting consequences for textual criticism. In early editing, emendation was mainly a matter of taste, and *de gustibus non est disputandum*. But later, with the development of theories of textual criticism, editions could be shown to be wrong from precept, independent of the editor's understanding of the works' linguistic milieu. Housman's excoriation of the application of the "best text" theory (36) is a good example. In the twentieth century, literary criticism, originally an important tool for the editors of classical and biblical texts for whom bibliographical evidence was not widely available, became subordinated to methodology. Methodology basically sought to get things right without the risk of individual critical evaluations. The assertion of the methodological basis of textual criticism, inescapably associated with scientific method, was preeminently an attempt to displace "taste" (i.e. unrationalized, nonideological editorial choices) with ideology. Subsequent derogation of textual methodology as "empiricist" and "positivist," which persists in McGann's essay, is partial and futile. The bibliographical elements of textual criticism necessarily operate on physical objects and cannot escape being empirical and positivist. (However, the truth of this does not prevent textual criticism from acquiring other characteristics as well.) Only an ideology that privileges immateriality over materiality can criticize textual criticism for employing the practices appropriate to its objective locus. Nevertheless, contemporary reaction to "science" and "positivism" must consequently reassert the importance of literary criticism for textual criticism, but a literary criticism not grounded on literary taste as before but on ideology, i.e., literary theory. This may authorize editions and, even more important for editors, establish a secure frame for the containment of editorial choices.

The necessary importation of literary theory into editing (or, the recognition of its influence there, if one wishes) raises questions too large for the essays to which I have responded to answer. One most important problem, given that there is vigorous competition amongst new literary theories and that several of them are fundamentally irreconcilable, is to determine the extent to which any of them can influence the production (rather than the reception) of an edition. Then, it would be interesting to learn how far an edition that had been prepared under the influence of any particular literary theory might differ from an edition prepared according to a different theory of literary criticism.

Finally, when competing ideologies or theories act to paralyze editorial judgment, it is good to be reminded of Schlözer's dictum, which Kenny characterizes as the "one universally valid principle of textual criticism" *cf Greetham* (677): each case is special. *P- 94*

Works Cited

Greg, W. W. *Collected Papers*. Ed. J. C. Maxwell. Oxford: Clarendon Press, 1966.

Housman, A. E. *Selected Prose*. Ed. John Carter. Cambridge: Cambridge UP, 1962.

Howard-Hill, T. H. "Playwrights' Intentions and the Editing of Plays." *Text* 4 (1988): 269–78.

Kenny, E. J. "Textual Criticism." *New Encyclopedia Britannica*. Chicago: Encyclopedia Britannica, 1988. 20:676–82.

McGann, Jerome J. *A Critique of Modern Textual Criticism*, 1983. Chicago: U of Chicago P, 1985.

Pebworth, Ted-Larry, and Ernest W. Sullivan II. "Rational Presentation of Multiple Textual Traditions." *Papers of the Bibliographical Society of America* 83 (March 1989): 43–59.

Thomson, George. "Marxism and Textual Criticism." *Wissenschaftliche Zeitschrift der Humboldt-Universität du Berlin Gesellschafts -und Sprachwissenschaftliche Reihe* 12 (1963): 43–52.

4

Textual Product or Textual Process: Procedures and Assumptions of Critical Editing

– cf
Shillingsburg
27 etc

PAUL EGGERT

HEN, HALF-LISTENING TO THE RADIO in February 1988, I hear the Australian minister for foreign affairs refer to "these calls for the death of the author" I immediately thought how blasé about the poststructuralist idea we are all getting when even a politician can refer to it with such easy acquaintance. But, as Senator Gareth Evans went on, I realized that the issue was in fact the Ayatollah Khomeini's death threat to Salman Rushdie. It was a brutal underlining of what, in a less strident form, is still a fact of life in the West: that, by and large, people continue to hold authors responsible for what they write and continue to read biographies of authors and artists and interviews with them.[1] But if that gives comfort I should hasten to say that neither form necessarily caters to preconceptions about the individuality and creative autonomy of the artist.

Even in Roger Berthoud's recent, rather defensive biography of the sculptor Henry Moore, the preconception is clearly in trouble. Moore's sculptures are such a familiar sight partly because he was long-lived, a shrewd businessman not incapable of sharp practice, and well organized as a producer, his assistants in his studios at Hoglands in Kent producing enlarged plaster copies of his small maquettes—the originals he made—with craftsmen in Berlin and Italy producing the versions in marble taken from the plaster copies, and often also producing and even finishing the casts in bronze. The extent of his supervision varied from his completely finishing off a plaster enlargement an assistant had brought to within two inches of where the surface would finally be, to making only a subtle adjustment in the angle of the head in a bronze casting prior to welding. This was in his mature years; in his old age he did less and less. The degree to which Henry Moore sculptures were actually the work of the artist is a nice question.

Certainly he was adamant that that all castings and copies were his property to dispose of. On one occasion an artisan in Italy employed to make large copies in marble of two of Moore's sculptures took it into his head to make an extra one of each for himself. The authorized two were to be sold in the usual way as sculptures by Henry Moore; the other two, though literally from the same artisan's hand, must have been considered by Moore to have been unauthorized fakes for he stormed down to Italy and took to them with a hammer (Berthoud 385).

To maintain that the first two copies were Henry Moore sculptures and the next two were not illustrates, neatly for editors, the unholy alliance of textual authority and textual property that underwrites our metaphors of purity and corruption used to characterize variant readings. The situation also points to a strain of sentimentality—a willed optimism—in the traditional notion of creative genius as an autonomous thing, only working through or possessed by individuals and manifested in their works of art. Distinctions between the terms *artist* and *artisan, art* and *craft* begin to blur as we allow our attention to stray past the finished work of art to encompass the actual facts of production. Berthoud's reiterated plea, that it does not matter much by which methods the end product is achieved provided it emerges as intended, ignores by a naive act of faith the production histories he has disturbingly and honestly cited; and the defense identifies the essence of the sculpture with the artist's intention, putting to one side the (inconveniently but indisputably) collaborative processes by which it came into being. The phrase "the work of his hand" is a potent metaphor related to the editorial term *autograph manuscript;* unfortunately it generates expectations that Moore's case usually did not substantiate.[2]

Leonardo da Vinci was one of the first to claim special privileges for the artist. In his notebooks he is a propagandist for a contemporary change in social status for craftsmen-artists; he wants to claim that the occupation of painting—"which is the sole imitator of all visible works of nature"—is that of a gentleman, whereas sculpting, a strenuous and dirty manual skill, is that of a tradesman (quoted in McMullen 52–53). At the beginning of the sixteenth century "religious pictures were still being produced under contracts that specified the traditional details and colors that were wanted, and allegories were often painted according to programs that were supplied by the patrons" (McMullen 50). But change was in the air; a demand became fashionable for paintings and statues that allowed the artist to demonstrate his talents, or virtu. Roy McMullen speculates that Leonardo's deliberately enigmatic rendering of the Mona Lisa was an attempt at a purely personal creation, teasingly untied to established iconographic traditions. In this situation the only way of understanding the painting, he argues, is to investigate its tangled history of intertextual relationships with other paintings—with copies and adaptations taken from it by painters visiting Leonardo's studio while it was in its probably very long period of gestation, and with further and later developments of those copies.

"Works of art," McMullen observes, "like people, often look enigmatic merely because they are marked by past lives—and discarded accessories—of which we know nothing" (66). This same assumption lies behind the recent Rembrandt exhibition at the National Gallery in London, one of the most well attended the gallery has ever mounted. The brief was fascinatingly simple: to use new techniques of X-raying paintings so as to allow partial recovery of the early attempts and false starts underlying the painting on the surface. Early versions of the composition of the subject, and a cross-section of the colors used, could be seen, and in some cases the place where Rembrandt's own work started and that of assistants finished could be identified (see Bomford, Brown and Roy). But clearly the object of fascination for the crowds of visitors was that such well-known paintings could be seen anew by recovery of part of their production history. People could see it for themselves. Process could be appreciated together with the finished and familiar product.

The economics of cultural production have for a very long time, perhaps always, tended to narrow our attention as viewers of works of art (or readers of works of literature) to the object that would sell most readily: the finished product. The idea has become so thoroughly naturalized that it has helped in turn to naturalize exaggerated doctrines about individual inspiration and execution, doctrines born probably in the Renaissance but of course later greatly stimulated by the climate of Romanticism. Such doctrines sanction the isolation and enshrining for canonical analysis of the finished state of classic works of art and literature, helping to foster distorted notions of the artist, the work, and the processes of creative production.

This is the lost innocence which the recent attackers of Hans Gabler's edition of *Ulysses* seem to be hankering after.[3] Not far below the surface of the various reviews and articles which appeared in 1988 a basic intolerance can be detected. It reads to me as something of a knee-jerk reaction, a resentment at having the sacred turf encroached upon—not by aggressive literary theorists this time, but by editors who, in the past, could have been trusted to resurface that turf reliably and let critics get on with the game. But now the editors are wanting to expose the textual subsoil as well. Irritation is revealed in the language used by Roger Shattuck and Douglas Alden in their review in the *TLS* of some new editions of Proust's *À la recherche du temps perdu*. Their praise is of the begrudging kind; they refer to the "impressive yet labyrinthine machine" offered by one edition, to another's system of notes as "an imposing intellectual gadget," and to various kinds of "scholarly paraphernalia": praise offered with one hand is withdrawn with the other (640–41). But the complacency of their point of view emerges in their comment that one edition of *Swann's Way* "provides the ideal form in which to read Proust—large type, a comprehensive introduction, all the notes one needs, and two red ribbons. Every Proust-lover should have one such handsome volume" (641). The red ribbons give the game away; despite the eminence of the two Proustians, one can detect here no real interest in or even tolerance for the new stimuli and information bibliography might offer. Although they profess marked interest in a 138-page deletion Proust made in *Albertine disparue,* they will not allow it to alter their understanding of the boundaries of the text. They refer to the deletion as "Proustian apocrypha" and declare that the function of good Proust editors should be "to tell us how far the true text of *[À la recherche]* extends and where the ruins begin. . . . Proust's most miraculous accomplishment was to create out of a confusing succession of abandoned and recuperated projects a single work" (641). This endorsement of miracles strikes me as an act of faith; the reviewers' desire, apparently, is for the unambiguous transcendence of product—"the single work"—out of process, for the innocence (in an older terminology) of the Verbal Icon, an innocence to which editors are *still* supposed to give their sacerdotal blessing.

Well, I suspect the reviewers are not going to get it, or at least not for much longer. That is not my sense of where modern editing is going—although the sort of comfort they want has traditionally, if unintentionally, been provided by critical editions. That comfort—whence it springs and how editors have traditionally provided it—are what I wish to reflect on in the first half of this paper. Having, as it were, done an apprenticeship editing *The Boy in the Bush* in a Complete Works series of D. H. Lawrence, I fell the need to step back a few paces and cast a deliberately skeptical eye on the habits of language and thought, and the practices, of modern scholarly editing—which has, of course, seen as its highest aim the establishment of a reliable reading text: a single, finalized textual product. The danger of a deliberately skeptical stance is unfairness, but I think of it as a tactical necessity if a genuine rethinking is to happen.

The great series of editions of American literature is perhaps the first model which comes to mind. The aim was assumed to be the cleaning up and thus preservation of the texts of the canonical works of American literature. Editing the work of literature would be like restoring an old painting whose overlayers of varnish and smoke discoloration would be stripped away to reveal the true object. The job when completed would have been done once and for all; government funds poured in to finance this heady ideal. After a rigorous collation of surviving states of a work, a reading text—that is, a single, finalized text—was prepared by choosing one state (often an early one) as base text, incorporating into it all revisions for which the author was deemed to have been responsible and also correcting other readings deemed to be errors.

With a scientific rigor, texts were in this way to be rid of "contamination" and made "pure": the newly established text without the apparatuses would be available for republication in student and popular editions; and New Critical analysis, its working methods essentially unchallenged, could then proceed, confident that comments on the sensitive phrasing or rhythmic movement of a particular line of poetry or prose would not turn out to be the ingenious emendation of a typesetter. The critical edition itself would sit on library shelves in splendid isolation; those opening it would find its apparatus designed to attest to the honesty and probity of the editor by having, usually as its first apparatus, the list of editor's emendations allowing the reader to follow, and contest if he wished, every emendation the editor had made to the base text (MLA 8–9). A collation of substantive variant readings might follow, though rarely one for accidentals. But no adjudication between what was authorial and what was not was attempted in the apparatus, so that the reader was faced by a forbidding list containing authorial revisions jostling for shoulder room with compositional and scribal trivia. Excavation was difficult, so that it was easier for the reader to accept the positivist assumptions of the edition's working methods and retreat to the safety of the CEAA-attested reading text.

The child of a positivist age, textual bibliography intimates that it has no limiting context, but that the scientific habits which it aims to implement—being utterly rigorous, systematic and as far from subjective as possible—should guarantee its trustworthiness. Editions can be faulted if these criteria are not met: for example, if the collation has not been done accurately. Willfulness or impressionism on the part of the editor are condemned, for there is assumed to be an absolute distinction between author and editor—the editor is supposed to be the servant of the author's intentions, not a co-writer.

Even if the ideal of objectivity had not been generally discredited in scientific circles as impossible of achievement, some potentially disruptive implications of the reigning editorial ideals had all along been lurking outside the circle of light. I refer to the worrying facts: that the editor creates an eclectic text that has had no prior historical existence; that it is a synchronic representation of a textual process that was in fact diachronic, in some cases spanning in composition and revision as many as thirty or forty years; and that the edited text was not ready by the author's contemporary audience *or* seen by the author. Thus it can only be a collaboration of author and editor—which the American habit of making the list of editor's emendations the primary apparatus implicitly confirms. To me, the editor's claim to be able to work out and restore what the author intended to write had he or she had perfect control over the production of the work—that is, the doctrine of final intentions—does not satisfactorily counter these objections. For one thing the doctrine sanctions a fairly strict replacement by the editor of earlier readings by the author's chronologically later revisions—assuming that there was no miscopying. Under this convention, revision is accorded the same importance as composition despite the likelihood that the author will often have been more intently engaged with the text when first writing it. Put another way, composition starts from scratch whereas revision is done to an existing text; at the time of revision the author is subject to a crucial textual influence—the existence of a manuscript—that was lacking when he or she first put pen to paper. "Revision," of course, is another submerged editorial metaphor (it is distinguished from the author's "correction" of scribal miscopyings); "revision" implies a "reseeing" of the text when the author may only, in a given instance, have been scanning and not involved at anywhere near the requisite depth. D. H. Lawrence put the distinction this way when giving advice in a letter to Mollie Skinner: "Write when there comes a certain passion upon you, and revise in a later, warier, but still sympathetic mood" (21 April 1925; Moore 840). To treat the (textual) results of a passion and a mood as the same (as you pretty well *must* in traditional editing) is the price of editorial consistency.

There are other editorial metaphors and habits of argument that also point to the limitations of the modern eclectic edition. They range from its characteristic nineteenth-century bourgeois metaphors of filial descent, textual purity, and corruption to an attempted invisibility on the part of the editor; from a desire for brevity and a preference for foregrounding factual evidence and keeping expression of belief or impression modestly in the rear, to a marshaling of evidence so that the appearance is given that the only possible, or only defensible, or the *inevitable* conclusion has been reached. I call this the rhetoric of strenuous inevitability. The aim is to shepherd the reader into a position where no other conclusion seems reasonable—whereas in fact different procedures, different editorial choices, as Peter Shillingsburg argues, might also be reasonable if there were a realization and open declaration in both cases of what critical ends the edition was serving (*Scholarly Editing*). However, the rhetoric of modern editions characteristically implies that the edition is not serving any critical ends, but is above and beyond them.

Take explanatory notes for instance. The aim is said to be to explain what is obscure to the average reader, to document biblical, literary, and historical allusions, and so on. The usual method is to appeal to fact by providing a citation, quotation, dates, or a recapitulation of what, in the particular case, is generally accepted to be true; the editor will have his or her literary critical opinions but he must keep them to himself. However, I have come to be suspicious about the factualness of "facts." Indeed I rather doubt there are any, at least in the absolute sense. In compiling explanatory notes one finds that historians quote other historians who quote original documents which, when one tracks them down, turn out to be contested personal interpretations of contemporary events. I have learned to think, with Sir Philip Sidney, of the historian as "loaden with old mouse-eaten records, authorising himself (for the most part) upon other histories, whose greatest authorities are built upon the notable foundation of hearsay" (105).

Textuality is inescapable it seems; even birth and death certificates are writings that offer opportunity for deception about age or varnishings of social status. At every turn interpretation is unavoidable for the editor. The decision of which readings to gloss is itself an intervention and the result of a more or less reasoned choice subserving a notion of what is important in the text. And it is not, I think, generally recognized that precise and concise wording—generally taken as the ideal in explanatory notes—is a calculated art allowing the editor to bring the reader to the very brink of seeing the point he or she wishes to make, but without actually stating it: this is another example of the scholarly rhetoric in action.

Editions' procedures may have been "naturalized," but they are not natural. This does not prove that the procedures are invalid, but it does strongly suggest that they are neither inevitable nor ideologically inno-cent, and that they take color and character from the contexts they inhabit. Until recently the context most usually overlooked was the commercial one. The inordinate length of time critical editions usually take to prepare might seem to place them beyond the pale of commercial considerations since they are clearly not done to make a fast buck. But they constitute nevertheless an intervention in the literary critical, teaching, and general book-reading marketplaces. The text that the editor constructs will be reproduced in cheap editions; it will make its way onto undergraduate and then secondary school syllabuses; and in time it may represent the work—it may *be* the work—for the bulk of its actual and potential readership. The editor may intend the intervention to be solely intellectual in character, but it is ineluctably economic as well. The original prepara-tion of an edition that is part of a series will have been preceded by negotiations between the publishing house, the series' general editor, and the owners of the copyright; and decisions about the most desirable layout and presentation of textual matter are likely to have been con-strained in advance by commercial pressures.

The burden of these observations is this: far from being free of con-textual constraint and coloration, critical editions only exist within them. Indeed the physical format of the book, to adapt a phrase of Peter Shil-lingsburg's, provides a situational context for any actual reading of it ("An

Inquiry" 65). In the case of a critical edition its manner of declaring the seriousness and respectability of the enterprise, its place within a series, its handsome and sober hardback presentation, all send signals to the reader. And before the reader opens the volume decisions for the series have been made, in the light of commercial considerations, which have established the volume's hierarchy or delimitation of textual readings. This hierarchy imposes, in turn, constraints on the readership's access to the work and therefore their knowledge and understanding of it. No such decisions are "natural" or inevitable; all are open to questions and should be questioned.[4]

My point, let me emphasize, is not that the eclectic edition no longer has a place but that it should not be considered the automatic or the natural choice; if it is proposed for the solution of the textual problems presented by a particular work, then it needs also to be defended in light of objections to it. We should not accept as an unargued given that a single textual product must be extracted from what was often a series of fascinatingly rich engagements of the author with the developing work. Warrant for doing so has usually been taken to be an author's bending his efforts toward publication, and thus preparing a single sequence of words and punctuation—a potentially saleable product—for the publisher. But while readings introduced by the author's coadjutors in the commercial production process—scribes, compositors, and editors—are treated as errors or contamination, the determining commercial context that required a single reading text is accepted and duplicated (in a cleaned-up form) without question. The editor reads each state of the work before editing it; he or she is often the first and last reader to do so. The pity of it is that a range of stimuli to a new understanding of the imaginative activity of the author as the literary work developed from state to state is buried in the apparatus at the back of the book, doomed to an unregarded senescence.

The conventional single-reading-text critical edition has reinforced what I believe was always an illusion: that the writer wrote a series of finished and thus essentially separate works in which his or her development or deterioration can be adequately studied. This is what I think of as the mountain peaks method of literary criticism: seen from afar, the works, like mountain peaks, are beautifully distinct—so what better method would you *want* to adopt but to treat them as individual works? But seen close up—

and the editor is forced to see them close up—the clear distinctions you saw from farther away begin to dissolve. The materials of which the peaks or "finished" literary works are composed are seen to be interlinked, symbiotic, and in continuous, interrelated flux. Once reveal and make available for the reader the earlier states of a novel say, and this dense linkage would begin to become clearer, more obvious. But this kind of analysis is not encouraged by critical editions which intimate, by their very construction of a single reading text, that the work is sufficiently represented by it.

Textuality will be better understood, I believe, when it is opened out—not only when different textual states of a developing work (let us say, a novel) are compared to one another but also when elements of them are compared to other things the author was working on while the novel was in progress: reviews, poems or essays perhaps, letters, maybe short stories or early states of another novel also in progress. These relationships within and between the author's writings form, as it were, an *authorial* intertextuality, a continuum of authorship, itself part of a larger biographical flux that takes its changing shapes in response to the pressures of the social, cultural, and other environments the author inhabits. The author's ability to organize, shape, and articulate or otherwise respond to those influences is manifested in the activity of authorship which is the part of that continuum we can most readily engage with. Editing intervenes in this activity; it privileges the agent and the moment of writing, and it documents the writing process. Or, rather, it has the capacity to document the process; but its habit hitherto of constructing a single reading text and providing an apparatus to serve *it* has catered to the illusion that imaginative activity gives rise in almost every case to a stable textual product. This has in turn fueled, by failing to challenge, the poststructuralist tendency to marginalize the author in order to give a free rein to the multiplicities of textuality and reconstruction. Editing procedures have tended to cast into the background the knowledge that literary works are not fixed but are, rather, unstable and problematic from the very start. Literary works usually consist of multiple, often competing, texts in all of which the author may have been intimately involved. Editions containing full textual disclosure with its wealth of evidence of changes of mind while the work was in progress point eloquently to the authorial agency of textuality. For the reader of such an edition the notion of authorship is unavoidable, and the manifestations of the author's imaginative activity too intriguing to be tempted to analyze them away.

The various poststructuralisms have argued for other kinds of textuality than the one I am describing; they have tried to show how textual meaning is infinitely deferred, unstable, or indeterminate. According to the practitioners of the New Historicism, because texts are constituted by interventions—critical readings, textual establishments, and other reconstitutions reflecting the ideological forces of a historical period—there can be no such thing as the ideal text. That is something that claims to rise above history, which is impossible. So far so good, but these theorists then pursue their insight about the historically context-bound nature of literary works to the point where they want to disconnect the author from textual production altogether. Jonathan Goldberg, for instance, refers to "the texts that we miscall Shakespeare's but which are and always have been the product of textual and critical interventions" (214). In a 1988 issue of *Textual Practice* Margereta de Grazia objects to what she calls the "boundaries" and "limitations" (81, 80) imposed by accepting the author as the source of textual authority—as what she calls, quoting Foucault (159), "the principle of thrift." She wants a form of edition that treats the text as "a wide array of collective and extended contributions and transformations" (82). She very carefully does not say collective authorship, because for her the text is a site of ideological conflict in which the author has no especially privileged place. However, if she were to set to work and edit from this premise, then she would be faced, as all editors are, with dealing with a diaspora of textual traces, all the responsibility of various people. The traces, in sixteenth-and seventeenth-century writings, are found in successive printed editions with stop-press corrections, and sometimes there are also foul papers and prompt copies or fair copies extant; in later periods, autograph manuscripts and corrected and uncorrected typescripts and proofs may be available.

Shakespeare (I mean the actual person, not the author we "reconstruct") wrote and probably either revised or wrote different versions of some of his plays that were subject to partial reconstitution on stage, in actors' memories, and on subsequent commitments to paper, so that what he originally wrote is not recoverable in full. De Grazia makes a great deal of the fact that Shakespeare's manuscripts are lost; she claims that they are a convenient idealism used by editors, a metaphysical mystification used to prop up the authorial source of textual authority. But if printing history confirms as a norm the progression from manuscript to stage to print, with various intervening complexities of transmission, then the lost manuscript is an idealism only in the technical sense that it is no longer extant. In comparison, de Grazia's view of the text as an ideological site is the idealism here; and while she contests the need for "boundaries" in editing, she herself puts the "single authorial consciousness" out of bounds (81).

Editing without boundaries is also an idealism, for basically there are four choices facing the editor, each with a boundary: either to design the edition so as to try to get as close as possible to what Shakespeare wrote (two or more texts of a play may be necessary); to try to exhibit as fully as possible the textual traces of the scribes, compositors, adapters (all are "involved"), and editors involved in the transmission of his texts; to document both sources of textual variation in a variorum rather than a critical edition; or, lastly, to mix and match the different versions according to the editor's aesthetic preferences. If the editor chooses the last alternative, then he will have to convince readers that his aesthetic preferences are more interesting than Shakespeare's likely textual decisions and more interesting than the habits and preconceptions of Shakespeare's contemporaries and his adapters, publishers, and editors of later periods. But at the end of the day textual traces are what the editor will have to sort, distinguish, and exhibit—whether possessed of a theory or not.

A New Historicist edition would presumably take the second alternative, documenting what Shakespeare's textual coadjutors found it necessary to adapt, rewrite, or transform as the work went through its various stages of transmission—that is, the interest would lie in what Shakespeare wrote only in its interactions with other people. I am assuming the need for a critical edition rather than a simple reprint. New Historicists cannot avoid critical editing because of the fact of multiple typesettings and expurgated and abridged versions all being available: all having, that is, historical positioning: having different audiences and different production histories. Not to edit critically would be a confession of helplessness, for New Historicists as well as anyone else. The editorial effort—a considerable one—would be to identify and distinguish the probable sources of those textual transformations and display their different manifestations over a period of time (say, till 1619; or perhaps concentrate only on the eighteenth century). "Shakespeare" (the reconstructed historical text) is such a capacious and wonderful phenomenon that such editions might well offer the critic interested in political and cultural cross-currents valuable stimuli for reflection. But as an editor dealing with any given textual trace, an individual person would have to be deemed responsible (though usually he could not be named, his function in the means of textual production could). The person may have been acting as the functionary for decisions taken corporately (say, the secretary of a troupe of actors, or a press-corrector implementing the policy of a printing house), but in either case the editor can only go by what has been written—its actual or inferred material presence. Hypothesizing intention in explaining textual variation would be part of the New Historicist editor's job too, except the focus might be, say, the compositor's intention. Arguments leveled against traditional critical editions concerning the irrecoverability of (authorial) intention would not be avoided by the New Historicist editor who would have to face the fact that the compositor was just as dead as the author.

I have tried to imagine whether a New Historicist edition of a D. H. Lawrence novel would be useful, and I think the answer is, it might be—in one case at least. I refer to *Lady Chatterley's Lover* and also to its first version, *The First Lady Chatterley*. The publishing history of *Lady Chatterley* is a saga in itself. An edition set up to illustrate it would detail the eccentricities, ambiguities, and crazy contradictions caused by its first typesetting in Italy by printers who knew no English, its multiple piracies, its posthumous first English and American publication censored to satisfy customs authorities but authorized by the Lawrence estate, and finally its uncensored publication in the U.S. in 1959 and England in 1960, again authorized by the estate, as well as the other uncensored printings that were not authorized. The usual cut-off date for reporting textual variation in the apparatus of a Lawrence edition—his date of death—would be beside the point in an edition that sought to document the succession of textual transformations performed by the various publishers, printers, and legal representatives. I have a copy of *The First Lady Chatterley* set up in type and printed in Sydney in 1944 at the same time as the novel was first published in New York—it was evidently safer to publish locally than try to get it through customs. The novel was banned temporarily in New York, and the Australian edition was separately censored by its publisher "to match local requirements," as the half-title page says. It was not published in England till 1972. Critics and literary historians interested in what could and could not be printed in the three countries in 1944 might get some use out of an edition that documented the novel's production history.

If the editor decided to privilege the production side in a novel that did not have the tang of banning to liven it up, what would such an edition have to offer the reader? Were it a Lawrence novel, one could say with certainty, because of the abundant evidence we now have, that the reader would find that typists and typesetters were subject to the usual fallibilities of eyeskip, inattention, and the instinct to correct to conventional usage and house style; that businessmen-publishers and even typesetters censored many short passages of Lawrence's prose; that magazine editors chopped up his short stories to suit their own assessment of likely audience reaction and available space in the issue; and that in the case of *Sons and Lovers* a publisher's reader reduced the length of the novel by 10 percent. All these influences, at least on the general level, might offer useful examples for the reader interested in the history, economics, and sociology of book production, in the theory and practicalities of collaboration, in the history of a standard English as reflected in the house styles of various publishers on either side of the Atlantic, in the rise of syntactic punctuation and its displacement of the older rhetorical style, and in the history of taste and the depiction of sexuality.

This interest might hold on the general level, but I am unconvinced that it would hold on the local—which is where an edition must prove itself. Once the reader had seen the predictable kinds of eye-skip operating, would he be any the wiser if he accepted the edition's invitation to read and consider the next thirty cases? Change eye-skip in that question for the house styling of punctuation[5] and it becomes obvious that its documentation would be overwhelmingly otiose—there would be a couple of thousand cases in *The Boy in the Bush*. I find it difficult to believe, however unfreighted of Romantic ballast the notion of authorship has become, that many readers would prefer an edition that foregrounded the production side. I doubt that many would wish to forgo the benefits of however impaired contact with what is usually the most significant textual agency—the author.

If authorial agency remains the principal source of textual interest for readers, then given the reservations I have sounded about the status and characteristic rhetoric and practices of the modern critical edition, does it make sense to continue to prepare and publish them? My answer is, I think, a heavily qualified yes; but my qualifications may be more important than the yes. The first one, which Peter Shillingsburg's work has crystallized for a lot of people, is that the critical edition is indeed critical: that is, that it corresponds to a particular rather than inevitable notion of which text should be assembled from the diaphanous continuities and the opaque and confusing disruptions of composition, revision, and production. It is possible, then, for an eclectic edition to come clean as it were, acknowledging and defending its assumptions about text. But even if that were done, would critical editions *then* make sense?

In 1975 Hans Zeller pointed to a major deterrent against considering eclectic editions for the presentation of (especially) poetry. Each state of the text, he argued, forms a discrete semiotic system, and every time the poet comes back to revise the poem he creates a new system whose textual elements now take up a different system of relationships to one another. For the editor to select only the new changes made in each successive state and to incorporate them back into the first version is to treat those systems of relationships as if they had not existed for the poet as he revised each state. The same argument may also apply to the novel. When a novelist is presented for revision with a scribal, typed, or proof copy of his manuscript, he makes textual decisions—deletions, corrections of error, and additions—on a copy which may contain perhaps a thousand or more miscopyings, the bulk being ones of punctuation. According to the Zeller idea, the author's revisions are now tied to those copyist errors, making their elimination in an eclectic text questionable.

This argument is one that I find impresses me more on the general level than it does on the particular: the eclectic edition has found ways of making pragmatic adjustments that partially evade the argument's clutches. In the Cambridge University Press series for instance, where Lawrence has revised a state of the text later than the base text, the revised reading is preferred and the base text emended accordingly. Where Lawrence has revised a passage that had been miscopied, the editorial tendency is to reinstate if possible the earlier reading on the grounds that the novelist did not have the opportunity to revise his own work. But where such a revision is linked thematically to other changes, especially if they are nearby, then it will also be accepted. The beauty of this pragmatic compromise is that it takes into account the intermittent nature of the bursts of engagement with the developing text that Lawrence characteristically had. However, were this practice to be converted into a *principle,* then the eclectic edition would become impossible, for an argument along Zeller's lines could conceivably be put that almost any later revision in one state of the text was related to all the others in that state, and thus that any revision of any of those substantive readings in a later state could not supersede its earlier counterpart in the reading text for fear of breaching the relationships between them. But, at least in regard to fiction, eclectic procedures deal cleanly and, I think, sensibly with those instances where at a given place in manuscript, typescript, and proofs the author can be seen revising and re-revising a particular idea or expression within an otherwise invariant context. To accept Zeller's inhibiting argument and refuse to incorporate the last revision on the grounds that the second last relates to similar revisions elsewhere in that state which the editor has accepted is to ignore this obvious effort on the author's part to get that idea out right.

This is a fact that Hershel Parker in *Flawed Texts and Verbal Icons* is reluctant to admit: the eclectic edition, if intelligently handled, can produce an authorial text that has some claim to be represented as the culmination of a process of compositional development. When that process is tightly defined chronologically, it makes sense to say that the author maintained his involvement in it rather than returning to the text more or less as an outsider (as Henry James did when revising for publication the New York edition of his novels). In the case of *The Boy in the Bush*, Lawrence wrote the manuscript in California and Mexico from September to November 1923, revised the typescripts in January 1924, and the proofs—which have only sparse revision—in April. The revision of the typescripts involved the writing of a new last chapter, a radical adjustment to the characterization of the hero and the emergence of one of the women characters as a potential new heroine. These changes of mind on Lawrence's part can be traced to the effect on him of the people he met and what he was reading on his return to England in December 1923. He certainly kept control of the developing novel in its larger design—the culmination of which is embodied in the reading text I have established.[6] Chronologically of course it is a patchwork quilt—where Lawrence did not change the manuscript readings I have not changed them, but where he subsequently did, I have nearly always followed suit. While my reading text captures, I hope, a textual culmination in a way that no previous printing has done, it necessarily conceals the early and distinct conception of the novel Lawrence was evolving as he wrote the manuscript before returning to London from Mexico.

It is clear in this case that the textual apparatus becomes of crucial importance in documenting the concealed phase. Here I get to the second qualification to my tentative yes about whether it makes sense to persevere with critical editions. It seems to me that where a critical edition is committed to the production of a reading text readily transferable into ordinary commercial format, then of all the single texts that could be extracted from the processes of composition, revision, and production, the traditional eclectic text will at least be a worthwhile one. But as the critical edition is also intended to serve the literary critic interested in the compositional development of the work, the layout of the apparatus assumes an importance in the edition at least equal to if not greater than that of the text itself. Indeed it may be that, in years to come, it will be the textual apparatus (and perhaps the notes and introduction) rather than the established text itself that readers find most useful. The apparatus in the Cambridge Lawrence series represents an advance, I believe, on the usual American system. Operating independently of the CEAA, the series has developed, and refined to a remarkable extent, its own modes and procedures while sticking to a traditionally constructed reading text. Only one textual apparatus is presented, and it is a very economical record of all variants subsequent to the base text whether authorial or not, including any editorial corrections. Where an editorial correction coincides with that of one state of the text, then that state is given as the source of the reading—a way of minimizing the appearance (though not the actuality) of editorial involvement in the text and a response to the unwitting CEAA tendency to underline the involvement of the editor.

Most large editorial undertakings undergo an evolution in their understanding of their task. Though it has experienced some changes of personnel, the editorial board of the Lawrence series has always seen the primary aim to be the provision of reliable texts to which the apparatus would be strictly secondary. This reflects the fact that the Edition's *Prospectus for Editors* was published in 1977, and that the poststructuralist challenge to Anglo-American editing procedures did not begin to take effect till the early 1980s, further catalyzed by the publication of Hans Gabler's edition of *Ulysses* in 1984. In the early years of the Lawrence series—the late 1970s and early 1980s—it was felt that, where both a manuscript of a work and a later state that had been revised by Lawrence were extant, the later version should normally serve as base text; where that base text had miscopied Lawrence's punctuation in the manuscript, the manuscript readings would be retrieved, but there would be no systematic recording of (other) variant readings in the manuscript. The textual apparatus was to record chronologically forwards, not backwards: it would not, therefore, be complete. This may now seem difficult to defend, but the decision to prefer later-state base texts shortened the apparatus considerably and so saved setting and printing costs;[7] and anyway, it must have been thought, if the primary aim of the edition was to present a reliable reading text, what would be the point of providing the whole textual record of every state of the work?

By the time I presented my proposal to edit *The Boy in the Bush* in 1983, opinions were changing in the direction of full textual disclosure, with the result that the Cambridge apparatuses now usually allow full access to the developing work at every point—with the exception of certain categories of silent emendation.[8] Other refinements have come with time and a deepening understanding of the possible uses to which the apparatuses might be put. Initially they functioned as a way of checking what emendations the editor had made to the base text; later, after the reading in every state began to be given, it was realized that there was a point in recording all three readings a typescript can bear at any one point: the typed reading, Lawrence's revision, and the copyeditor's correction or house styling. In other words the edition now distinguishes (using appropriate symbols) between a state of the text and the sources of the text within that state. The recording is not just documentary but interpretative; the authorial is distinguished from the nonauthorial, thus helping to explain the editor's preferences in the reading text and allowing the reader to construct the sequence of alterations within the one state.

This is to say that despite the cramping constraints of having the apparatus serve the reading text, the series has been developing the apparatus into a recording instrument that gets at least within coo-ee of the ideal I would propose for a critical edition: one that would make it possible for the reader to know *both* the processes of composition and revision *and* the textual product that resulted. To know the work of literature as both textual process and product and to get into touch with the authorial flux it inhabits may be to know the familiar work anew. And it might be to know authorship more clearly too, without having to give adherence to exaggerated Romantic notions of creativity on the one hand, or to resort to poststructuralist destabilization on the other. We may come to appreciate the ways in which the text was unstable, unfinished, under the strains and pressures of its authorial location, all along.[9]

Notes

This essay is a revised version of a paper given at a conference, "Editing in Australia," in April 1989 (and published in its proceedings volume with the same name) at University College, Australian Defence Force Academy, Canberra.

1. Interviews with authors are a modern form dating, in England at least, only from the c. 1880s; biographies are older of course, but both forms are undergoing a boom in the poststructuralist era.

2. When Moore died all work on enlargements then in progress at Hoglands ceased as Moore had stipulated they should. Berthoud comments, "This gave the rather misleading impression that he had exercised some supervision in [the previous three years, following an operation]. It is true that from time to time an assistant would bring a working-model-sized piece into the sitting room and stand it on a table for him to see; and on occasion a large polystyrene model was trundled to the window for his inspection. But Moore was in no state to suggest or make any changes. 'Very good my boy,' he might say, pleased to know that the good work was going on" (417). The anecdote reveals an assumption underlying a lifetime's practice; doubtless artists' workshops have always been run much this way.

3. I cannot comment on the charge of inaccuracy in Gabler's transcriptions; wherever such a charge is sustained, no editor would argue with the need for correction. My concern is with questions of theory.

4. This does not mean I support the sort of objection raised by Shattuck and Alden (641) and John Kidd (32) in relation to the edition of *Ulysses,* and Charles Ross in respect of the Cambridge University Press (CUP) *Women in Love.* The allegation is that editors are players in a game primarily intended to establish a lucrative new copyright. In my experience academic editors are not usually so canny; certainly the Lawrence Works series, which is not in receipt of any governmental or university subsidies, does not make profit; but neither does it lose money. Its editors and general editors are all paid for their efforts, if far from handsomely. Of the sixteen volumes produced since the first one appeared in 1980, sales have usually been between 1,500 and 2,000, except for the newly discovered novel *Mr Noon,* which sold 10,000. When CUP decided to undertake the edition a contract was negotiated with the Lawrence estate (consisting of grandchildren of Frieda's first and third husbands; no money from the estate goes to any blood relative of Lawrence). The estate is ably represented by Gerald Pollinger, a well-known London literary agent. He spares no efforts to maximize income for the estate and was successful in his negotiations with CUP, who at first believed that the new edition would be genuinely popular. He secured a sizeable percentage of the royalties despite the fact that the copyright was about to run out (in 1980, for most but not all of the previously published material). In return CUP got what it had to have if the series was to run to completion: unlimited access for its editors to all Lawrence manuscript material and the right to publish without interference, competition, or further negotiation newly established texts of the complete works including the letters (a good percentage of which had never been published) and all other unpublished material. The estate and CUP claim that the eclectic texts constitute a new copyright; so far the claim has not been tested in court.

If the facts of the case with *Ulysses* are at all similar to the CUP example, then the commentators' allegations are a simplistic response to a situation that is more complex than they appreciate. They are in effect demanding not only a textual innocence (as I have argued) but a commercial one as well. This is to pose an impossible ideal and then fault the editions for failing to satisfy it.

5. Lawrence's publishers seem not themselves to have developed house styles; rather, printers did it for them.

6. See Introduction (Eggert, *The Boy in the Bush*) for the novel's composition and production history; Lawrence's manuscript is his rewriting of an unpublished novel by Mollie Skinner.

7. See the Kalnins, Vasey and Worthen editions.

8. Because the Lawrence Edition treats nonauthorial variation as textual corruption and thus of subsidiary importance, the decision was taken to shorten the apparatus by not including multiple instances of identical cases of house styling and other variants where the categories could be exclusively defined. The list of these, which is sometimes extensive, appears in the note on the text in each edition.

9

Works Cited

Berthoud, Roger. *The Life of Henry Moore*. London: Faber, 1987.

Bomford, David, Christopher Brown, and Ashok Roy. *Art in the Making: Rembrandt*. Catalogue of an exhibition. October 1988–January 1989. London: National Gallery Publications, 1988.

The Cambridge Edition of the Works and Letters of D. H. Lawrence: Prospectus and Notes for Volume Editors. Cambridge: Cambridge UP, 1978 [November 1977].

de Grazia, Margareta. "The Essential Shakespeare and the Material Book." *Textual Practice* 2 (1988): 69–86.

Eggert, Paul. "Textual Product or Textual Process: Procedures and Assumptions of Critical Editing." In *Editing in Australia*. Ed. Paul Eggert. English Dept. Occasional Paper 17. University College ADFA, Canberra. Distributed by New South Wales UP, 1990. 19–40.

———, ed. *The Boy in the Bush*. By D. H. Lawrence and M. L. Skinner. Cambridge: Cambridge UP, 1990.

Farmer, David, Lindeth Vasey, and John Worthen, eds. *Women in Love*. By D. H. Lawrence. Cambridge: Cambridge UP, 1987.

Foucault, Michel. "What Is an Author?" *Textual Strategies*. Ed. Josué Harari. Ithaca: Cornell UP, 1979. 141–60.

Gabler, Hans Walter, ed. *Ulysses: A Critical and Synoptic Edition*. By James Joyce. 3 vols. New York: Garland, 1984.

Goldberg, Jonathan. "Textual Properties." *Shakespeare Quarterly* 37 (1986): 213–17.

Kalnins, Mara, ed. *Apocalypse*. By D. H. Lawrence. Cambridge: Cambridge UP, 1980.

Kidd, John. "The Scandal of *Ulysses*." *New York Review of Books* 35 (30 June 1988): 32–39.

Lawrence, D. H. *The First Lady Chatterley*. Sydney: Peter Huston, 1944.

McMullen, Roy. *Mona Lisa: The Picture and the Myth*. Boston: Macmillan, 1975.

Modern Language Association. *Statement of Editorial Principles and Procedures: A Working Manual for Editing Nineteenth-Century American Texts*. New York: Modern Language Association, rev. ed., 1972.

Moore, Harry T., ed. *The Collected Letters of D. H. Lawrence*. 2 vols. London: Heinemann, 1962. Vol. 2.

Parker, Hershel. *Flawed Texts and Verbal Icons*. Evanston: Northwestern UP, 1984.

Ross, Charles. "The Cambridge Lawrence." *Essays in Criticism* 38 (1988): 343–51.

Shattuck, Roger, and Douglas Alden. "Searching for the True Text." *Times Literary Supplement* 10–16 June 1988: 640–41.

Shillingsburg, Peter. "An Inquiry into the Social Status of Texts and Modes of Textual Criticism." *Studies in Bibliography* 42 (1989): 55–78.

———. *Scholarly Editing in the Computer Age: Lectures in Theory and Practice*. English Dept. Occasional Paper 3. Duntroon, Aus.: Faculty of Military Studies, University of New South Wales, 1984. 2d ed. Athens: U of Georgia P, 1986.

Sidney, Sir Philp. *An Apology for Poetry or The Defense of Poesy*. Ed. Geoffrey Shepherd. Manchester: Manchester UP, 1973.

Vasey, Lindeth, ed. *Mr Noon*. By D. H. Lawrence, Cambridge: Cambridge UP, 1984.

Worthen, John, ed. *The Prussian Officer and Other Stories*. By D. H. Lawrence. Cambridge: Cambridge UP, 1983.

Zeller, Hans. "A New Approach to the Critical Constitution of Literary Texts." *Studies in Bibliography* 28 (1975): 231–63.

5

The Manifestation and Accommodation of Theory in Textual Editing

D. C. GREETHAM

 SHORT WHILE AGO, AT A SESSION called "Sex, Text, and Context," I asked the American historians of the Association for Documentary Editing foregathered at their annual convention in Charlottesville whether they could envisage what would happen to the material manifestations of textual theory and practice—the textual page, the apparatus, notes, and so on—if a genuine feminist ethic were to be employed in the construction of historical textual editions. The response of the panelists and audience was a mute incomprehension: how could such a question be asked, and what did it mean anyway? Pressed, I suggested that one such manifestation might be the inversion (or subversion) of the authority of the "central," intentionalist text of the textual page by the incursion of the "rejected authority" of textual variants, perhaps sporadically or even globally, in a dissipation of the traditional hierarchical structure of the eclectic edition. In the typical eclectic edition, the privilege embodied in the textual page proper is set against the repressed role of the rejected variants, which are usually printed in smaller type, sometimes at the bottom of the page, but often, in these cost-conscious days, relegated to the outer fringes of the edition, at the end, or even in a separate volume, to be purchased only by the textually curious while the real business of scholarship and criticism begins and ends with the received text of the textual page proper. Again, mute (or not so mute) incomprehension. Why

would anybody want to do such a thing? Well, the exchange might not have been productive then, and I was, in any case, somewhat aware of the political impropriety of seeming to question the feminist credentials of a mostly female panel by suggesting how a feminist credo might work. But in a session on "Sex, Text, and Context," with its highly provocative title, the speculative interrogation of feminist textual principles and methods did not seem out of place, even to a professional organization that considered feminism in editing to be largely a question of an affirmative-action response to the subjects and personnel of editing: as long as one had balanced editions of the great white fathers with those of female historical figures with suitably voluminous private papers to be published, and as long as one had made sure that some of the editorial staff (and ideally a general editor or two) were women, then the feminist agenda had been encountered and satisfactorily dealt with. This was a reduction of ideology to the marginalia of editing—its demographic breakdown—but such a concern should not be disparaged, especially in a discipline like textual scholarship, which is still overwhelmingly staffed by males.

But the demographics notwithstanding, the greater intellectual and ideological problem resides in some form of that innocent question asked of the ADE: how does a textual theory impinge upon the actual business of editing? What negotiations with author and text(s) must be undertaken to reflect this ideology? And how may we observe the manifestation of the theory in the concrete formal features of an edition? All too frequently, textual critics have assumed that there is really *no* theory behind the mechanics of editing, that constructing a text is wholly empirical, that operations may be conducted well or ill, but that there is no need to justify the operations themselves, only their particular success in the present case. Thus, until very recently there was an automatic assumption in Anglo-American editing that the recovery of an author's intentions was the sole aim of the editorial enterprise, and the only room for editorial maneuvering or negotiation was whether these intentions could best be fulfilled by, say, an adoption of a Greg-Bowers-Tanselle attitude to copytext or that of a Thorpe-Gaskell, often simplified to the intentionality of initial accidentals versus the intentionality, or what Shillingsburg calls the "expectations" (*Scholarly Editing* 44–55), of publication normalization. Such an argument took for granted that auctorial presence and desire were données of the editorial responsibility, leaving only the question of where this presence and desire could be most easily arrested and displayed.

But the times are more contentious now, as the professional and public debate over both Jerome J. McGann's "social textual criticism" (Howard-Hill; McGann, "Bones," "Critical Editing," *Critique*, "Monks and Giants"; Tanselle, "Historicism," 19–27) and Hans Walter Gabler's edition of *Ulysses* ("Process," "Synchrony," *Ulysses* (ed.); Kidd, "Inquiry," "Scandal"; Rossman) demonstrates. The text and the editor's involvement in and production of that text are part of public awareness now in a way that they have not been for centuries. That both Professors McGann and Gabler are contributors to this volume of essays is therefore quite proper to such a collection, and in the first part of this essay I would like to take advantage of their presence by briefly examining how (in the case of Gabler) a concrete and complex edition may be "read" theoretically and how (in the case of McGann) a theory may or may not produce particular concrete manifestations. Thereafter, I will consider in more detail what might happen to our textual assumptions if we were to negotiate in terms of a particular theoretical approach (psychoanalytic criticism) and what effect such negotiation might have on our estimation of the significance of the actual appearance of "critical" editions.

What, then, does it mean, to seek evidence of the operations of theory in the physical forms of an edition, and what are the negotiations which the editor is likely to undertake in the production of these texts? To some extent, my denigration of the mere demographics of editing may be too prejudicial in answering these questions, for while it is clear that one does not produce a poststructuralist edition simply by hiring a few members of the hermeneutical mafia to write the notes (any more than one produces a feminist edition by having female editors), the sensibilities of an editor can obviously affect both the theoretical procedures and the physical form. Thus, Donald H. Reiman rightly cites the "historical context in which modern editors and their readers live" (357) as grounds for the policy adopted by *Shelley and His Circle* of allotting major essays on the women in the circle to female scholars, without thereby compromising the role of male scholars also contributing to the series; and in describing the ways in which an editor of eighteenth-century diaries must edit male and female entries differently, Elaine Forman Crane illustrates how "a gender-conscious editor can contribute as much to the revision of women's history as the historian or literary scholar who uses the documentary material for the basis of a book" (381). Reiman and Crane (panelists on that ADE discussion) show that "feminism" in editing can have an important social function, although my concern is more with the formal aspects of ideology.

The evidence I am seeking for the manifestation of theory is thus more materially, concretely textual than personally idiosyncratic, and is perhaps parallel on a *formal* basis with Gary Taylor's charting of the identities of editions and editors by analyzing their rhetoric ("Rhetoric"). Where Taylor is concerned with the *diction* and inherent persuasive strategies adopted in editing—even down to the rhetorical value of a table of contents (46)—I am curious about the ideology embedded in form and method.

I will begin by examining some of the possible "traces" (an appropriately Derridean term) of theory in Gabler's edition of Joyce's *Ulysses*. As is well known, the diachronic rather than synchronic rationale and procedure for a genetic edition such as the Gabler *Ulysses* inevitably challenges the authority of intentionality, or at least that intentionality which has motivated the typical Greg-Bowers eclectic edition. I realize, incidentally, that Tanselle argues that a synoptic edition such as Gabler's cannot properly be called genetic, since it does not attempt a reconstruction in the synoptic apparatus of a single document ("Historicism" 38, n72). It is easy to understand (or account for) Tanselle's dissatisfaction: as a defender of a copytext theory, he must feel his theoretical grounds undercut by an editorial proposal that admits of *no* single copytext in the traditional sense, but rather a seamless web of alternative readings not measured or tested against the "indifference" of a control document. But as I have already argued ("Theory" 20, n39) that Tanselle's taxonomy is unduly restrictive, I will proceed as if synopticism is a form of geneticism.

I believe that Philip Cohen and David Jackson in this volume are correct in ascribing a structuralist ethic to geneticism, particularly in the mapping of the temporal rather than spatial relationships of the states of a text, but, as I have suggested elsewhere ("Theory" 9), I would maintain that it is the bipolar oppositions of structuralism, the effects of a series of off/on "switches" embedded in a synoptic apparatus, whereby only one lection can be selected at any one moment of reading, which subverts any remaining singular intentionality in such a text. It is, finally, the lack of the typical hierarchical construction of the eclectic text, the importation of the apparatus into the body of the textual page, that renders such singularity impotent by reversing what I term the *necessary* and *problematic* (base and superstructure) of the text's conception, in a manner I describe more fully later in this essay. But therein lies the problem with the "opening" (in the bibliographical sense) of the Gabler edition, for the *recto* page of an opening of the Garland critical edition displays such a singularity, and appears to mark at best a concession not only to the hobgoblin of readability but also to that very single-state, eclectically constructed intentionality which the synoptic text sought to mute and at worst an inconsistency of purpose that renders the whole enterprise suspect.[1]

However, it could be argued that the openings of the Gabler edition display not conceptual or methodological inconsistency but an attempt to wed two formerly incompatible ideologies—Anglo-American intentionalist eclecticism and European geneticism. This conclusion is the more plausible given the polymathic and cross-cultural history of the *Ulysses* editor, a continental editor familiar with the genetic tradition but working on one of the major multiwitness texts of English-language literature and a student of Fredson Bowers, the foremost eclecticist of the century. Gabler's *Ulysses* is thus a forceful international statement, but it depends for its success on the willingness of the reader to effect a double reading of the text—a suspension of critical interrogation of the text in the acceptance of the purified formal features of the recto and an active employment of this same interrogation in a continual manipulation of the structuralist "switches" of the verso. Such a dual reading (and a dual theoretical rationale for such reading) is obviously discouraged by the separate publication of the "Corrected" text in 1986, but the duality is no more than that democratic pluralism that Shillingsburg has espoused as the only possible textual credo in these days of critical and intellectual diversity ("Literary Theory").

I have to admit a quibble, however, to this neat dichotomy, for the verso genetic text may be seen (especially in Tanselle's bibliographically restrictive sense), not as a structuralist demonstration of oppositions or interrelationships, but rather as a spatial coding of that linear, temporal process that we call "com-position," a series of separately identifiable but closely connected documentary states, with a very discernible chronological beginning, middle, and end. It is this view of geneticism that is propounded by Albert von Frank, in claiming for the genetic text the demonstration of a "poetics of editing" that is itself a reflection of the poetics of the compositional process. He argues, for example, that the interrelated sequentiality of the variants in an Emerson lecture must be preserved in the reading (and criticism) of the text, so that each separate opposition of variants cannot be *dealt* with separately but must be held up to the developing matrix of the "work" as a whole, as it moves from one conceptual stage to another (8). Perhaps this emphasis on the intertextuality of the individual lection is no more than a restatement of Zeller's structuralist position (241) that a change in one lection alters the fabric of the entire texture of readings that comprise the text, but I think that von Frank's privileging of processional, linear poetics is much closer to Poulet's phenomenological attempt (44) at the sharing and replicating of the "thoughts of another" (i.e., the putative and now resuscitated "author") than it is to a technical and cumulative recording that does not demand an auctorial consciousness as its motivation. Von Frank's emphasis on the linearity of consciousness is indeed very similar to the phenomenological evidence accumulated by Steven Mailloux, although Mailloux draws this evidence into the service of a reader-response rather than a phenomenological ethic (114–15). A genetic edition such as Gabler's *Ulysses,* particularly one with such estranging openings, may therefore be more complex theoretically than we (or perhaps even its editor) had supposed, and an easy or consistent identification of its options may require a series of reading postures. Gabler's edition may be more important as an editorial gesture of pluralism than as an embodiment of the sort of local textual feuding carried on by John Kidd and others (e.g., Rossman), and for this gesture, complex and provocative, all textual theorists and practitioners should be grateful.

The work of Jerome McGann and the implications of social textual criticism are being considered more fully by other contributors to this volume. I will concentrate, therefore, only on the specific problem of materialization, noting that McGann has generally been less than sanguine about the possibility of even an electronic hypertext's ability to store and present the multivariate conditions of bibliographical coding ("Contemporary Literary Theory"). But this bibliographical code is only the second of the two semiotic systems ("Critical Editing") that McGann finds in all texts and their transmission, and the first (the linguistic code) offers fewer representational problems to electronic or even nontraditional print production. For example, Derek Pearsall (105) suggested some years ago that, considering the multiple levels of auctorial intention and scribal reworking present in the surviving manuscripts of *The Canterbury Tales,* the only proper way to reflect this compositional and social history was through a loose-leaf binder edition, with a core of fixed tales but otherwise open to the reader's desire to represent the "creative involvement" of the Chaucerian editor/scribe in the reshuffling and continual reconstruction of the text.

Further it might be possible to argue that *any* traditional edition with a full historical collation presents an account of the "social" transmission of the work, according to McGann's or Pearsall's rationale. It is theoretically possible for a scholarly reader of such an edition to construct any state or state of the texts from the evidence preserved in the apparatus. But there is a significant difference in emphasis, for while the historical apparatus may indeed contain the variants from all states, these variants have been rejected from the textual page proper by the imposition of the textual theory on which the edition has been constructed—best-text, eclectic, or whatever. The historical collation cannot be said to represent the ontology of the text (its mode of being) but rather its dissemination, corruption, and destruction (its unbeing or unmaking) according to the traditional rules of stemmatic dissolution of privileged meaning, whereby the *codices descripti* have no independent authority and may be dropped as "witnesses" to the text. Even Pasquali's rule of "recentiores non deteriores" (41–108) does not change the basic assumptions of authority and corruption, it merely identifies the two components of the text's history at other parts of the transmission than those envisaged by orthodox Lachmannians, and does not satisfy the requirements of a social theory of the text for a completely unprivileged charting of variation as a function of readerly rather than writerly activity. It goes without saying that even such apparently technical/objective constructions as Quentin's "positive critical apparatus" (Severs 71), based on a statistical coding of variants in triads, or Vinton Dearing's "rings" and "rules of parsimony" (92–97, employing symbolic logic to resolve the problems of cross-fertilization of collaterals) do not address McGann's concerns for a social-driven model of text whereby auctorial presence is simply one (the "originary") moment of transmission and not of itself superior to other moments that have had a collaborative role in the viability of a *textus receptus*.

It may therefore be that Pearsall's loose-leaf (or its electronic equivalent, a series of "windows" on a CRT) really is the medium for the presentation of a social text, and this would be quite proper since his suggestion occurred in a collection edited by McGann. It may also be that the critical variorum (for example, the *New Shakespeare Variorum*) is a textual manifestation of that form of social history known as *rezeptionästhetik*, since the variorum charts and codes the entire history of readerly responses to a text, usually without editorial interpretation or intervention. But McGann is still right to suppose that these several vehicles already available or soon to be so would conserve only the linguistic code, not the bibliographical. It may therefore be that we have not yet seen a fully realized social textual edition, although it is tempting to suggest that such programs as John Miles Foley's HEURO, formulated to present and *continue* the formulaic reworking of Yugoslav oral epic, could be modified to (re)present the bibliographical aspects of text production, as could a facsimile (but loose-leaf) critical edition on the Pearsall model.

The "play" involved in Pearsall's suggestion—or in G. E. Bentley Jr.'s similar suggestion for editing Blake—inevitably has Derridean overtones, for could it not be argued that if a reader may (re)construct texts through the caprice of a loose-leaf binder (as a means of reflecting what Pearsall calls the "history of literary taste" 104) so may the same reader manipulate the features of a text according to the whimsy of *his* own history of taste, a form of the deconstructive *jeu,* the play *in* the text that continually defers a fixable meaning or form to that text and instead allows, indeed promotes, an indeterminate, and continually deferred, meaning according to the requirements of *différance?* In fact, it may be ironic that it is only as a result of the technical advances in the most traditional of disciplines—textual scholarship—that the full critical implications of the Derridean *jeu* can be textually demonstrated. Texts may indeed be spliced and erased, they may be reconstituted and grafted onto other texts, marginalized and (en)folded with an electronic ease that would seem to make the worst nightmares of a New Critic confronting poststructuralism come true! It is important to emphasize this technical potential, for until recently the capacity of textual scholars to produce editions that did not represent best-text or eclectic text ideologies was limited by the bibliographical constraints of publication. Pearsall's "loose-leaf" is a somewhat primitive premonition of the technical change, but the solid, opaque appearance of orthodox textual editions (with a privileged textual page augmented by the clearly inferior status of apparatus and historical collation) has perhaps encouraged a belief among critics that textual scholarship must subscribe only to a fixity of text, a definitive text that authorizes criticism by releasing an orthodox reading to the critic. But for the poststructuralist, the apparent definitiveness of the textual scholar's work may seem remote from the current business of criticism and to represent an illusion of control no longer tenable. But in such suppositions the poststructuralist is employing a model of textual scholarship that has been challenged by the textual scholars themselves and in large measure displaced by a more fluid, less authoritarian paradigm. Thus, when Richard Lanham recently warned an audience of literary critics that they might one day have to confront texts that were not mono-dic, simple-state representations of auctorial intention, he was unaware (as was most of his audience) that the work of such textual scholars as Michael Warren, John Miles Foley, and Gary Taylor was already producing texts of this multivariate type. Further, as the symposium of literary and textual scholars sponsored by the Society for Critical Exchange demonstrates (*Textual Scholarship*), most literary theorists simply assume that there have been no procedural, ideological, or theoretical advances in textual scholar-ship in the last few decades—just as Fredson Bowers found of the literary critics in the fifties (4–5).

Therefore, I would now like to suggest some points of convergence where the issues typically faced by textual scholars can be reinvested by a consideration from "other" theoretical dispensations, using the vocabu-lary and conceptual assumptions of these dispensations. While some allu-sion will be made to several recent ideologies, I will concentrate on an area where both concept and terminology are both perhaps more "comfort-able" to the practicing textual critic, namely, psychoanalytical criticism, from Freud to Lacan to Bloom and Kristeva. This will be a test case of how, even at a necessarily superficial level, some of the recognized ele-ments of even such traditional editorial methods as Greg-Bowers eclecti-cism can be read "against the grain" by theorists of other persuasions, to produce quite different characterizations of the textual evidence and tex-tual procedures than those presumably posited by the eclectic editors themselves. In a sense, I am therefore offering a Bloomian "strong mis-prision" of eclecticism, filtering it through psychoanalytical criticism, in order to demonstrate the ideological fluidity of the medium we textual scholars work in.

Once one invokes the idea that an editor's main responsibility is the recovery of an author's "intention," scholarly editing may be seen as a form of psychoanalysis, but there has been comparatively little work done on the technical aspects of twentieth-century psychoanalytical theory that might apply directly to the formal features of an edition and the process of editing. Even in his study of parapraxis, Timpanaro is content primarily with an attempt to discredit Freud's theory of the "slip" by attempting to demonstrate that the best-known citations of the slip in the psychoanalytical literature can in fact be adequately explained by using the methods textual criticism has traditionally used to recover "lost" texts. Shillingsburg (*Scholarly Editing* 27) does include the "Freudian slip" as one of the components of textual "error" or "variance" that might disturb intention but does very little with the opportunity.

But what if we were, for example, to consider the major feature, or "originary text," of Freudian analysis—the dream—as a "text" in *our* sense of the word? Would it not then be possible to perceive the role of scribe/printer as the "ego," responsible for the sorting and organization of the unpublished and unpublishable text for general consumption? Could we not see that textual conflation in the structuring of texts is analogous to the process of "condensation," or *Verdichtung*—the superimposition of dream elements (Freud, *Interpretation* VI A)?[2] And could it not appear that the variant (or perhaps most specifically the error of "homoeoteleuton") is a form of the dream's "displacement"—*Vershiebung*, the "transvaluation of physical values" and the change of context to effect internal censorship (*Interpretation* VI B)?[3] Similarly, the "day's residue" theory of dream production, whereby the significant or insignificant events of immediate experience are melded into an apparently coherent form in order to marry various disparate situations into a viable (if highly figurative) narrative (Freud, *Interpretation* I C) could be seen as the same process— and the same motivation—whereby, on the one hand, texts suffer contamination from disparate sources to produce an apparently uniform synthesis (according to the skills of the contaminator in hiding his tracks), *or*, on the other, texts either occur in or can be traced to a series of "fragments" of auctorial imagination, most easily observed in the "remaniement" school of textual criticism in Slavic studies (Fennell) or in much recent work on Middle English texts, especially Chaucer (Pearsall, Hudson).

Taking the analogy further, could we not maintain that the developing states of text common in multiple-witness works are in fact various forms of the "latent content" (what Freud calls the "dream-thoughts") of the work entire, and that eclecticism imposes the "dreamwork" on this latent content, to produce the "manifest content" ("dream-content") of the features of the dream as narrative (Freud, *Interpretation* VI, 311–12)?[4] The introduction of normalization, perhaps to ensure the "readability" of a text would correspond to the "secondary revision" (*Bearbeitung*, Freud, *Inter-*

pretation VI I) practiced by the dreamer during the dreamwork to ensure the "uptake" of the dream. That is, the irrational dream sequence (the apparent self-contradictions and illogicality of the evidence of the multiple witnesses taken as a whole) is sorted into a more familiar and more logical order through a selection of dream or textual variants to form an "intelligible pattern." Freud specifically likens this process to a reader's ignoring a "misprint," so strong is the desire for uniform harmonious narrative.

But while these obvious features of standard editing practice can be seen to embody several of the characteristics of classical Freudian dream theory, it is when we turn to the relations of the analyst and the analysand that the parallels become more pertinent. It is, after all, Eugene Vinaver's claim that the very term *textual criticism* implies a mistrust of texts (352), which need to be subjected to a rigorous interrogation by the editor if their "true" meaning is to be recovered, and we are all familiar with, indeed live in a period of, the "hermeneutics of suspicion" in which this querulous, interrogative attitude of textual criticism finds its perfect accommodation. Vinaver himself provides a psychological model for the charting of the process of error in the act of scribal copying in medieval scriptoria (353), and it is through the employment of such a model that the analytist/editor recovers the analysand's repressed text in order to satisfy and overcome the natural suspicion of the "manifest" content of texts. The technical medium whereby the manifest content is displaced is, of course, the act of "transference" (and "countertransference"), common enough in phenomenological criticism, in which the figure of the analyst (editor) begins to assume the psychological conflicts of the analysand (author) to gain a "privileged" insight not otherwise available. It is precisely this "privilege" that such intentionalist editors as Kane and Donaldson claim as their prerogative in their editing of Langland (212–13). That is, through a subtle and wide-ranging "reading" of the manifest content of the *Piers Plowman* manuscripts—all of which are by definition corrupted or displaced representations of the latent content that is Langland's "dream" text (literally so in this case)—the editor/analyst achieves knowledge of, indeed *becomes,* the psyche of the putative author and can thereafter use this knowledge, gained through transference, in the interpretation of the manifest content and the reconstruction of the latent content, even when there is no direct evidence for the latter. One could argue, in fact, that Kane and Donaldson proceed to make diagnoses of textual corruption on much less substantive evidence than that enjoyed by most analysts (often on directly contradictory evidence [Fowler], where it is assumed that the manifest content is inevitably and deliberately "lying"—or misrepresenting the latent content—and *can do no other*).

The intentionality that is the cover for such editorial devices does depend upon privilege—the privilege of what is usually identified as id-psychology, the concentration on the expression of repressed meaning. Its counterpart, ego-psychology, is analogously employed by the "affective" or "sociological" critic or textuist, who concentrates, not on the recovery of the "originary moment" (regarding this as only one, and that not a particularly significant stage in textual transmission), but on the checks, balances, controls, normalizations, and regularizations that enhance the text as it is prepared and modified for its public presentation. The egos of the normalizers and regularizers are obviously involved in this process, although they will usually claim obeisance to an author as their motivation; but even if they were not, this stage would still be an aspect of the *text's* ego, as it is refined and put through a secondary revision in order to make itself more "legible."

During this process, however, not all the features of the latent content will be satisfactorily repressed or concealed by refinement, and the analyst will therefore look for the "symptomatic loci" (Freud, *Interpretation* VI, 527–29) that point to shifts in narrative where the latent content shows through. Similarly, the bibliographer (most typically and appropriately the *analytical* bibliographer) looks for the same features, called in his case "bibliographical disturbances," where the "seams" of the manifest content (for example, the doubling of speech heads in dramatic texts) display a faulty join attempted at the ego stage of refinement. Identifying such moments and then dis-covering what they imply about the layers of text beneath them are central to the dogma and technique of analytical bibliography. Usually this is deemed a representation of that discipline's basically historical orientation (i.e., the setting out of the processional nature of textual transmission in a concrete medium), but it can just as easily be seen as a psychological process, where the compositors, acting as the text's ego (in an attempt to prepare it for public viewing), may have slipped in their creation of a perfectly seamless bibliographical artifact, and some evidence of their work remains *despite their attempts to hide it*. That is, the double speech heads for Proculeius in the famous "bibliographical disturbance" of the First Folio *Antony and Cleopatra* (Hinman xvii) were not *intended* by the compositors, but were slips committed in their eradication of material repressed in order to refine the textual appearance of that outer leaf in the folio gathering, which needed to lose text to be accommodated to the constraints of the casting-off of copy.

Thus, it can be observed that many of the accepted features of classical Freudian psychoanalysis mirror procedurally and productively the similarly classical features of eclectic editing and related textual disciplines. And eclecticism can also be seen in more recent psychoanalytical methods. For example, the historical editor generally works from a sense of his own "belatedness," in Bloomian terms, and while he would generally resist the charge of a "misprision" of the auctorial text in the act of editing, this is often what happens in fact, particularly among those editorial schools (from Alexandrian analogy through to modern eclecticism) who have sought a "swerve" (or *clinamen*) from the document lection for the sake of "improvement" upon the original (19–45). Similarly, one could argue that the current fashion of fragmentalism (especially among medievalists) is an acknowledgment of Bloom's stage of *tessera* (49–73), the desire to reduce the work to pieces so that it then needs the successor poet (the editor) to put it together again in a coherent form. We could also marshal the contingents in the "old spelling"/"normalization" quarrel around Bloomian terms—with the old spellers seeking a prohibition against a sullying of the "original," a prohibition that marks the first stage in the identification of an anxiety of influence, and the modernizers or normalizers working to emasculate the precursor, to render it harmless and reduce it to a document available in one's own terms. Thus, the historians who were the target of Tanselle's attack in "The Editing of Historical Documents" were charged with precisely this offense—that they had sought a misprision of the author and his text for their own purposes, which were to hedge it around with annotations and commentary designed for the modern reader and thus to detract from the originary force of the author's language and to render the text as a whole safe by encumbering it with belatedness.

Similarly, the typical eclectic tendency to divide textual page from apparatus can be fraught with ideological contention. For example, we could argue the rejection of the "significance" (in both senses) of the variants as a quite *literal* Lacanian sliding of the signified beneath the signifier (*Speech and Language* 31, 113–14; *Écrits* 149, 154). Lacan inherits the Saussurean formula for representing "meaning" but inverts it: Saussure (113) had expressed the arbitrary combination of the signifier (morphological or phonological unit) and signified (conceptual referent) in the formula $\frac{S}{s}$ with S = signifier and s = signified). Lacan, however, while calling into question the entire security of the collocation, demonstrates the dominance of the paternal signifier (the "law") over the signified, by rewriting the formula with the signifier "on top" $\frac{S}{s}$ with the understanding, however, that the rejected, unconscious signified is unstable and may shift unpredictably, each shift occupying a different aspect of the continued negotiation between the Imaginary and the Symbolic in their construction of the Real. Since (again in Saussurean/Lacanian terms) all signifiers achieve identity only by their *difference* from other signifiers and by the *lack* or *absence* of the signified, we can observe the operations on the eclectic textual page in a Lacanian mode. Thus, it is the surface features of the textual page, full of selected morphemes (signifiers) displayed prominently and authoritatively, that first command our attention. But these signifiers have their current identity not only because they are *not* other signifiers in the author's idiolect, but also because they are *not* the rejected signifiers of the apparatus, which now operate as the lower term (signified) of Lacan's formula. This may sound a fanciful way of making the distinction, but we should recall that for Lacan all discourse is, through the agency of metonymy and/or metaphor (*Écrits* 154–58), a sort of "slip" (of tongue, of pen) which the signifieds in the apparatus represent, and that texts suppress their means of production through precisely the sort of "smoothing" that the eclectic textual page aspires to. Moreover, for Lacan desire is an endless movement from signifier to signified, and a sense of a resulting *lack* which this movement creates (*Écrits* 156–57). The eclectic editor has been through this same movement, back and forth from text to variant to text, deciding (as he or she hopes) which is which, and desiring an end that is artificially produced by the apparent hierarchical construction of the typical eclectic edition. The "radial reading" McGann has noted as the proper readerly posture for critical editions ("How to Read") duplicates this editorial movement in similarly Lacanian terms.

However, just as one of the characteristics of modernism is to make the "act of enunciating" the very medium of discourse, to display the process of production by a formalistic "baring of the device," so too have more recent editors grown uneasy with the silent repression of variants (or their muting through an apparatus), characteristic of eclectic editing, and have sought to bare their own device of variance prominently by importing the rejected signifieds back into the matrix of the signifiers. In this way, the

Lacanian unconscious as the sliding of the signifieds under the signifiers is not arrested (for the endless desire for completion still goes on *within* a synoptic or diachronic text just as it did in an eclectic one), but the axis of that desire is revealed rather than being repressed—in an acknowledgment both that multivariate texts cannot be so easily controlled or reduced and that the devices, the interrogation of the text by the reader/editor, cannot be disguised by hierarchy.

Finally, we could note that Kristeva's development of Lacan, especially in her distinction between the "semiotic" and "symbolic" stages of language acquisition, may also have textual ramifications. For example, the function of Kristeva's pre-Oedipal "semiotic" component in her theory is to act as the "other" of formal language, a presyntactic flux of not-yet-identified phonemes which record the "pulses" that go on under the "law" of language system and order (29–30). The semiotic thus prefigures and potentially undermines the syntactic order of the texts that are our formal "language," achieved at the "symbolic" stage of language acquisition. Viewed against the patriarchal authority of that syntax (logical and coherent and "identifiable" and usually represented in the definitive text of the eclectic reading page, which is rigorously "syntactic"), this semiotic stage is clearly a feminist threat to that authority. Semiosis thus has the same fluidity and pluralism as the variation *considered as a whole,* i.e., the complex of pulses that resists the structuring of variance into symbol (lection) and seme (variant). Instead of such structuring, semiosis promotes that "creative excess over precise meaning" that makes the variant so distressing to the eclecticist, whose aim is to privilege the very precision (or at least the appearance of it) that the semiotic variant subverts. It is, again in Kristevan terms, something "left over" (the "pluralization" of the "thetic doxy"), the "unexpressed" text that tends toward anarchy in language and must thus be constrained by the symbolic medium in which most editors work (60).

But not all editors. John Miles Foley's experiments with fluidity and excess in his computer editing of Yugoslav epic texts display the potential for anarchy (an endless and ultimately formless permutation of fixed units) that Kristeva's semiotic pulses embody. To be fair, we have to acknowledge that Foley's editing does have a "program" (called, appropriately, HEURO), a series of predefined constraints that link the object text with the variants (85–89); but the editor/reader at the terminal confronted with these relationships has a potentially limitless number of combinations to create and work with *and* does not produce a text that is composed entirely of textual-page signifiers and rejected apparatus-signifieds. In place of the conventional textual page, Foley's HEURO produces a continuous matrix (hovering between textual page and apparatus, and partaking of the characteristics of both) of signifiers *and* signifieds, or rather of total variations that function somewhere between the semiotic and symbolic levels.

Kristeva's analysis thus poses two possibilities—the multiple "authority" of the semiotic stage, feminist and fluid, and the "definitive" authority of the symbolic stage, patriarchal and fixed. The latter is more comfortable to most editors, particularly those of an eclectic or "best-text" disposition, since it confirms the authority of the symbolic "law" embedded in the edition; but the former is more creative, since it allows an infinite free association of textual components, a flux that keeps all options of textual contamination and conflation open and continuously *usable*. Clearly, symbolic-stage editing (with permanent lections selected as symbolic representations of the underlying "meaning" of the text) has dominated traditional textual scholarship, particularly those areas or genres concerned with a public posture for the work (novels, poems, histories, essays). But, as recent editorial experimentation of the Foley, Warren, Taylor type demonstrates, semiotic-stage editing may prove attractive in genres where the private (or semipublic) gestation and re-presentation of the work are its characteristic ontological mode (for example, letters, journals, drama, oral literature, or *drafts* of any of the genres in the symbolic stage). Such "semiotic" editing in these genres could perhaps take the form of a geneticism in which the normative chronological thrust was replaced by a free-floating index of states, with a combinatory power that would not be restricted to reproducing only one stage of a document (or documents) at a time. It would (literally) "incorporate" all lections, all aspects of a variation, into this textual flux, but would go beyond the reader-produced documentary variance promised by Pearsall's method of combination. The very concept of "error" would have to be abandoned, for that is a product of the later, "symbolic," logical and hierarchical stage of language, and the syntactic rules (derived from this stage) for sentence or clause structure—and even for individual morphemes—would have to be held in abeyance in favor of an acceptance in these semiotic genres of imperfected utterances, spelling inadequacies or aberrations, dislocated and disjointed phraseology. To some extent, these values are partially manifest in current genetic method, but this method usually observes a documentary delineation and "discretion" that would be inappropriate to semiotic editing, and may also retain the concept of "error" within such documentary states—as does the Gabler *Ulysses*.

The Kristevan psychological ethic can be viewed editorially as a way of producing a feminist deconstruction of traditional or eclectic method. By reversing (or rather ignoring) the hierarchies inherent in such traditional editing, it fulfills the feminist agenda for a subversion of patriarchal formulae embedded in canonical texts and the presentation of these canonical texts in canonical editions. Kristeva could therefore answer the question posed at that ADE session on "Sex, Text, and Context," or rather answer it in the *formal* terms in which it was posed, not in the social or demographic terms in which it is usually answered. Freudian and Bloomian editions we already have—the eclectic, hierarchical, phenomenological attempts to reconstruct a consciousness and its intentions, well documented in the major products of the Greg-Bowers editorial enterprise. And, since Lacan occupies something of a middle ground between Freud and Kristeva, we might observe that the standard genetic refusal to accept the permanent status of the rejected readings of the "signifieds" in the apparatus, and the similar genetic insistence on their reimportation into the body of the textual page, reflects both the Lacanian deconstruction of Saussure's formula for the sign and the Lacanian movement of language "desire" as the continually deferred "lack" that this fluctuating relationship between signified and signifier speaks to. Thus Freud is already with us, Lacan with us in part, and Kristeva may be with us shortly now that we have the technological ability to represent flux rather than determinism.

But so what? A traditional, "nontheoretical" textual critic or bibliographer might declare: you've shown us all this fancy new language and invoked a pantheon of new authorities (usually foreign) in place of the "strict" bibliographers we're familiar with, but this cannot possibly have any bearing upon the way I do my business of editing. In general, of course, the traditional textual critic is right—theory (literary or textual) does not impinge upon the *business* of editing because that business has largely considered itself theory-proof: its theory has been that there is no theory, only method, and that this method succeeds or fails on the skills of the editor, not on the validity of the method itself. This tendency to localize and render specific the empiricism of editing is perhaps best exemplified in the textual adage that "all [textual] problems are different." If they are all different (in kind, not just in severity), then each one must be solved independently of the others—indeed, as if the others did not exist. But this assumption is contradicted by the doctrine of the "skills" of the editor in these little local moments, for if success of method depends upon skill of manipulation, then the accumulated knowledge that creates that skill becomes a theoretical matrix against which to test the specific problem being considered. This matrix of knowledge may be as technical as a growing awareness of the orthographic characteristics of an author's (or scribe's) manuscript or as subjective as the increasing identity with the putative author's psyche and likely linguistic choices—as in the example of Kane and Donaldson's Langland. Theory in both these cases is theory in the scientific sense: not something which is unproved ("only a theory" as the creationists love to charge Darwin), but a *system* of organized empirical knowledge arranged in such a manner as to be able to account for the data so far gathered and to be able to *predict* other likely results of the manipulation of data. In this sense orthographic theory would be able to predict that a given author would be more likely to have spelled an apparently indifferent word one way rather than another in specific contexts (of, e.g., meter), and psyche theory would be able to predict that Langland would have preferred a "perfected" alliterative stave to a scribally deficient one. Such theories—and their immediate textual results—may, of course, be highly contentious, and other textual critics may offer rival matrixes to accommodate (and predict) the data. This has certainly been the case with Kane/Donaldson's *Piers* (see Fowler), but does not detract from the charm of the comprehensiveness of its theory. It is this comprehensive quality in general theory that W. J. T. Mitchell draws attention to in his listing of the theoretical attributes of "[1] reflection, [2] fundamental principles, [3] models, schemes, systems, [4] large-scale guesswork, [5] metaphysics, [6] speculation, [7] intuition, [8] abstract thought" (6). These attributes are opposed (in parallel series) to an "empiricist" list of "[1] immediate perception, [2] surface phenomena, [3] things in themselves, [4] small-scale certainty, [5] physics, [6] traditional wisdom, [7] discursive reading, [8] concrete experience" (6). In the case of the Kane-Donaldson *Piers,* the irony is that they have employed the predictive accumulation of empirical data based on the skills matrix, while their general theory of consciousness (to which they have putative access) would be sufficient grounds for their principles of emendation. They are thus trying to have it both ways—and perhaps succeeding.

But it is because more traditional textual criticism has seemed to be so concerned with the components of Mitchell's *second* list (perhaps especially the "surface phenomena" of individual lections and the "small-scale certainty" of the specific crux and its solution) that the discipline's reliance upon components of the first list (especially on "fundamental principles" and "speculation") has been obscured, not only to its rivals in the "critical" camp but even to its own practitioners. I would hold, however, that this characterization is changing, for the work of Tanselle on intentionality, external fact, historicism, and so on, while appearing to offer encyclopedic and discursive surveys of practical problems in editing, also responds to a series of "fundamental principles" (e.g., that in most cases there is such a thing as "final intentions" and that seeking them out is a desideratum in textual scholarship), and it delineates a "model" or "scheme" whereby the "small-scale certainty" of the individual editor can be predicted or tested. It is true that, on occasions, Tanselle has seemed resistant to theory, as for example in his criticism of Parker's "full intentionality" model used to reject eclectic editing of American fiction ("Historicism" 27–36). But I fancy that this resistance is to theoretical postures that seem implausible or invalid, not to theory as a general means of explication and clarification. Tanselle's most recent work (e.g., his Rosenbach lectures published as *A Rationale of Textual Criticism*) marks indeed a refinement and distillation of his theoretical argument, for it offers not encyclopedic empiricism but taxemes of "fundamental principles," largely without exemplary citation (for example, that archival and editorial activities are equally "textual," that "work" is immanent in, but not identifiable with "text," and that McGann's bibliographical code is generally not part of the intended text, but only of that text's cultural history).

Further, the recent work of Gabler, McGann, Shillingsburg, Mailloux, and others has called into question whether the Greg-Bowers-Tanselle concentration on intentionality is the only or the most desirable "fundamental principle" for textual criticism. This resistance has had the effect of demonstrating (a) that intentionality is not necessarily a *donnée* of the discipline and (b) that intentionality is not only "*only* a theory" but also a "system" of "abstract thought" whose existence and recognition as such gives allowance (and perhaps credence) to other theories. Like M. Jourdain, in *Le Bourgeois Gentilhomme*, who discovered that he had been speaking prose all his life, our current textual critic has discovered that he has all along been a theorist *malgré lui*.

But this new allowance does not quite answer the earlier question attached to the presence of "foreign" theory (e.g., psychoanalytical criticism), for the Tanselle/Gabler/McGann debate is still centered around the validity or otherwise of intentionality, despite McGann's attempts to move it elsewhere, and such "systems" as psychoanalysis (or poststructuralism or speech-act theory or whatever) may not seem "native" to the questions of text and textuality as they have been conceived of by practicing textual critics. Here, I think, likes the problem and its resolution—the *conception* of what is "native." The "native" or "natural" ideology of text is one in which the critic postulates a "base" (in quite Marxist terms) of what is historically and conceptually "necessary" to the comprehension and evaluation of a discipline, and then gives allowance to a "superstructure" of resulting forces that creates the problematics for that discipline. In Hegelian philosophy, the accepted "base" was, of course, thought and the laws of reason, with materialism as the "superstructure" for its expression. In reversing the relationship (by making materialism and socio-economics the base, and thought—or specifically political thought and ideology—the superstructure), Marx reconceives of the "necessary" or "native" component and gives a quite different "allowance" to the problematics.

In traditional textual criticism, the "base" has similarly been thought, but the thought of a highly personalized conception of the individual creative consciousness, and the linguistic codes of text and texts have been the most obvious elements of the superstructure. These codes have proved to be the problematics of the discipline, the contentions around which arguments pro- and con- "meaning" have arranged themselves, while all along assuming the solid "base" of the auctorial psyche. Judged purely in these terms of necessity and problematics, the traditional textual-critical relationship of base and superstructure hardly needs any adjustment to accommodate the supposedly "foreign" theory of psychoanalytical criticism I have briefly alluded to above, for the problematics of both text(s) and edition(s), and the various linguistic codes they embody, bear a fairly stable relationship to the "necessity" of the putative psyche that functions as their base. The temporary discomfort caused by a nonnative vocabulary can therefore function rather like a "bibliographical disturbance": it alerts the practitioner to the very practice he has been operating under by showing him where the "seams" (or "semes"?) of argument lie hidden, and forces him to reconsider the characteristics of the "base" (the psyche) that has given him the allowance for these operations. But it does not cause a reconfiguration of the base/superstructure or necessity/problematics relationship itself and can therefore be comparatively easily accommodated, to produce (I would hope) a more interrogative mood in the construction and evaluation of the psyche in the edition and the edition in the psyche.

This was perhaps the reason I selected psychoanalytical criticism as a brief test case of reconception, for the rereading it requires is a less-threatening, while more interrogative, reinvestment of our traditional base and superstructure. But such a reinvestment is nonetheless a product of having read the discipline against the grain (by the employment of a disjunctive terminology that may or may not reinforce one's presumptions), and the process of rereading through the other ideologies (structuralism, phenomenology, and the rest) is not different in kind from that offered by psychoanalysis and its conventions. Such a series of rereadings, with evidence more fully developed than the rather cursory survey suggested here, is obviously beyond the scope of a short, speculative article, but it is the subject and method of the larger study on which I am now engaged. It will inevitably involve a reconsideration of the characteristics and identity of a series of differing bases, not all of which will prove quite so amenable to the predispositions of current textual criticism. For example, one can predict that a complete reversal of base and superstructure would be required to deal effectively with most structuralist and post-structuralist theories, for if the "author" becomes at best a *product* of and not the *cause* of text and reading, then such an "author" is moved from base to superstructure, and the reading and text, instead of being the resultant problematics, become the causative necessity of the base. But the study will, I trust, demonstrate that the challenge of theory both native and foreign is one that can no longer be ignored by the "strict and pure" bibliographers.

Notes

1. I would therefore share Tanselle's unease about the presence of the reading text: "Why, one is bound to ask, should there be a separate 'reading' text if all the variants are an essential part of the work? Why should 'the object of scholarly and critical analysis and study' (which is 'the totality of the Work in Progress') be seen as 'opposed' to 'a general public's reading matter'? If the 'work of literature possesses in its material medium itself, in its text or texts, a diachronic as well as a synchronic dimension' . . . , does it make sense for the 'general public's reading

matter' to be something less than the whole work? Is Gabler saying that scholars and critics need the real work, but ordinary readers can make do with what amounts to an abridged version, offering less than the full aesthetic pleasure that the work in its entirety provides?" ("Historicism" 39). But my emphasis would be different, drawing attention to the synthesis rather than the consistency of the two modes, while recognizing that they are clearly *different*.

2. In fact, Freud notes that "the work of condensation in dreams is seen at its clearest when it handles words and names," giving as an example "It's written in a positively *norekdal* style," where the "monstrosity [norekdal] was composed of the two names 'Nora' and 'Ekdal'—characters in two well-known plays of Ibsen's," a linguistic process directly equivalent to the textual definition of conflation (*Interpretation* VI, 330–31).

3. Freud concentrates on what he calls "artificial interpolations" (*Interpretation* VI, 342), whereas homoeoteleuton (or eyeskip) would appear to offer the *opposite* result—omission rather than insertion of material. But Freud makes clear that the process is the same—the opening up of a "difference between the text of the dream-content and that of the dream-thoughts" (343) through a displacing of the original elements and their replacement, or representation, by a differently ordered narrative structure. The task of the analyst and the editor is then identical—to discover where the "seams" in the new narrative occur, and to use these seams as an indication of the original "value" of the elements.

4. Freud likens the surface of the dream (the latent content) to a "pictographic script, the characters of which have to be transposed individually into the language of the dream-thoughts" (312)—a concept very similar to Saussure's attempted distinction between signifier and signified (see below), later deconstructed by Lacan.

Works Cited

Bentley, G. E. "Blake's Works as Performances: Intentions and Inattentions" *Text* 4 (1988): 319–41.

Bloom, Harold. *The Anxiety of Influence: A Theory of Poetry.* New York: Oxford UP, 1973.

Bowers, Fredson. *Textual and Literary Criticism.* Cambridge: Cambridge UP, 1966.

"Contemporary Literary Theory and Textual Criticism." Society for Textual Scholarship Conference Session. New York, 7 April 1989.

Crane, Elaine Forman. "Gender Consciousness in Editing: The Diary of Elizabeth Drinker." *Text* 4 (1988): 375–83.

Dearing, Vinton A. *Principles and Practice of Textual Analysis.* Berkeley: U of California P, 1974.

Fennell, John L. I. "Textology as a Key to the Study of Old Russian Literature and History." *Text* 1 (1981): 157–66.

Foley, John Miles. "Editing Oral Epic Texts: Theory and Practice." *Text* 1 (1981): 75–94.

Fowler, David C. "A New Edition of the B Text of *Piers Plowman*," *Yearbook of English Studies* 7 (1977): 23–42.

Freud, Sigmund. *The Interpretation of Dreams*. Trans. James Strachey. London: Hogarth/Institute of Psychoanalysis, 1953. Rpt. New York: Avon, 1965.

Gabler, Hans Walter. "The Synchrony and Diachrony of Texts: Practice and Theory of the Critical Edition of James Joyce's *Ulysses*." *Text* 1 (1981): 305–26.

———. "The Text as Process and the Problem of Intentionality." *Text* 3 (1987): 107–16.

———, Wolfhard Steppe, Claus Melchoir, eds. *Ulysses: A Critical and Synoptic Edition*. By James Joyce. 3 vols. New York: Garland, 1984.

Greetham, D. C. "Literary and Textual Theory: Redrawing the Matrix." *Studies in Bibliography* 42 (1989): 1–24.

Hinman, Charlton, ed. *The Norton Facsimile: The Shakespeare First Folio*. New York: Norton, 1968.

Howard-Hill, T. H. "Theory and Praxis in the Social Approach to Editing." *Text* 5 (in press).

Hudson, Anne. "Middle English." In *Editing Medieval Texts: English, French, and Latin Written in England*. New York: Garland, 1977.

Kane, George, and E. Talbot Donaldson, eds. *Piers Plowman: The B Version . . . An Edition in the Form of Trinity College MS B. 15. 17*. London: Athlone, 1975.

Kidd, John. "An Inquiry into 'Ulysses: The Corrected Text.'" *Papers of the Bibliographical Society of America* 82 (1988): 411–584.

———. "The Scandal of *Ulysses*." *New York Review of Books,* 30 June 1988, 32–39.

Kristeva, Julia. *Revolution in Poetic Language*. Trans. Margaret Waller. Paris: Seuil, 1974; New York: Columbia UP, 1984.

Lacan, Jacques. *Écrits*. Trans. Alan Sheridan. Paris: Seuil, 1966; New York: Norton, 1977.

———. *Speech and Language in Psychoanalysis*. Trans. Anthony Wilden. Baltimore: Johns Hopkins UP, 1968.

Lanham, Richard. The Future of Doctoral Programs in English. MLA/Ford Foundation Conference, Minnesota, April 1987.

Mailloux, Steven. *Interpretive Conventions: The Reader in the Study of American Fiction*. Ithaca: Cornell UP, 1982.

McGann, Jerome J. Discussion, "Contemporary Literary Theory and Textual Criticism" Session. Society for Textual Scholarship Conference. New York, 7 April 1989.

———. *A Critique of Modern Textual Criticism*. Chicago: U of Chicago P, 1983.

———. "How to Read a Book." Paper presented at "New Directions in Textual Studies" Conference, Austin, Texas, 30 March–1 April 1989.

———. "The Monks and the Giants: Textual and Bibliographical Studies and the Interpretation of Literary Works." In *Textual Criticism and Literary Interpretation*. Ed. McGann. Chicago: U of Chicago P, 1985. 180–99.

——. "Shall These Bones Live?" *Text* 1 (1981): 21–40.

——. "What Is Critical Editing?" *Text* 5 (in press).

McLaverty, James. "The Concept of Authorial Intention in Textual Criticism," *The Library,* 6th ser. 6 (1984): 121–38.

Mitchell, W. J. T. "Pragmatic Theory." In *Against Theory.* Chicago: U of Chicago P, 1985. 1–10.

Parker, Hershel. *Flawed Texts and Verbal Icons: Literary Authority in American Fiction.* Evanston: Northwestern UP, 1984.

Pasquali, Giorgio. *Storia della tradizione critica del testo.* 2d ed. Florence: Monnier, 1962.

Pearsall, Derek. "Editing Medieval Tests: Some Developments and Some Problems." In McGann, *Textual Criticism and Literary Interpretation* 92–106.

Poulet, Georges. "Criticism and the Experience of Interiority." Trans. Catherine Macksey. In *Reader-Response Criticism.* Ed. Jane P. Tompkins. Baltimore: John Hopkins UP, 1980. 41–49.

Quentin, Henri. *Essais de critique textuelle (ecdotique).* Paris: Picard, 1926.

Reiman, Donald H. "Gender and Documentary Editing: A Diachronic Perspective." *Text* 4 (1988): 351–60.

Rossman, Charles. "The New 'Ulysses': The Hidden Controversy." *New York Review of Books,* 8 December 1988, 53–58.

Saussure, Ferdinand de. *Course in General Linguistics.* Ed. Charles Bally and Albert Sechehaye. Paris: Payot, 1972. Trans. Roy Harris. La Salle, Il. Open Court, 1986.

Severs, J. Burke. "Quentin's Theory of Textual Criticism." *English Institute Annual* (1941). 65–93.

Shillingsburg, Peter. "Key Issues in Editorial Theory." *Analytical and Enumerative Bibliography* 6 (1982): 3–16.

——. "Literary Theory and the Work Itself." *Critical Exchange* (in press).

——. *Scholarly Editing in the Computer Age.* Athens: U of Georgia P, 1986.

Tanselle, G. Thomas. "The Editing of Historical Documents." *Studies in Bibliography* 31 (1978): 1–56.

——. "The Editorial Problem of Final Authorial Intention." *Studies in Bibliography* 29 (1976): 167–211.

——. "External Fact as an Editorial Problem." *Studies in Bibliography* 32 (1979): 1–47.

——. "Historicism and Critical Editing." *Studies in Bibliography* 39 (1986): 1–46.

——. *A Rationale of Textual Criticism.* Philadelphia: U of Pennsylvania P, 1989.

Taylor, Gary. "The Rhetoric of Textual Criticism." *Text* 4 (1988): 39–57.

——, and Michael Warren, eds. *The Division of the Kingdoms: Shakespeare's Two Versions of "King Lear."* Oxford: Oxford UP, 1983.

Textual Scholarship and Literary Theory. Special issue of *Critical Exchange* 24 (Fall 1989).

Timpanaro, Sebastiano. *The Freudian Slip: Psychoanalysis and Textual Criticism.* Trans. Kate Soper. N.p.: La Nuova Italia, 1974; London: Verso, 1985.

Vinaver, Eugene. "Principles of Textual Emendation." *Studies in French Language and Mediaeval Literature Presented to Professor Mildred K. Pope.* Manchester: U of Manchester P, 1939. 351–369.

von Frank, Albert. "Genetic versus Clear Texts." *Documentary Editing* 9 (December 1987): 5–9.

Warren, Michael, ed. *The Complete "King Lear."* Berkeley: U of California P, 1989.

Zeller, Hans. "A New Approach to the Critical Constitution of Literary Texts." *Studies in Bibliography* 28 (1975): 231–64.

6

Notes on Emerging Paradigms in Editorial Theory

PHILIP COHEN and DAVID H. JACKSON

UCH CURRENT EDITORIAL PRACTICE RESTS on a New Critical conception of literature, combined with the very *un*–New Critical identification of authorial intention with textual authority. Editors have often either ignored the issue of literary ontology (the aesthetic problem of how a work exists) or offered remarks on the subject that reveal a conventional New Critical theory of literature.[1] This procedure doubtless owes much to Romanticism, the New Criticism's precursor, with its literary and psychological assumptions about the individual and autonomous artist. It also reflects modern book production and publication. After all, a book published by an author and his publisher suggests a very different literary ontology from differing manuscripts circulated by a Renaissance poet or a set of folk materials inherited and embellished by an ancient bard.

Recently, a number of writers have questioned these two theoretical bases of editing, and their attacks on the conservative ontology and intentionalism of the Anglo-American school have pointed to new ways of editing literary works. Few such editions have yet appeared, and the main example—Hans Walter Gabler's *Ulysses*—has been enveloped in controversy. Nonetheless, the theoretical discussions and methodological proposals of these writers bear analysis and suggest a paradigm shift in editing— one that will marry bibliography with contemporary literary theory.

Because the doctrine of final authorial intention—Fredson Bowers's significant elaboration of W. W. Greg's famous "Rationale of Copy-Text" (1951)—has received so much attention, we will focus primarily on the less-remarked question of literary ontology. We will discuss intention to the extent that it is interconnected with questions of how literature may be said to exist. Our main argument, however, is that an editor's assumptions regarding literary ontology, or the assumptions on which the editor's chosen method is based, determine the stages of the editorial process as well as the form of the edition itself.

The more recent writings we examine generally dissent from the Bowers school on the question of authorial intention and *do* comment on the issue of ontology. Interestingly, they do so in ways that suggest correlations with the interpretative assumptions and ontological conceptions of literary works found in contemporary literary theory. These recent editorial suggestions restrict the criterion of authorial intention in text-constitution. Some of these proposals even indicate a shift from spatial to temporal conceptions of the work, from a single and autonomous well-wrought urn to a diachronous series of interrelated sign systems. Such a shift parallels the evolution in literary theory from modernist and New Critical to postmodernist, semiotic, and poststructuralist conceptions of literature. After a brief discussion of the ontological assumptions of traditional editorial theory and practice, we will review the challenge mounted by some recent editorial work by Steven Mailloux, Jerome J. McGann, Hans Zeller, Hans Walter Gabler, and Peter Shillingsburg in the light of this conceptual shift.

Because editorial theory draws its key concepts and terms from literary theory, our discussion, like accounts of literary theory from Frank Lentricchia to Terry Eagleton, begins with the New Criticism. On the issue of literary ontology, the prevailing school of Anglo-American editing is unabashedly New Critical. The central documents of the Anglo-American editorial tradition represented by Fredson Bowers and G. Thomas Tanselle to support W. K. Wimsatt's assertion in "Battering the Object: The Ontological Approach" that a "poem is an utterance which . . . is hypostatized as an object, and metaphorically as a spatial object" (73–74). Bowers and Tanselle belong to this commonsense school of Anglo-American literary theory, a school that rarely looks beyond the conservative ontological generalities of the New Critical tradition.

Despite a variety of provocative and forceful challenges to its supremacy, Anglo-American editorial theory has been dominated by the criterion of authorial intention at least since the appearance of Greg's seminal "Rationale."[2] Since then, Fredson Bowers, Greg's foremost American advocate, has contended in numerous articles, books, and editions that by following Greg's rationale an editor may produce an eclectic single best text that approximates the ideal text an author finally intended to make public. When Bowers asserts in "Textual Criticism," his essay for the 1970 Modern Language Association volume *The Aims and Methods of Scholarship in Modern Languages and Literatures,* that "a critical edition . . . pursues and recovers the author's full intentions wherever found, and correctly associates them in one synthesis," his assumptions about literary authority (auctorial) and ontology (spatial) are apparent. Similarly, in "The Editor and the Question of Value: Another View," he writes that "a properly emended single text or a critical synthesis of multiple authorities will ordinarily produce what is known as an 'ideal text,' or critical reconstruction superior to the evidence (text) of any one document" (57).[3] Bowers never concedes that equally legitimate literary texts might be constituted on the basis of assumptions that vary from his own spatial and authorial orientations. On the issue of whether authorial intention is the only scholarly orientation one may take to the various texts of a literary work, Tanselle sides with Bowers in "Textual Scholarship," his essay for the 1981 Modern Language Association volume *Introduction to Scholarship in Modern Languages and Literatures:* "Of the various directions that editorial intervention could take, the one of scholarly interest is that which leads toward the text intended by the author" (37). "One is interested, after all," he adds later, "in what the author, not the publisher's editor, wrote" (42).[4]

In the most discussed statement of the traditionalist position, "The Editorial Problem of Final Authorial Intention," Tanselle unhesitatingly reifies the work-to-be-edited. He admits a variety of possible meanings for a given work. Like Bowers, however, he valorizes only one of these: the intended meaning the author deposits in the work. Our guide to this most privileged meaning, Tanselle argues, is "the text itself": "the most reliable source of information about the author's intention in a given work is the work itself" (321). Tanselle defines "the work" in straight formalist terms—granted, with an intentionalist twist. The work embodies "the intention of the author to have particular words and marks of punctuation carry a particular meaning or meanings" (324–25).

While intention is the authority on which Tanselle bases his practice of assembling eclectic critical texts of literary works, the source of this authority is the work itself, in its ideal, spatially whole, structurally integrated, New Critical state. For Tanselle, the work is a historical act of intention, an ideal and enduring configuration created by an author but embodied (inevitably) in a flawed form. Like Wimsatt, Tanselle uses spatial metaphors to analyze the literary work. The editor, Tanselle cautions, must "examine both the author's intention to use a particular word and the author's intention to mean a particular thing in the work as a whole" (317). The "work as a whole," Tanselle points out, might have passed through different versions, which he tellingly characterizes: "If one may think of a work in terms of *a spatial metaphor,* the first [kind of revision] might be labeled 'vertical revision,' because it moves the work to a different plane, and the second 'horizontal revision,' because it involves alterations within the same plane" (335, emphasis ours). Ultimately, Tanselle sees intention as mental stasis. Quoting Michael Hancher, he defines "active intentions" as "the actions that the author, at the time he finishes the text, understands himself to be performing in that text" (317). For Tanselle, the ideal configuration of the work eternally reflects the author's understanding of his or her creation.

An afternoon spent perusing the textual notes of scholarly editions approved by the Modern Language Association's Committee for Scholarly Editions reveals that almost all the texts have been prepared according to criteria and assumptions well within this Anglo-American editorial tradition. The editors of the Virginia Crane and the Northwestern/Newberry Melville editions have privileged authorial intention, especially final intention, in selecting and critically emending copytext to produce a single clear reading text and a separate critical apparatus. On the other hand, editors of works never intended for publication—such as journals, notebooks, and letters—have followed the dictates of documentary rather than critical editing. Thus the Harvard Emerson and the Princeton Thoreau editions import the critical apparatus into the text in order to preserve errors, cancellations, and variants. Only the Cornell Wordsworth is noticeably different in terms of assumptions and execution from the typical CSE edition. Aiming to present all the manuscript readings and the changes in the authorized editions of Wordsworth's printed poetry, as well as provide accurate texts of his poems as they stood at the time of their completion, the editors have supplemented their clear reading texts and critical apparatus with full transcriptions of the manuscripts along with photographic reproductions of the most important and difficult texts. When different versions of the same poem exist, as in the volume on the 1798 *Prelude,* they appear on facing pages.

Many contemporary literary theorists, however, have rejected New Critical spatial assumptions about the literary work of art and also, at the same time, continued the modern tendency to banish the author and his intention from any serious discussion of literature. These trends, as we will shortly see, are reflected in some current editorial theory. Pressing the linguistic analogy, structuralist critics have argued that literary meaning arises less from authorial intention than from the relations between elements within intrinsic and intersubjective textual structures. Thus Roland Barthes proposes in his aptly titled essay "The Death of the Author" that "the voice loses its origin, the author enters in his own death, writing begins [when] a fact is *narrated* no longer with a view to acting directly on reality but intransitively . . . finally outside of any function other than that of the very practice of the symbol itself" (142). Unlike the New Criticism's emphasis on the literary artifact itself, much structuralist theory also stresses the temporal process by which a reader resorts to interpretative conventions and codes to make sense of a text. Meaning, Jonathan Culler contends in *Structuralist Poetics,* is less the product of a conscious subject like an author than the result of a reader assimilating a text by means of linguistic and literary conventions, which are culturally and institutionally determined. Stanley Fish has put the reader-response case more polemically in *Is There a Text in This Class?:* "I challenged the self-sufficiency of the text by pointing out that its (apparently) spatial form belied the temporal dimension in which its meanings were actualized, and I argued that it was the developing shape of that actualization, rather than the static shape of the printed page, that should be the object of critical description" (2).

Posing an even greater challenge to editorial reliance on authorial intention is the work of Jacques Derrida, for whom meaning is continuously dispersed along an endless chain of deferments, each sign leading to another sign rather than to a determinate meaning. In this model, language becomes more ambiguous and slippery. Meaning is also radically unstable, for Derrida, because writing lacks speech's fit between intention and utterance: the original author and his meaning are thus irrecoverably absent. In "Signature Event Context," he even reverses the traditional

privileging of speech over writing by arguing that writing's iterative
structure produces meaning independently of author, reader, and context
and that this "essential drifting" characterizes spoken discourse as well
(316). For many contemporary theorists, literary works result from temporal interactions among texts and readers and larger discursive systems.

Although contemporary theory has generally not concerned itself with
the theoretical issues underlying the genesis, transmission, and reconstitution of literary texts, some recent editorial proposals have either challenged or sought to refine the traditionalist position by beginning with
similar theoretical premises. Although the logic and versatility of the
Greg-Bowers rationale for scholarly editing is not in question, there *are*
other ways to edit texts.[5] And the differences between these proposals and
the traditional schools can be traced to ontological models and the editorial procedures those models suggest. These approaches are quite distinct from each other, yet each holds one or both of the following tenets:
first, the temporality of the work's creation, being, and reception; and
second, the community-based nature of its existence. These dissenting
approaches reject the notion that the work is the temporal, spatial, and
exclusive creation of its author. In this sense, they may be seen as par-
ticipating in a paradigm shift in literary theory away from the textual
ontology of the New Criticism.

Steven Mailloux acts as a mediator between traditional textual criticism
and contemporary literary theory in *Interpretive Conventions: The Reader
in the Study of American Fiction* (1982). Mailloux declares his reader-
response orientation by viewing the literary work as temporal rather than
spatial and by locating the work in the perceptive processes of the reader.
Mailloux's theory of literature has roots in the continental school of
phenomenological criticism and issues from the mainstream of reader-
oriented literary theory: "All reader-response critics," he writes, "share the
phenomenological assumption that it is impossible to separate perceiver
from perceived, subject from object. Thus they reject the text's autonomy,
its absolute separateness, in favor of its dependence on the reader's creation or participation. . . . reading is not the discovery of meaning but the
creation of it" (20). In this model, textual authority is conferred by the
author's understanding of what the work does to the reader during the
temporal process of literary apprehension.

The reader-response approach that Mailloux takes has important implications for the editor's policy of copytext emendation. Mailloux is

willing to accept the orthodox goal of fidelity to authorial intention, but he redefines authorial intention from the perspective of reader-response and speech-act theory in order to save the concept. He reconceptualizes intention to accord with the philosophical and interpretative premises of the reader-response school. In particular, the goal of "final authorial intention" is replaced with the category of "inferred intention." Authorial final intention now becomes "the critic's description of the convention-based responses that the author . . . understands he will achieve as a result . . . of his projected reader's recognition of his intention" (99). This inferred authorial intention is recoverable because authors and readers share a number of interpretative conventions. Mailloux's notion of authorial intention recognizes the need to produce a critical interpretation of a text before actual editing commences by referring to the structure of the reader's response and to the relevant historical, biographical, and bibliographical evidence. Mailloux rejects the uncritical acceptance of all authorial revisions, but he is more explicit about the interpretative nature of deciding when the creative process has ended: "The interpreted 'moment' of completion determines the relevant final revisions" (112). This is an aesthetic rather than intentionalist basis for editorial authority, and, according to Mailloux, it can lead to "validly overrul[ing] the author's chronologically final intentions" (121). Although Mailloux does not give full credit to the complexity of Tanselle's discussion of the term *final* in "The Editorial Problem of Final Authorial Intention," even a liberal reading of Tanselle would not permit Mailloux's disregard for chronology or his complete shift from intention to aesthetics.

Mailloux's proposal thus has the virtue of frankly recognizing that authorial intention is a construct formulated before the editorial process begins. Moreover, he rests these assertions upon a coherent, convention-based theory of interpretation that explains how inferred authorial intention can be reconstructed. One is still tempted to assert that literature differs from speech acts because no speaker is present to provide cues and feedback for interpretation. Mailloux might strengthen his position by confronting as rigorously as he presents his own case the Derridean argument that writing's indeterminacy precedes and constitutes speech. Certainly, an intentionalist theory that draws so heavily upon speech-act philosophy needs to refute this argument. Surprisingly, Mailloux does not exploit the full potential of his temporal reader-response conception of a literary work. Thus, spatialist assumptions survive in his adherence to a *single* best text that approximates inferred final intentions. Finally, we should point out that Mailloux is a literary critic and theorist rather than an editor—he has evinced no interest in producing a scholarly edition according to his reader-response principles. Because no editor has undertaken an edition based on Mailloux's proposal, the practical virtues and drawbacks of his editorial theory cannot be assessed.

Like Mailloux, Jerome J. McGann rejects the intrinsic model of the literary work. In *A Critique of Modern Textual Criticism* (1983), McGann speaks scornfully of a "hypnotic fascination with the isolated author" that "has served to foster an underdetermined concept of literary work" (122). He has firm views on what our "concept of literary work" should be: we now require, he argues, "a socialized concept of authorship and textual authority" (8). The traditionalist school "so emphasize[s] the autonomy of the isolated author as to distort our theoretical grasp of the 'mode of existence of a literary work of art'" (8), he writes, invoking Wellek's classic formalist analysis of literary ontology.

From this New Historicist position, McGann draws a range of theoretical and practical conclusions. To begin with, textual authority is "a social nexus, not a personal possession. . . . it takes place within the conventions and enabling limits that are accepted by the prevailing institutions of literary production" (48). Therefore, contrary to Tanselle's concept of the discrete, autonomous text, "the 'work' [is] a series of specific 'texts,' a series of specific acts of production, and the entire process which both of these series constitute" (52). The process of publication, far from being a likely source of contamination, is essential to the work's attainment of full ontological status: "'Final authority' for literary works rests neither with the author nor with his affiliated institution; it resides in the actual structure of the agreements which these two cooperating authorities reach in specific cases" (54). In short, the changes that happen within a work as it moves from manuscript to printed version are an essential as well as inevitable part of that work's "training . . . for its appearance in the world" (51).

These views lead McGann to some familiar objections to the traditional school, most importantly as regards copytext selection. Although numerous prepublication documents abound in the modern period, his argument runs, Greg is not applicable to post-Renaissance texts. Writers share authority with the institutions of literary production; therefore, manuscript is rarely if ever to be preferred as copytext. Only when a work passes into a first edition has it been properly "trained" for the world. Before publication it quite literally does not exist in its fullest state.

McGann chides textual critics for remaining "relatively innocent of the large theoretical issues and problems which have recently come to light" (9). And he declares that his "book tries to develop a fully elaborated argument for a socialized concept of authorship and textual authority" (8). Yet McGann's "fully elaborated argument" turns out to rest on an assertion—that literary works must be "trained" for their "appearance" in the world. While McGann repeats the assertion often, he does not explain or defend it. Old-school New Critics like René Wellek, and new-school theorists from structuralism and its various "post's," generally achieve a higher and more persuasive level of critical discourse than McGann.

McGann attacks the notion that authors have "autonomy," and he derides Bowers's and Tanselle's alleged "hypnotic fascination with the isolated author" (122). In taking this polemical tack, he overlooks Tanselle's discussion of collaboration in "The Editorial Problem." Tanselle fully admits of instances where collaboration with editors and others should be acknowledged and factored into copytext selection and emendation. Tanselle diverges from McGann by insisting on the exercise of editorial judgment to determine in which cases the collaborative interpretation is appropriate and in which cases the prime authority of authorial intention should be assumed. Less programmatic than McGann, Tanselle stands firmly in the Greg tradition of demanding a free reign for editorial discretion.

Despite his rejection of eclectic editing in the case of multiple legitimate texts, McGann's editorial work does not appear to be that radical a departure from the Anglo-American editorial tradition. Although the first volume of his edition of Byron's *Complete Poetical Works* appeared in 1980, only three years before *A Critique of Modern Textual Criticism,* the traditional aspects of McGann's editorial practice may surprise those familiar with the polemical nature of the *Critique.* In his edition McGann reproduces "correct" single reading texts that are faithful to Byron's intentions (1.xxviii). He maintains a flexible case-by-case attitude toward the selection of copytext, taking "as copy text the latest edition of these works which it can be shown, or reasonably deduced, Byron himself corrected" (1.xxxiv). While this position is consistent with Greg's rationale, McGann rejects Bowers's and Tanselle's preference for the manuscript as copytext, especially as regards accidentals, because Byron repeatedly looked to friends and the house editors for his publisher for assistance in pointing, frequently complained to his publisher about errors in punctuation in the printed texts, and often corrected punctuation in proof.

One may see here the beginning of the *Critique*'s collaborative and sociological bent, but McGann's editorial practice seems still to rest on an authorial definition of textual authority, which he broadens to include the concept of collaboration and delegation. Thus he adheres to authorial intention in emending copytext: he accepts variants from another text only "when Byron can be shown to have specifically called for revisions after the establishment of copy text" or "when it can be shown that the present copy text has not faithfully reproduced what Byron wanted to be printed" (1.xxxvi). Except for its deliberately less-than-complete textual apparatus, *Lord Byron: The Complete Poetical Works* could have been approved by the CSE. Although authorial intention is only one of several authorizing factors in his *Critique,* McGann's reversion to a modified form of it in practice undermines his theoretical insistence on the social nature of the production of literary works of art. McGann's theoretical position is, nonetheless, provocative. The now-familiar call for selecting as copytext early printing editions, rather than manuscript versions, deserves all the discussion it will bear. The time has now come to explore fully the theoretical premises and practical applications of the "social school" of editing, and McGann began the discourse that enables this exploration.[6]

Moving beyond Mailloux's and McGann's adherence to a single best text derived from new notions of textual authority, the German historical-critical school charts a course between documentary and critical editing, retaining an authorial definition of authority but rejecting authorial intention as a criterion for adjudicating among multiple authorial versions. Indebted both to structuralism and semiotics, Hans Zeller's "A New Approach to the Critical Constitution of Literary Texts" (1975) conceives of a text as a system of signs that authorial revision transforms into another system: "Since a text . . . does not in fact consist of elements but of the relationships between them, variation at one point has an effect on invariant sections of the text" (241). The editor of the nineteenth-century Swiss poet and novella-writer Conrad Ferdinand Meyer, Zeller rejects eclectic copytext editing because it contaminates the textures of a work's different semiotic systems of authoritative versions (237). This approach also stresses the difficulty of recovering authorial intention, especially when writers defy editors by continuing to revise their works. Zeller's theoretical position permits emendation only of unequivocal errors. What he labels a "textual fault," an intermittent suspension of authorization, occurs when a particular reading "admits of no sense in the wider contextual setting, or . . . contradicts the logic specific to the text" *and* when analytical bibliography confirms this conclusion (260).

In emphasizing the editor as historian rather than critic, Zeller's concept of minimal emendation thus attempts to purge literary interpretation from the editorial process. Although Zeller presents no theory of reading for determining whether violation of sense or logic has occurred, his limited concept of emendation restricts considerably an editor's exercise of his interpretative skills. In leading him to posit a series of spatialized authorial artifacts of equal value, Zeller's semiotic and structuralist assumptions also destabilize the traditional notion of a single best text.

Working from a similar theoretical foundation, Hans Walter Gabler proposes a similar nonintentionalist editorial rationale for the new edition of James Joyce's *Ulysses* (1984). In his 1981 essay "The Synchrony and Diachrony of Texts," Gabler reveals the origins of his assumptions in continental genetic editorial theory and shows himself to be one of the rare editors interested in discussing literary ontology and its relation to editorial practice.[7] He extends Zeller's structuralist conception of the individual text but renders nugatory the latter's fear of version contamination by viewing the text as a totality comprised of all its authorial versions in temporal succession: "By such definition, the work attains an axis and extension in time from earliest draft to final revision. Its total text presents itself as a diachronous structure correlating the discrete synchronous structures discernible, of which that conferred by publication is only one" (309). Given that the literary work contains both axes, we can look to the documentary forms (the texts) in which the work historically appeared for its complete manifestation: "The synchronous and diachronous structures combine to form the literary work in the totality of its real presence in the documents of its conception, transmission, and publication" (325).

His dynamic conception of the text is a temporal one, integrating individual authorial versions into a larger sign system. Consequently, Gabler's theoretical position leads to a form of textual apparatus that is quite distinct from that advocated by the traditionalist school. Whereas most CEAA/CSE editions discuss textual history in an introduction and then in textual notes comment on variant readings from different versions,

Gabler has adopted a "show" rather than a "tell" posture toward apparatus in his edition of *Ulysses*. Gabler's edition prints, on the verso in the integral apparatus of a synoptic edition, the emended continuous manuscript comprising the Rosenbach Manuscript holograph, the typescripts, the *The Little Review* serializations, the proofs for the 1922 first edition, and the first edition. The form of apparatus, the synopsis, ingeniously visualizes in a synchronic image the diachronic axis of the work's existence, displaying through an elaborate system of diacritical marks the growth of the "continuous manuscript text" of the novel. Gabler takes pains to explain how we should read its diacritical marks and other symbols because authority is conferred by the total work as it occurs in this continuous-manuscript text. This synopsis is only one possible form of apparatus that can stem from Gabler's theory. He admits other forms, so long as they illustrate what modern German editing calls "integral apparatus."

This continuous-manuscript text of *Ulysses* extending over a sequence of various documents also serves as Gabler's copytext in the traditional sense because there is no "unified holograph manuscript at a state of development corresponding to the first-edition text" (3:1895). Thus the right-hand side of the edition presents a critically established clear reading text that is "based with the greatest possible consistency on the author's manuscripts" and "does not follow the departures of typescripts and proofs from the text in autograph" (1:vii). This reading text corresponds to the final level of revision of the continuous-manuscript text, the first edition text purged of transmissional corruption.

Surprisingly, pre–fair copy authorial variants, which would be useful to scholars, are not included although Gabler concedes that he has referred to those drafts for purposes of emendation (3:1895). Nevertheless, their absence seems arbitrary and inconsistent with the theoretical notion of a continuous manuscript. Gabler's temporal model is also somewhat schematic: revision is not a process of discrete stages, nor do his divisions recognize that surviving documents may not reflect other stages. More importantly, the presence of a critically established clear reading text is a curious retreat from his earlier theoretical insistence that "the object of scholarly and critical analysis and study . . . is not the final product of the writer's art alone, but beyond this, the totality of the Work in Progress" ("Synchrony" 325). Yet Gabler's theoretical discussion is also compromised by an unwillingness to do away with intentionality completely: he argues at one point that "we never come closer to an author's willed structuring of design and meaning than through his conscious choices of language, expression, and style" (309). Indeed, Gabler's theoretical foundation is most problematic in its attempts to blend the historical emphasis implied by limiting the text to its *authorial* versions with the ahistorical emphasis of his structuralist and nonauthorial conceptions of the text. In preparing his edition, Gabler may have yielded to commercial pressures for such a reading text. Nevertheless, his assumptions and his edition represent an odd, perhaps untenable, combination of Anglo-American and continental editorial traditions: he both views all the authorial versions of *Ulysses* as constituting its complete text *and* uses the continuous-manuscript text as his copytext in order to produce a single reading text as the new, critically established text of *Ulysses.*

cf
Greetham
82 &
Gabler
165 n4

    Controversy surrounding Gabler's edition does not undercut the *theoretical* interest of his approach. Charles Rossman recently revealed in the *New York Review of Books* that members of the Academic Advisory Committee—Richard Ellmann, Philip Gaskell, and Clive Hart—had doubts about Gabler's work. Gabler's most relentless critic, John Kidd, confuses the theoretical and practical aspects of the edition by attacking them indiscriminately in "The Scandal of 'Ulysses.'" Kidd's attacks on Gabler's notions of a continuous-manuscript copytext and a synoptic edition, and on Gabler's tendency to grant maximum authority to the Rosenbach Manuscript holograph, seem differences of editorial opinion. Kidd renders these differences in an excessively polemical way. More legitimate are Kidd's charges concerning Gabler's consistent and accurate application of his principles. For instance, Kidd asserts that Gabler consulted only facsimiles rather than the original documents; wrongly posited and reconstructed now-lost final working drafts for some chapters that Joyce revised after he made his fair copies from the drafts; occasionally ignored Joyce's preferred spelling and punctuation; emended silently at times; and failed sufficiently to explain some of the emendations he does note.

    We agree with those who, like Tanselle, find these charges quite serious. If Kidd and Gabler's other critics are right, the world will have to wait for a more reliable application of Gabler's theoretical ideas. The ideas themselves, however, have an important role in editorial discourse. His edition exhibits both a real influence by a major contemporary theoretical school and a refreshing awareness of the importance of ontology to the editorial task.

    Drawing upon contemporary and traditional arguments against its recuperability, Zeller and Gabler seek to discredit the use of authorial intention in selecting or creating a single best text. This criterion survives only in the narrowest sense for discriminating between authorial variants and transmissional corruption. Both editors may underestimate the critical dimension of these discriminations, since neither of them sets forth a theory of interpretation that explains how an editor determines whether a given reading violates a text's logic or sense. Presumably a structuralist editor needs a theory of reading as much as a traditional editor does. Although they have not fully recognized the roles of individual and social interpretative conventions in creating literary works out of texts, their proposals still mirror literary theory's curtailment of authorial intention and the more deliberate shift from spatial to temporal conceptions of the literary work.

A laudable attempt to accommodate the diversity of current editorial commentary can be found in Peter Shillingsburg's *Scholarly Editing in the Computer Age* (1986). Shillingsburg's critical pluralism admits reader-response critics, structuralists, and deconstructionists to the literary clubhouse rather than checking first to see if they are card-carrying historical, biographical, and textual critics. His tolerance proceeds from an awareness that various definitions of textual authority result from different but legitimate orientations toward literary texts. He aptly distinguishes different definitions of textual authority and their relation to the different textual orientations—aesthetic, historical, authorial, and sociological—an editor can have toward the forms he or she edits. Although each theoretical orientation leads ultimately to a different kind of scholarly edition, Shillingsburg rejects the argument that one orientation is intrinsically superior to the others. He also refuses to identify the literary work with any one of its physical embodiments in a text, arguing instead that the fundamental nature of texts is to be indeterminate and multiple and that the work is a nonphysical entity implied by all of its authoritative texts. Thus he cautions against thinking "that the work is a platonic ideal which the author strives to represent in some final or best version. While the text may be monolithic in some specific instances, it cannot be assumed to be so always" (46). One might respond that this notion of the literary work as a nonphysical entity implied by all its authoritative texts still smacks of so much Platonizing.

Like Zeller and Gabler, Shillingsburg also develops a much-needed attempt to limit the criterion of authorial intention. Because authorial intention, even on the level of recording a specific linguistic sequence, is always shifting from recording one such sequence to recording a modification or complete transformation of it, he argues that only an author's intention "to record on paper, or in some other medium, a specific sequence of words and punctuation according to an acceptable or feasible grammar or relevant linguistic convention" can be recovered more or less conclusively (36). Far less objectively recoverable is an author's intention to mean something by that sequence or to prefer one authorially intended variant or version over another. Consequently, "the author's 'intention' itself is probably not one thing that can be adequately represented by a single or simple authenticated text" (39). When traditional editors conflate or discriminate among authorial variants and versions for some finally intended text, Shillingsburg contends, they are almost always performing a critical task, one that is the product of their implicit or explicit theories of language, literature, and reading. Although editors with an authorial definition of authority have often theoretically conceded that their efforts are critical, their practice has not always reflected this admission. Editorial apparatuses, for example, are not always organized so as to enable a reader easily to construct different texts out of a literary work's various authoritative forms.

Implicit in Shillingsburg's comments is the rejection of the traditional, spatial conception of the literary work. He seems to mirror the current theoretical trend toward viewing the literary work as a temporal process: "I am trying to establish the concept of a work as fluctuating in its composition and multiple in its versions" (48). Emphasizing a literary work's existence as temporal rather than spatial, Shillingsburg points out, undercuts not only those literary critics and theorists who are either oblivious to textual matters or seek one reliable and authoritative text with which to work but also those editors in the tradition of Greg, Bowers, and Tanselle who edit critically to approximate the single ideal text which an author finally intended to appear before the audience.[8]

The authenticity of Shillingsburg's democratic impulse is evidenced by his reformulation of editorial theory and practice so as to produce scholarly editions for a profession characterized by critical pluralism. He wants to shift "the emphasis from 'the right text' to 'the whole work'" and have "the editor . . . prepare the text according to his preferred orientation and provide an apparatus usable by persons with other preferences" (55). Emphasizing apparatus over reading text, Shillingsburg proposes a historical edition based on the narrower definition of intention only, an edition that separates authorial readings from transmissional corruptions and shows the historical development of the authoritative authorial texts through their variants. The beauty of this type of edition is that a reader would be urged to construct the literary work of art out of the available historical texts according to the reader's own theoretical assumptions: "Presenting information in an orderly form, not just establishing a single 'authenticated' text, is the editorial function" (42).[9] Readers of *Scholarly Editing in the Computer Age* will soon see the practical implications of Shillingsburg's proposal when Garland begins publishing its Thackeray edition (projected 18 to 21 volumes) under his general editorship. *Henry Esmond,* edited by Edgar F. Harden, appeared in 1989 and *Vanity Fair* will soon follow.

The editorial theorists we have discussed clearly state their position on how the work-to-be-edited may be said to exist. McGann asserts that literature is social, not individual. Mailloux also presents a community-based model of literature, but in addition stresses its temporal dimension. Zeller and Gabler add a temporal, or diachronic axis, to the spatial, or synchronic, axis emphasized by the New Criticism. And Shillingsburg's editorial pluralism seeks to accommodate different theoretical premises. The most important implication of these theoretical challenges to the traditionalist school of Bowers and Tanselle is a new way of handling the three most important stages of the editorial process, the stages where the editorial process is most visible: the selection of copytext; the emendation of copytext; and the formation of the textual apparatus.

The differences of method and editorial result that we have been discussing illustrate the importance of the theoretical premises that undergird the editorial task. Textual and literary criticism may be seen as distinct fields of inquiry, yet editors stand only to benefit from investigating one of the philosophical problems with which literary theory has long been concerned: how are we to define the nature and existence of the work? The answer to this question is a crucial early step in the assumption of editorial authority.

Although it may be premature to predict the direction textual criticism will take in the future, a paradigm shift appears to be in progress. We are clearly in the midst of a combative period with a number of gauntlets being thrown down. At the heart of this challenge to the spatial assumptions of the New Critics and their disciples lies the fundamental question of literary ontology. The skepticism regarding the use of authorial intention in text-constitution and the shift from spatial to temporal conceptions of literary works in some recent editorial proposals parallel similar developments in literary theory. The editorial theorists under discussion realize that any edited text is, to a certain extent, the product of interpretative, even ideological conventions, and that authorial intention is only one of several possible orientations toward a set of historical documents. In stressing the text's intrinsic instability within a determinate set of historical forms, these textualists are on a track parallel to the literary theorists.

Textual scholarship thus appears, at least in theoretical discussions, to be moving toward assumptions about the nature of the literary work that are more in accord with current theories of literature. No new approach to editing as yet offers the methodological rewards or theoretical consistency of the traditional approach of Bowers and Tanselle. Yet the uneven results of these challengers should not be held against the endeavor to update the theoretical foundation of literary editing. On the contrary, it would be surprising if such a revolutionary undertaking did not have a rocky start.

One reason to applaud the recent work in editorial theory is that it has tended to reconcile textual scholarship and literary criticism. For too long literary critics and theorists have ignored the fact that texts are unreliable and that different versions of many famous literary works have long been in circulation. By the same token, editors have habitually ignored the lively debate among literary critics—a debate, as we have seen, that has the most serious ramifications for the selection and emendation of copy text.

As the study of the humanities expands, the establishment of texts, editing's historical role, will become increasingly important. Editing will continue to perform an important service: it will, as it has for centuries in biblical and classical studies, provide reliable texts for critics to interpret. But editing and textual scholarship can also contribute to the growing debate about the nature of discourse. Foucault observes in his renowned essay "What Is an Author?": "A theory of the work does not exist, and the empirical task of those who naively undertake the editing of works often suffers in the absence of such a theory" (144). As far as this goes, it is correct. However, the most recent work on editing shows that a theory of the work cannot exclude the process in which it comes into the world, the process with which textual scholarship is now and has always been centrally and fruitfully concerned.

Notes

1. The review of editorial theory included in the bibliographical section of the CEAA's 1972 *Statement of Editorial Principles and Procedures,* for example, lists only six articles which "may be useful . . . in helping an editor to clarify his own thinking [about] the nature of works of art" (18). Editorial discussion since 1972 has generally disregarded the issue of ontology.

2. With the exception of Morse Peckham's "Reflections on the Foundations of Modern Textual Editing," the voluminous criticism of Greg's "Rationale" has not challenged the essay's implicit intentionalist assumptions. See, for example, Donald Pizer's "On the Editing of Modern American Texts"; John Freehafer's "Greg's Theory of Copy-Text and Textual Criticism in the CEAA Editions"; and Philip Gaskell's *A New Introduction to Bibliography* 338–42; and Tom Davis in "The CEAA and Modern Textual Editing."

3. Bowers's statements about final authorial intention appear in "Some Principles for Scholarly Editions of Nineteenth-Century American Authors" 60; "Textual Criticism" 30–31; and "The Editor and the Question of Value" 51. Greg and Bowers's conception of divided authority for accidentals and substantives, their procedures for eclectic editing, and their underlying assumptions concerning literary ontology and authorial intention were adopted by both the Center for Editions of American Authors (1963–1976) and the Center for Scholarly Editions (1976–). See, for example, the CEAA's *Statement of Editorial Principles and Procedures* 4–6; and the CSE's "The Center for Scholarly Editions: An Introductory Statement" 384. While the term *final authorial intention* is not used in these last two documents, it is, nevertheless, implicit in their adoption of Greg's rationale.

4. Tanselle's adherence to the standard of final authorial intention can be found in "Greg's Theory of Copy-Text and the Editing of American Literature" 284–88; "The Editorial Problem of Final Authorial Intention" 321–25; and "Recent Editorial Discussion and the Central Questions of Editing" 60–64.

5. The principle of diversity of approach is endorsed by the CSE in its *Introductory Statement:* "The CSE is not interested in endorsing any one position; different approaches are defensible in different situations" (4). And Greg, Bowers, and Tanselle have all placed the execution of editorial judgment before bibliographical dogma of any kind. See Greg's famous remark in the "Rationale": "These, however, are all matters within the discretion of an editor: I am only concerned to uphold his liberty of judgment" (28).

6. In fairness, we should note that McGann's editing of the five Byron volumes that have appeared so far follow a strict format for the Oxford series of English poets. At a recent meeting of the Society for Textual Scholarship (April 1989), he announced that he began formulating his ideas about textual criticism while preparing the Byron edition and that he would edit future projects differently. McGann said, for example, that he hoped to publish multiple historical versions of a text rather than an emended eclectic version. Such a move would be a practical consequence of the principles enunciated in the *Critique.*

7. For brief introductions to the French editorial school known as *critique génétique*, see Louis Hay's "Genetic Editing, Past and Future" and Klaus Hurlebusch's "Conceptualizations for Procedures of Authorship" (103–5). Developing out of French structuralist theory in the 1970s, genetic editing concerns itself with the growth of a literary work through its various textual stages. Believing that meaning arises from relationships within a text and between different versions, genetic editors produce synoptic editions that destabilize the notion of a single best text. Clearly, the geneaology of this approach begins with, but moves beyond, Lachmann.

8. In "Textual Criticism in Nineteenth-Century Studies," Donald Reiman offers a similar criticism of the Anglo-American editorial tradition for conflating "several different states of the text with conjectures in a mishmash that represents no version that the author ever approved or that earlier readers who admired and were influenced by the work ever saw" (16). Because an author's intentions are always shifting and because critical editing interferes with the primary documents, Reiman recommends that scholars rely not on a critically established text but rather on accurate reproductions of each major version of a text.

9. Of course, it is a beauty visible only to other textual scholars. For classroom teaching and for general reading, a single "clear" text will always be required. The vitality of New Critical interpretative, theoretical, and editorial approaches stems from this simple unalterable fact that the greatest market demand is for classroom texts.

Works Cited

Barthes, Roland. "The Death of the Author." In *Image-Music-Text*. Trans. Stephen Heath. New York: Hill and Wang, 1978.

Bowers, Fredson. "The Editor and the Question of Value: Another View." *Text* 1 (1981): 45–73.

———. "Some Principles for Scholarly Editions of Nineteenth-Century American Authors. *Studies in Bibliography* 17 (1964): 223–28. Rpt. in *Art and Error: Modern Textual Editing*. Ed. Ronald Gottesman and Scott Bennett. Bloomington: Indiana UP, 1970.

———. "Textual Criticism." In *The Aims and Methods of Scholarship in Modern Languages and Literatures*. Ed. James Thorpe. 1963. 2d rev. ed. New York: Modern Language Association, 1970. 29–54.

"The Center for Scholarly Editions: An Introductory Statement." *PMLA* 92 (September 1977): 583–97.

Culler, Jonathan. *Structuralist Poetics: Structuralism, Linguistics, and the Study of Literature*. 1975. Rpt. Ithaca: Cornell UP, Cornell Paperbacks, 1976.

Davis, Tom. "The CEAA and Modern Textual Editing." Review-Essay of CEAA Editions. *Library* 32 (1977): 61–74.

Derrida, Jacques. "Signature Event Context." 1971. In *Margins of Philosophy*. Trans. Alan Bass. Chicago: U of Chicago P, 1982. 309–30.

Eagleton, Terry. *Literary Theory: An Introduction*. Minneapolis: U of Minnesota P, 1983.

Fish, Stanley. *Is There a Text in This Class?* Cambridge: Harvard UP, 1983.

Foucault, Michel. "What Is an Author?" In *Textual Strategies: Perspectives in Post-Structuralist Criticism*. Ed. Josué V. Harari. Ithaca: Cornell UP, 1979. 141–60.

Freehafer, John. "Greg's Theory of Copy-Text and Textual Criticism in the CEAA Editions." *Studies in the Novel* 7 (Fall 1975): 375–88.

Gabler, Hans Walter. Letter. *New York Review of Books*, 18 August 1988: 63.

———. "The Synchrony and Diachrony of Texts: Practice and Theory of the Critical Edition of James Joyce's *Ulysses*." *Text* 1 (1981): 305–26.

———, Wolfhard Steppe, Claus Melchior, eds. *Ulysses: A Critical and Synoptic Edition*. By James Joyce. 3 vols. New York: Garland, 1984.

Gaskell, Philip. *A New Introduction to Bibliography*. London: Oxford UP, 1972.

Greg, W. W. "The Rationale of Copy-Text." *Studies in Bibliography* 3 (1950–51): 19–36. Rpt. in *Art and Error: Modern Textual Editing*. Ed. Ronald Gottesman and Scott Bennett. Bloomington: Indiana UP, 1970.

Hay, Louis. "Genetic Editing, Past and Future: A Few Reflections by a User." Trans. J. M. Luccioni and Hans Walter Gabler. *Text* 3 (1987): 117–33.

Hurlebusch, Klaus. "Conceptualisations for Procedures of Authorship." *Studies in Bibliography* 41 (1988): 100–35.

Kidd, John. "The Scandal of 'Ulysses.'" *New York Review of Books*, 30 June 1988: 32–39.

Lentricchia, Frank. *After the New Criticism*. Chicago: U of Chicago P, 1980.

Mailloux, Stephen. *Interpretive Conventions: The Reader in the Study of American Fiction*. Ithaca: Cornell UP, 1982.

McGann, Jerome J. *A Critique of Modern Textual Criticism*. Chicago: U of Chicago P, 1983.

———, ed. *Lord Byron: The Complete Poetical Works*. 5 vols. Oxford: Oxford UP. 1980–86.

Peckham, Morse. "Reflections on the Foundations of Modern Textual Editing." *Proof* 1 (1971): 122–55.

Pizer, Donald. "On the Editing of Modern American Texts." *Bulletin of the New York Public Library* 75 (1971): 47–53.

Reiman, Donald. "Textual Criticism in Nineteenth-Century Studies." *Nineteenth-Century Contexts* 11 (1987): 9–21.

Rossman, Charles. "The New 'Ulysses': The Hidden Controversy." *New York Review of Books*, 8 December 1988, 53–58.

Shillingsburg, Peter. *Scholarly Editing in the Computer Age*. Athens: U of Georgia P, 1986.

Statement of Editorial Principles and Procedures: A Working Manual for Editing Nineteenth-Century Texts. 1967. Rev. ed. New York: Center for Editions of American Authors, Modern Language Association, 1972.

Tanselle, G. Thomas. "The Editorial Problem of Final Authorial Intention."

Studies in Bibliography 29 (1976): 167–211. Rpt. in *Selected Studies in Bibliography*. Charlottesville: UP of Virginia, 1979. 308–53.

———. "Greg's Theory of Copy-Text and the Editing of American Literature." *Studies in Bibliography* 28 (1975): 167–229. Rpt. in *Selected Studies in Bibliography*. 245–307.

———. "Historicism and Critical Editing." *Studies in Bibliography* 39 (1986): 1–46.

———. "Recent Editorial Discussion and the Central Questions of Editing." *Studies in Bibliography* 34 (1980): 23–65.

———. "Textual Scholarship." *Introduction to Scholarship in Modern Languages and Literatures*. Ed. Joseph Gibaldi. New York: Modern Language Association, 1981. 29–52.

Wimsatt, W. K. "Battering the Object: The Ontological Approach." In *Contemporary Criticism*. Ed. Malcolm Bradbury and David Palmer. London: Edward Arnold, 1970. 60–81.

Zeller, Hans. "A New Approach to the Critical Constitution of Literary Texts." *Studies in Bibliography* 28 (1975): 231–64.

7

The Rhetorical Politics of Editing: A Response to
Eggert, Greetham, and Cohen and Jackson

STEVEN MAILLOUX

FTER SEEING AN AD FOR THE new film version of *Phantom of the Opera*, my ten-year-old daughter asked if she could see the movie. I told her no; it's a horror film rated R. She then declared in her most earnest voice, "But Dad, I *love* the Phantom of the *Author*."

"Loving the phantom of the author" can serve as the motto for the following comments. The phrase signifies the problematic status of the author among some contemporary critical theorists, but it also suggests the commitment, the enthusiasm, and, yes, even the joy felt by scholars and critics who continue to use the "author" as an interpretative category organizing their literary studies. Nowhere is the question of the author more crucial for the institutional politics of the discipline than in the area of textual study and editorial theory. Here the stakes for theoretical practice are clear, at least at first glance: Should editors establish their texts based on a theory of an individual author's final intentions or on some other theory that refuses to privilege the individual author?

The essays in the present volume show how complicated this question becomes when the fields of textual editing and critical theory are brought together in productive dialogue. The three essays I will discuss provide especially intriguing examples of this conversation. Paul Eggert's piece presents a rhetorical reading of editorial theory and proposes to supplement traditional "product" metaphors with those of "process." Philip

Cohen and David Jackson also demonstrate an informed sensitivity to the rhetoric of editing. They describe the parallels between the tropes of New Critical formalism and traditional editing theory and then suggest that traditional editors should pay much more attention to the new antiformalist metaphors now available in various poststructuralist theories and in some recent new editorial paradigms. And in D. C. Greetham's essay we find a figural reading of editing itself from the perspective of psychoanalysis.

"Textual Product or Textual Process" is the most explicit in its rhetorical analysis. Eggert reads editing theory from "within," highlighting the tropes it uses to get its work done. He points out, for example, the significance of the "metaphors of purity and corruption used to characterize variant readings." He notes how the "phrase 'the work of his hand' [in discussions of sculpture] is a potent metaphor related to the editorial term, *autograph manuscript*." He usefully remarks on "revision" as "another submerged editorial metaphor" and suggests how it sometimes functions misleadingly to attribute later authorial changes to a writer's "reseeing" the text rather than to something more accurately labeled a "scanning." And he comments on editing's "characteristic nineteenth-century bourgeois metaphors of filial descent, textual purity, and corruption." He then combines this tropological reading of editing with an analysis of its "habits of argument," which he calls "the rhetoric of strenuous inevitability." Such a rhetoric works to "shepherd the reader into a position where no other conclusion [than the editor's single reading text] seems reasonable."

I find this rhetorical reading of editing to be quite persuasive, though I am confused by one argument Eggert makes. Why does he feel it necessary to set up an absolute opposition between a scientistic editing project based on reconstructing one single reading text based on an author's final intentions and a poststructuralist theory committed to giving "free rein to the multiplicities of textuality"? For Eggert, traditional editing privileges the determinate reading text, while poststructuralism rejects all privileging of any kind of determinacy. In one case, we have rigid, stable singularity and in the other unstable, infinite freeplay.

This depiction of traditional editing and poststructuralist theory makes them rather monolithic in themselves and absolutely opposed in their relation to each other. Such a depiction leads to problems in Eggert's essay. The first involves an overreaction to the reductive version of poststructuralism he has created. Suspicious of poststructuralist notions of radical indeterminacy, Eggert refers to the author as an "actual person" *as opposed to* something we "reconstruct." In light of Eggert's convincing arguments against other editorial phantoms, what does it mean to refer in the present to the "actual" author independent of a historical reconstruction made in the present? Historical reconstruction, when convincing, does give us the "actual person" or, better, it gives us the only author available, the only author that counts. It is a mistake to oppose the "actual person" to a "historical reconstruction" because any past person you point to will only count as such if the "historical reconstruction" you have proposed is convincing within the rhetorical context in which you propose it. The rhetorical context includes assumptions about the author's biography, interpretations of his or her texts, beliefs about the composing process, standards of what counts as evidence, acceptable lines of argument, and so on.

To make the theoretical claims I have just made about "historical reconstruction" is to take a position that can be identified loosely as poststructuralist (more precisely as rhetorical pragmatist).[1] Such a position sees the notion of infinite freeplay to be just as misguided as the idea of eternally stable meaning. Both notions suggest a state of textuality—either objective determinacy or absolute indeterminacy—that contradicts our lived history of rhetorical conflict over the editing and interpretation of texts. There are moments—sometimes long periods of time—in which a version of a text or the persuasiveness of an interpretation is widely accepted within a historical community. At such times claims for radical indeterminacy have little rhetorical purchase. However, the privileging of a textual version or interpretation is never in principle absolute or permanent. It can be and often is called into question as the rhetorical context shifts from one community to another, from one historical moment to the next. Eggert ignores this version of poststructuralism (or perhaps would not recognize rhetorical pragmatism as a poststructuralist theory) and views poststructuralism as monolithically declaring the end of all boundaries including authorial agency. Caught between a false opposition he has constructed—a simple notion of individual authorship versus an undesirable concept of radical indeterminacy—Eggert sometimes opts for the former position, which underlies the very rationale of traditional editing he has so persuasively criticized.

Most of the time, however, Eggert rejects "discredited Romantic notions of creativity" and develops a more nuanced concept of authorial agency. What strikes me as most significant about his process model of "authorial intertextuality" is the way he relates that model to the contemporary functions of the "author" in literary culture. He asks, "If authorial agency remains the principal source of textual interest for most readers, then given" his "reservations . . . about the status and characteristic rhetoric and practices of the modern critical edition, does it make sense to continue to prepare and publish them?" I am less interested here in Eggert's "heavily qualified yes" to this question than I am in his observation about the *uses* of the "author" by readers and editors. Throughout his essay, Eggert implies that editing's use of traditional tropes might be changed by adopting the instrumental trope of "use." To what use will a particular edition be put? What use is a clear reading text? What use is authorial intertextuality? To focus on the use of texts is to shift the question away from whether traditional intentionalism or radical indeterminacy more accurately reflects the essential nature of literature or authorship and to recognize the multiple uses editing serves inside and outside the academy. To come at the questions of editorial theory from this perspective is to avoid the trap of thinking that theory precedes practice rather than being an extension of it. Asking questions like "What is the correct theory of authorship in general and what are its implications for editing practice?" often leads to endless debates structured by such distinctions as objectively singular text versus absolute textual indeterminacy or unconstrained individual intention versus collective authorship. To avoid such theoretical ghosts there is a need to examine editing's historical accomplishments, the past interests it has served, its relation to the discipline of literary studies and the humanities more generally, the function of authors in a larger cultural politics, and so on. To focus on the uses of authors, texts, and editing sidesteps the theoretical arguments preoccupying many debates within textual scholarship. Sidestepping such theoretical deadends does not, of course, solve all the problems of practice.

Whereas Eggert's gambit is to read the tropes of editing from "within" that practice, Cohen and Jackson's essay, "Notes on Emerging Paradigms in Editorial Theory," reads the tropes at the boundary between editing and critical theory. In doing so, they have a more differentiated and thus ultimately more sympathetic view of poststructuralism than Eggert. Their strategy is to argue that editing theory needs to incorporate the tropes of critical theory into its domain much more explicitly and more self-consciously than it has done in the past. Like Eggert, they call for a new set of tropes for editing, and again like Eggert they find that the trope of use has an especially strong potential within the field.

Cohen and Jackson first establish the close relationship between the spatial metaphors used by the New Critics and those employed by the Anglo-American editing tradition represented by Bowers and Tanselle. Then in an impressive discussion of recent theory and editing, Cohen and Jackson show how spatial metaphors for the literary work are being replaced by temporal metaphors. I reveal my own pragmatist biases, I'm sure, when I find their talk about (an ahistorical?) "literary ontology" to be less helpful than their historical analyses of the rhetoric of editing and its tropes of use. On the latter, Cohen and Jackson's position is very close to that of Eggert. They mention in a note how classroom teachers and general readers continue to use a "single 'clear' text" and how such needs continue to determine aspects of editorial practice. They make the perceptive comment that the "stubborn vitality of New Critical interpretative, theoretical, and editorial approaches stems from this simple unalterable fact that the greatest market demand is for classroom texts." Like Eggert, they emphasize how editorial practices should be determined by the future contexts of use for the texts being edited.

Eggert and Cohen and Jackson examine the uses of tropes in editing and suggest the trope of use as a way of solving some of its practical problems. In "The Manifestation and Accommodation of Theory in Textual Editing," Greetham eventually takes an entirely different tack, using tropes from another discipline to read editing itself. First, however, he follows the strategy of Cohen and Jackson in focusing on the boundary of two fields, editing and literary theory, showing their complex affinities and differences. He usefully explores the theoretical assumptions underlying various editing practices, a project that extends the work of his excellent overview, "Textual and Literary Theory: Redrawing the Matrix."

But in the second half of the present essay, Greetham develops another relation between the fields of editing and theory. Here he works, as he puts it, against the grain of editing's self-representations and rereads editing according to the tropes of psychoanalytic criticism. He further complicates his reading by overlaying it with the Marxist trope of base/superstructure. This is a suggestive figuring of the enterprise of editing. It is important to note, however, that Greetham is not trying in this section to claim that his reading has direct consequences for editorial practices or even to suggest that it illustrates the manifestation of theory in that practice. Rather, Greetham's goal is more speculative: his recharacterization of editing might alert "the practitioner to the very practice he has been operating under by showing him where the 'seams' (or 'semes'?) of argument lie hidden." This rhetorical self-reflexivity is especially crucial at the present disciplinary moment when so many competing tropes and arguments are shaping the theories and practices of scholarly editing, poststructuralist theory, and their future interrelationship.

The theoretical analyses by Eggert, Greetham, and Cohen and Jackson all contribute to this rhetorical project, and in addition they encourage further discussions that might work within a slightly different line of questioning: Besides asking "How can editing use critical theory?" shouldn't we also be asking, "How can critical theory use editing?" I will conclude these comments by trying a little of my own speculative theorizing on the intersection of editing and theory, relying in part upon a rhetorical appropriation of the work of Michel Foucault.

Let me take the ongoing debate over the phantom of the author as my point of departure. As with many of this volume's contributors, I will use the names of Jerome McGann and G. Thomas Tanselle to stand in for two sides in one current controversy. The function of the individual author for the Greg-Bowers tradition of editing has been to serve as the source of final intentions that are to be represented in the text of an editor's critical edition. McGann has challenged this tradition by arguing that it contains "ideas about the nature of literary production and textual authority which so emphasize the autonomy of the isolated author as to distort our theoretical grasp of the 'mode of existence of a literary work of art' (a mode of existence which is fundamentally social rather than personal)" (*Critique* 8). The practical result has been the mistake that any "editorial intervention by a publisher or his agents between the author's manuscript and the published text" is "regarded as a corruption of the authoritative text" (*Critique* 20). McGann opposes this theory of the autonomous author with a more collaborative view of authorship, which argues that "the production of books, in the later modern periods especially, sometimes involves a close working relationship between the author and various editorial and publishing professionals associated with the institutions which serve to transmit literary works to the public" (*Critique* 34–35). Thus, the goal of editing should not be to reconstruct the text intended by the autonomous author but to recover the text produced by the original author-publisher collaboration. More exactly, McGann argues that in the choice of copytext "the presumption should lie with the first edition since it can be expected to contain what the author and publishing institution together worked to put before the public" (*Critique* 125).

G. Thomas Tanselle has defended the Greg-Bowers theory of final authorial intentions against this collectivist view of authorship. In doing so, he advocates what he refers to as "the primacy of unconstrained authorial intention as a guide for critical editing" ("Historicism" 127). Tanselle acknowledges the social aspects of authorship but argues that when there is a conflict between author and publisher, preference should be given to "an author's uninfluenced intentions" (127), "to what an author thought and wrote when not making concessions to pressure from others" (129). More generally, Tanselle claims that "an editor's guiding principle in textual decisions" must give priority "either to the author's intentions or to outside influences," and he agrees with the editors who "have regarded authorial intention as the more sensible choice for a scholarly edition" ("Historicism" 132–33).[2]

I cannot do full justice here to Tanselle's theory of authorship and editing or to his detailed response to McGann's critique.[3] Essays in this volume provide various glosses on the issues involved in this debate and on the consequences for editing of one side winning out over the other. I would simply like to gesture toward another way of framing the disagreement and mention some questions such a reframing makes more visible.

A Foucauldian notion of power rejects the usefulness of viewing the theoretical issue in editing as a choice between unconstrained author's intentions and an equally unproblematic collective authorship. Power, as a network of force relations, works positively as well as negatively, constraining and enabling the individual agent who is constituted as an authoring subject, one who is never "unconstrained" in the ideal Platonic sense Tanselle seems to be positing.[4] On the other hand, the social model of authorship does not offer a real theoretical alternative to a focus on the individual author because it is just as "arbitrary" to draw your boundary of inquiry at the author-publisher collaboration as it is to draw it around only the author itself, for the publishing apparatus is just as enmeshed in material and ideological social formations and networks of power as the author is.[5] The social model of authorship does, however, raise important questions about the assumptions concerning authors, assumptions that continue to organize the academic study of literature.

To reframe the dispute over authorial intention and authority in terms of a Foucauldian pragmatism is to resituate the issues so that the following questions become primary: Given the fact that the unconstrained author is an ungraspable phantom, a theoretical impossibility, which categories of power relations should we attempt to identify and what should we do with them in our editorial practice? What effect would these decisions have on other practices, such as literary criticism and history, composition and creative writing, within the discipline? If we continue to organize our discipline around the category of authorship, what do we gain and what do we lose? If we give up that category, where are we?

Especially for literary theorists, the debate over these and related editorial questions should be of primary importance, for they take up some of the most central issues presently dividing the discipline: the question of authors and authority; of intention and determinacy of meaning; of literary creativity and material, cultural production; and of aesthetics and historical reconstruction. Moreover, some crucial political issues are also being raised by these editorial debates. I'm not only referring to the institutional politics of how our discipline would be reconfigured if a collectivist notion of authorship became generally accepted in the profession. I'm also referring to the way that the political question of agency is being conceptualized within editorial theory.

What liberal humanism and traditional Marxism and feminism once gave us was a theory of agency to explain and promote political change of the status quo. The humanist concept of the free individual and the liberationist notion of the collective agent of history both established grounds for the development of effective rhetorical appeals and political strategies. Both raised the possibility of challenging socio-political formations that enforce domination and exploitation of marginalized groups in American society. Most poststructuralist theory, as radical as its rhetoric is, does not provide anything as useful for justifying a progressive form of political activism. Indeed, various Americanized forms of deconstruction and Foucauldian genealogy present powerful critiques of the autonomous individual and the unified self, of the grand narratives of liberation and global theories of power, without providing anything to replace the productive theories of agency based on these concepts and frameworks.

My suggestion here is not that such poststructuralist theory should therefore be ignored. Rather, at the present historical moment these challenges must be worked through. This work is currently being done in theoretical practices associated with such perspectives as materialist feminism, what Henry Louis Gates calls the "new black aesthetics movement," postmodern Marxism, and Cornel West's "prophetic pragmatism." And I've tried to suggest (and the present volume demonstrates) that this work is also being accomplished in an area of study often damned by faint praise or dismissed as atheoretical: the theoretical practice of editing.

Notes

1. For further discussion, see Mailloux, *Rhetorical Power.*

2. For further discussion of "outside influences" on authors, see Tanselle, *Rationale* 83–87. Also see Parker for detailed historical examples and suggestive analyses. The differences between Tanselle's and Parker's forms of intentionalism are evident throughout Parker (e.g., 226–28) and in Tanselle, "Historicism" 135–42.

3. This is especially unfortunate because I have learned so much from Tanselle's own attempts to represent other theoretical positions clearly and fairly. For example, his portrayal of my own previous work ("Textual Scholarship and 'Author's Final Intention,'" in Mailloux, *Interpretive Conventions* 93–125) succinctly and usefully states my case (Tanselle, "Historicism" 142–44). Of course, Tanselle sees his straightforward description as a refutation of my position (understood against the background of his larger argument), while I see it as simply a restatement of my persuasive case (which calls other parts of his argument into question).

4. On Foucault's concept of power, see, for example, Foucault, *History of Sexuality; Discipline and Punish; Power/Knowledge;* and Mailloux, *Rhetorical Power* 136–44. Foucault, "What Is an Author?" is relevant to issues raised throughout my comments.

5. For a sample discussion of this wider context for editing, see McGann, *Critique* 125–28; but also see Tanselle's criticisms of these pages ("Historicism" 130–33). See McGann, "Monks and Giants" for a helpful discussion of the role of editing in a more comprehensive socio-historical project that takes into account the larger social formations in which publishing and editing take place.

Works Cited

Foucault, Michel. *Discipline and Punish: The Birth of the Prison.* Trans. Alan Sheridan. New York: Vintage, 1979.
———. *History of Sexuality, Vol. 1: An Introduction.* Trans. Robert Hurley. New York: Pantheon, 1978.
———. *Power/Knowledge: Selected Interviews and Other Writings, 1972–1977.* Ed. Colin Gordon. New York: Pantheon, 1980.

———. "What Is an Author?" Trans. Josué V. Harari. In *Textual Strategies: Perspectives in Post-Structuralist Criticism.* Ed. Harari. Ithaca: Cornell UP, 1979. 141–60.

Gates, Henry Louis, Jr. "Introduction: 'Tell Me, Sir . . . What *Is* "Black" Literature?'" *PMLA* 105 (1990): 11–22.

Greetham, D. C. "Textual and Literary Theory: Redrawing the Matrix," *Studies in Bibliography* 42 (1989): 1–24.

McGann, Jerome J. *A Critique of Modern Textual Criticism.* Chicago and London: U of Chicago P, 1983.

———. "The Monks and the Giants: Textual and Bibliographical Studies and the Interpretation of Literary Works." In McGann. *The Beauty of Inflections: Literary Investigations in Historical Method and Theory.* New York and Oxford: Oxford UP, 1985. 69–89.

Mailloux, Steven. *Interpretive Conventions: The Reader in the Study of American Fiction.* Ithaca: Cornell UP, 1982.

———. *Rhetorical Power.* Ithaca: Cornell UP, 1989.

Parker, Hershel. *Flawed Texts and Verbal Icons: Literary Authority in American Fiction.* Evanston: Northwestern UP, 1984.

Tanselle, G. Thomas. "Historicism and Critical Editing." *Studies in Bibliography* 36 (1986): 1–46. Rep. in Tanselle. *Textual Criticism Since Greg: A Chronicle, 1950–1985.* Charlottesville: UP of Virginia, 1987. 109–54.

———. *A Rationale of Textual Criticism.* Philadelphia: U of Pennsylvania P, 1989.

West, Cornel. *The American Evasion of Philosophy: A Genealogy of Pragmatism.* U of Wisconsin P, 1989.

8

Issues of Identity and Utterance: An Intentionalist Response to "Textual Instability"

JAMES MCLAVERTY

THE DEATH OF THE AUTHOR—reported somewhat prematurely by Barthes over twenty years ago—now seems confirmed as he loses his grip not only on his meanings but on his text. "Iterability," which played such an important role in Derrida's deconstructive reading of the Austin-Searle theory of speech acts, has now found a strange bedfellow in the "instability" of the text. "Iterability" is different from "iteration," which might suggest the mere repetition of an original; there can be no signification, it is argued, without "iterability." As Derrida puts it in "Signature Event Context," "The possibility of repeating, and therefore of identifying, marks is implied in every code, making of it a communicable, transmittable, decipherable grid that is iterable, for a third party, and thus for any possible user in general" (315). In the best sustained attempt I have found to explicate Derrida's position, Samuel C. Wheeler III argues that as the iterability of representations is a feature that cannot be completely present, significant items are always referring to something else and deferring their meanings; thoughts and intentions, as representations, are nonpresent in just this way. Because intentions cannot be brought in to help out speech acts, and because context can never be exhausted, meaning remains indeterminate. "Iterability," Rodolphe Gasché points out in his study of Derrida (212–14), involves not only repetition but alteration: as Derrida himself puts it in "Limited Inc. abc,"

"Iteration alters, something new takes place" (175). This emphasis on iterability has interesting links with the more radical versions of the doctrine of "textual instability," a phrase I have borrowed from D. F. McKenzie's 1985 Panizzi lectures. This doctrine also derives its force from problems of repeatability and context. Just as it is impossible for the critic to settle on one single meaning for a text, so, it is claimed, it is impossible for editors to recover and present a single authoritative text. Authors often produce different versions of their works; and even when they don't, any attempt to repeat a text is likely to produce variation and will certainly project the text into a new context, inducing different reader responses. The attempt to get at an authorial version would, according to one version of the doctrine, be not only vain but wrong-headed: any text is so thoroughly shaped by the demands of the readership, the publisher, and the market in general that any attempt to purge it of the resulting characteristics would be a mistake. At its extreme this approach obliterates iterability in favor of alteration; poems become events, and each reading is a new event.

Although I am skeptical of the cogency of the arguments from iterability, I am simply going to sidestep them here. This paper is not concerned with establishing certainties on which the textual critic can rest but rather with suggesting lines of inquiry and how they might be pursued with consistency. John Searle has argued in his helpful review of Jonathan Culler's *On Deconstruction* that Derrida shares "the real mistake of the classical metaphysician," which was "not the belief that there were metaphysical foundations, but rather the belief that somehow or other such foundations were necessary" (78). My aim is to respond to the present debate in textual criticism as someone who wants to go on talking of authors and their intentions and meanings, but cannot ally himself completely with foundationalist theorists of authorial intention such as P. D. Juhl, Steven Knapp and Walter Benn Michaels, and, their equivalent in textual criticism, Hershel Parker.[1] In particular, I want to draw attention to the links between authors, texts, and editors on the one hand and mundane forms of human activity on the other. It is difficult to feel the appropriate frisson, a mixture of horror and excitement, at "textual instability" when it fits in so well to the general pattern of experience. I woke up this morning to find a few more grey hairs on my head, that my bicycle needed a new tire, and that Mrs Thatcher had changed her mind about the wholesomeness of the British egg—it has salmonella—though it is not yet clear what she intends to do about it. "Textual instability" is not a feature that shows the strangeness of literary texts but their ordinariness; and if we have been in the habit of thinking differently, it must have been from some last romantic longing for simplicity and foundations—or from the desire to maintain the power of editors. The problems surrounding "textual instability" are therefore susceptible of discussion in quite ordinary ways, and I suspect they can be boiled down to two questions. What do we mean when we say several versions belong to the same work? (This corresponds to the problem of bicycles with new tires.) And what should the editor be presenting to the critic for interpretation? (Something corresponding to Mrs. Thatcher's speech on the British egg.)

The problem the textual critic faces over versions is first and foremost a problem of identity. It is a fundamental problem because it is so difficult to explain what a version is. There are several versions of Hardy's *Tess of the D'Urbervilles,* one of which, that of 1892, I shall discuss later; each of these seems to be *Tess* and yet they are not strictly the same. If for A to be identical with B it is necessary for everything that is true of A to be true of B, then the *Tess* of 1892 is not identical with the *Tess* of 1895. This curious situation enables G. Thomas Tanselle's essay "The Editorial Problem of Final Authorial Intention" to raise the question when—perhaps always or never—we should regard a new version as a separate work (200–201). It seems a promising way out to ask how much the versions are *like* one another, but on closer inspection that will not do at all; in some respects all the versions of *Tess* are like *Jude the Obscure,* or *Middlemarch,* or even *The Winter's Tale,* and these are certainly not the same work. Nelson Goodman's strictures on similarity in *Problems and Projects* (437–46) should lead us to recognize that we lack the appropriate vocabulary and standards for discussing degrees of likeness.

Fortunately the case of *Tess of the D'Urbervilles* has a structure in common with a problem raised by Hobbes and much debated in modern philosophy, one that is usually illustrated by the case of Theseus' ship. I take my version from Andrew Brennan's *Conditions of Identity.* Theseus sets sail with a new ship, but before long it has to go in for repair; old planks, nails, and sails are taken out and replaced by new ones. Over a long period of time, through numerous repairs, all the old material is replaced by new, and the problem is raised: Is this the same ship that Theseus started out with? It has a continuous history, but not a scrap of the material that originally made up the ship remains. The best sort of solution to this problem is one that has already been offered to textual criticism from a very different tradition of thought by Hans Walter Gabler: it is to introduce a new dimension, that of time. Theseus' ship is a persisting thing; it exists through time; at time t, it is composed of such and such materials, at time t_2 it is composed of other materials. In *Ulysses* Stephen Dedalus sees in this a possible way of avoiding paying his debts, "Wait. Five months. Molecules all change. I am other I now. Other I got pound" (1:405), before moving on to consider other aspects of personal identity. Stephen toys with the idea that physical changes release him from debt, but a more acceptable view would be that he should pay up because his identity persists through time without being dependent on the continuing presence of the same physical material.

This solution to the problem of Theseus' ship succeeds through an appeal to continuity, from one stage to the next, of matter, structure, and function. Some material must survive from the refitting or we should say that Theseus had a new ship, though we might be skeptical of the attempts of some philosophers to fix the figure at, for example, two-thirds. Similarly there must be continuity of structure: a new pattern of decking, a change in the rigging, or even an improved shape of oar might not make a new ship, but a complete remodeling of the hull probably would. The point about structure is closely bound up with the requirement of continuity of function. A quite small change in material and structure may change the identity of an object if the function changes—Brennan's example is the transformation of a lamp into a robot-arm (184)—whereas much larger changes will be acceptable if the object continues to function in the same way: it *must* still be Theseus' ship if he's still sailing it from island to island.

The dependence on material, structure, and function provides opportunities for philosophers to create ingenious new difficulties. Suppose the ship has been completely renewed over a period of years and is in active service in the ownership of someone we will call, quite arbitrarily, Jerome McGann; but all this time the discarded pieces of the ship have been collected together and rebuilt into a ship strictly resembling the original by someone else we might call Fredson Bowers. Who is the owner of Theseus' ship, McGann or Bowers? There are now two claimants, one on the basis of the material at time t, and one on the basis of the function, still being carried out at time t_2. They are different, so they can't both be identical with Theseus' ship, identity being transitive. Interference with normal progress through time has produced an intractable problem similar to one raised in a famous essay by Bernard Williams in which two brothers both wake up with the memories of Guy Fawkes. Problems of this sort lead Brennan, taking a lead from Derek Parfit, to suggest that what really matters to us may not be identity but survival. Our account of identity depends on one stage of the ship surviving into another, and we may be clear about survival when we are unclear about identity. Theseus' ship survives authentically as both McGann's ship and Bowers's ship, but it may not be possible to identify it with either. In other words, the philosopher can only help the textual critic in this area by explaining why it is that issues of identity are so problematic, and suggesting that it might sometimes be helpful to talk about survival instead. As Brennan says over halfway through his book, "In saying these things, of course, we have still failed to give a decent theory of artefact identity. But by now it should be clear that we are unlikely ever to come up with one" (190).

The relevance of the case of Theseus' ship to textual criticism will already be clear. Different versions of a work can be taken to correspond to different stages in the renewal of the ship, and the key to the question of identity is whether one stage survives into another with regard to material, structure, and function. If we confine ourselves for the moment to published versions, where issues are clearer, it will be difficult to find cases where revision creates a new work without the author's supplying a new name. This is the convention we operate under. The retention of the name usually signals an adequate survival of material and structure in the form of words, punctuation, and so on, and it will usually signal continuation of the same function. At least it will signal the author's and publisher's attitude to identity; it would be open to readers to disagree, but I know no striking cases where they have done so. It is not difficult to invest cases where the author's decision might be challenged. Let us imagine, for example, that Swift himself prepared *Gulliver's Travels* in an edition for children: political allusion lost its role in the first two books; the satire on scientific method was softened in the third; and in the fourth book the behavior of the Yahoos, especially with regard to their table manners and the handling of their excrement, improved beyond recognition. *Gulliver's Travels* could not, I suggest, survive these changes; even if there was considerable continuity of material and structure, the function would have changed from that of a satire to that of a fairy story.

While questions of identity—when a version becomes a separate work—have not generally been raised by readers and critics, they have been raised by textual critics. I must resist the temptation of running through the well-known examples, bludgeoning them with the criteria of surviving material, structure, and function, but I should like to comment briefly on the two best known, those of Wordsworth's *Prelude* and James's novels, because they raise a generally neglected issue.

Neither the 1805 nor the 1850 *Prelude* was published during Wordsworth's lifetime and neither was given the name *Prelude* by him. Both were prepared for publication, however, so neither raises the special difficulties I shall discuss later. As I agree with Jonathan Wordsworth that the difference between the two versions of the *Prelude,* particularly with regard to the orthodoxy and conservatism of 1850, have been overstated (523–24), the issue of their status as works depends on their relation to *The Recluse,* the masterwork that Wordsworth never completed. A simple view would be that as 1805 was intended to be part of *The Recluse* and 1850 was not, these are two different works, and that the differences in theology and style are confirmation of this. But this does not seem to have been Wordsworth's view. His accounts of the poem he was writing in 1805 are remarkably consistent: it is a "tributary," or "portico," or "anti-chapel" to *The Recluse.* But as early as 6 March 1804 he says it will not be published "during my lifetime, till I have finished a larger and more important work" (531). The implication is that it will be published posthumously, even if *The Recluse* is never finished. This explains the language in which the 1850 version, actually completed in 1839, is discussed by Wordsworth and his family. Dora says her parents are "correcting a long Poem written thirty years back and which is not to be published during his life" (536), and Christopher says Wordsworth has "worked very hard, especially in the revising and finishing of his long autobiographic poem" (536). I suspect Wordsworth himself identifies the two versions in a letter of 11 April 1839 in which he talks about the 1805 poem and goes on, "That book still exists in manuscript. It's publication has been prevented merely by the personal character of the subject" (538). So for Wordsworth and his circle this is the same poem, but corrected, revised, finished. Whatever the difficulties in providing an apparatus, and whatever the problems raised for the final-intention school of editing, *The Prelude* looks like a Theseus' ship of a poem—first built as a dual purpose tug or cargo-boat and finally launched as a cargo-boat.

The theoretical problems raised by the New York edition of Henry

James's novels are remarkably similar. The author has a similar attitude to his changes, and once again the issue of the relation of one work to another, or to a set of works, is raised. This is perhaps the most neglected issue in textual criticism—the relation of the part to the whole, the item to the series, the single element to the collected works. James often talks of the prospective New York edition as if he were a painter wanting to add a brush stroke or two to the creation of youth: "My idea is, further, to revise everything carefully, and *to re-touch,* as to expression, turn of sentence, and the question of surface generally" (4:366). But in contrast to this, there are passages where he seems concerned with something like a change of function. He says, for example, that the shorter things "will gain in significance and importance, very considerably, by a fresh grouping or classification" so that they "conduce to something of a common effect" (4:366); the interest and value of the edition will "rest not a little on the proper association and collocation" (4:367) of the stories. In a hasty letter to Robert Herrick he explains that the edition's raison d'être "is in its being selective as well as collective, and by the mere fact of leaving out certain things . . . I exercise a control, a discrimination, I treat certain portions of my work as happy accidents" (4:371). The question of survival becomes the focus of attention as it does in Brennan's discussion of identity: some parts are to survive to the next stage but others are not. What detailed difference the new arrangements of James's novels and stories make to their operation I leave to the specialist, but two points emerge clearly: first, James believed that his works continued their life into the New York edition; second, he wanted the New York edition to be assessed as a whole. James was trying to see his output as a whole, not as a series of discrete utterances but as one utterance with many parts. It might even be that the editor concerned with a single work, as opposed to James's collected works, should make a quite different choice of reading text.

In dealing with James's novels I have already had to draw on the idea of an utterance, and I now need to develop this notion, because the answer to my second question, "What should the editor be presenting to the critic for interpretation?" is "An utterance." By an utterance I mean the product of any act that falls within the range of meanings the *OED* gives for *utter:* "to put forth, or put upon the market; to issue; to send forth as sound; to express; to reveal"—in short, anything to do with making outer or external. In eighteenth-century legal documents *utter* is often used as a synonym for *publish,* and publication is the most important form of utterance for modern texts. But a poem or story can be uttered without being published—it could be read to family, or friends, or the court—and it can be intended as an utterance when no one but the author ever sees it. There are two main arguments for the importance of utterance. The first comes from the need to make sense of the history of a work, something I have not yet shown to be possible. The second comes from the need to respect authorial meaning.

My discussion of the identity of ships and texts left out an important distinction between the two. When a new version of Theseus' ship set out to sea, the old one had vanished, its elements replaced by the new. It was necessary to indulge in a wild fantasy of someone having the dedication and energy to collect all the discarded materials and build them into a ship in order to get rival claimants to the title of being Theseus' ship. But no such fantasies are needed with texts; the New York edition of *The American* came into being and persisted alongside copies of the first edition, which were still capable of functioning, of being sold, lent, and read. This is because *The American* exists in a type-token way and not as a work-of-art particular, the material which is retained from stage to stage—words, punctuation, and so on—is instanced in any number of types, which need not change in order for a variant token and its types to be produced. A history of the literary work constructed on the same basis as that of the ship would not, therefore, be one of discrete stages; it would be one of overlapping versions and of coexisting rival claimants to be the work. Any intelligible history of the work, therefore, has to emphasize its utterances, or the prepublication stages that are sufficiently like utterances to provide a history. Any serious consideration of versions must take them as actions of the author that can be fixed to a particular time.

Utterance is so important that I am tempted to go further and challenge the notion that preutterance stages of the work, the process of composition, are part of the work at all. The history of the *Mona Lisa* begins when the artist finished the painting; the splashes and daubs on the canvas that constituted its earlier stages were not the painting because they did not have that function. I am reaching the same conclusion that Tanselle reached in "Historicism and Critical Editing" in what was even for him an exceptionally perspicacious footnote. His example was a vase, and he pointed out that in a session's pottery there will be earlier versions of this vase but they will be destroyed in making the final version. As he points out, this cannot mean that the whole work does not survive (43). The same, I believe, applies to an unuttered version of a text, and to those who would object that in this respect type-token works differ from particulars, I would point out that some early versions of a poem may exist only in the poet's head and are lost just as surely as the early versions of the vase. This leaves me with the conclusion, perhaps a trivial one, that Professor Gabler's edition of *Ulysses*, which I much welcome and admire, does not present us with the total text of *Ulysses* but with a very great deal that is not *Ulysses* at all.

The strongest arguments for the importance of utterance, however, do not come from these discussions of identity but from a concern with the interpretation of texts. It has been clear for a while now that the best underpinning for intentionalist criticism comes from the work of Paul Grice, John Searle, and those who have followed up their investigations of meaning and speech acts. Grice began this line of inquiry by admitting a much wider understanding of meaning than has been drawn upon by the hard-line intentionalists who have succeeded him. In his essay on "Meaning," he distinguished natural meaning (for example, "These clouds mean rain" or "These spots mean measles") from non-natural meaning (when a person means something by an utterance) (377–78). According to Grice a lot of human behavior falls into the category of natural meaning: there is an intention informing what I do, but I do not intend the other person to respond in recognition of that intention. One of Grice's examples will clarify the position: "I have a very avaricious man in my room, and I want him to go; so I throw a pound note out of the window. Is there any utterance with a meaning $_{NN}$ [non-natural]? No, because in behaving as I did, I did not intend his recognition of my purpose to be in any way effective in getting him to go. . . . If on the other hand I had pointed to the door or given him a little push, then my behaviour might well be held to constitute a meaningful $_{NN}$ utterance" ("Meaning" 384). Grice is far from wanting to restrict meaning to his non-natural meaning (of which speech acts are an important part); the fun of his paper comes in trying to distinguish one sort of meaning from another. The recent work on intention by Juhl and Knapp and Michaels has (in spite of typically scholarly concessions by Juhl) neglected this point, restricting meaning to the author's intended meaning and insisting on a logical relation between meaning and author's intention. I think this approach is doubly mistaken: it neglects Grice's identification of natural meaning (where the proper response is not dependent on recognition of the utterer's intention), and it is still bound in to a fundamentally anti-intentionalist habit of talking about meaning without reference to persons. The paradigm case of a non-natural meaning as originally presented by Grice, and modified by Searle in *Speech Acts,* suggests a two-way transaction: "S intended the utterance of *X* to produce some effect in a hearer *H* by means of the recognition of this intention" (43). But there can still be meaning when one side of the exchange is lopped off. As Searle himself has argued in "Meaning, Communication, and Representation," I can mean something by a representation even if there is no present or future audience, even myself (213–14). And, I suggest, something can have a non-natural meaning for me even though no one intended it (I thought Grice was telling me to leave, but he wasn't). I suspect criticism would profit by disallowing the question "What does it mean?" unless it is accompanied by the qualification "To whom?" Two examples should clarify these issues. The first is taken from Hirsch and developed by Juhl: "A hitherto faithful husband claims to be giving an evening seminar on eighteenth-century French literature, when in fact he is becoming all too familiar with Olga Olavsen, the new Swedish instructor. 'What did you discuss in class tonight?' his wife asks. '*Les liaisons dangereuses,*' he quickly replies. 'Again? I thought you did that two weeks ago.' The man blushes deeply and hesitates" (30–31). The point of the story is that the husband means he was in class, but the wife may interpret what he says differently and thereby reach the truth. There are two ways she might do this. She might think the husband intends to admit his liaison; in that she would be mistaken, but it would be the non-natural meaning for her. Or she could be interpreting the husband's behavior as the unconscious revelation of his infidelity—a correct interpretation of the natural meaning of his behavior. Both of these are meanings but neither is his meaning. The second example comes from D. F. McKenzie's Panizzi lectures, in which he gives an example from Maori culture of a landscape that is replete with meaning, such that physical features have a narrative function (31–32). This contrasts ironically with the use by Juhl and Knapp and Michaels of an example in which rock erosion produces Wordsworth's "A slumber did my spirit seal," an example with which they hope—in vain in my case—to persuade us that there must be someone to intend a meaning. All they succeed in showing, I think, is that when we interpret something as an utterer's intended meaning, we are assuming someone has uttered it. McKenzie's example shows that there can be rich and powerful meanings in a landscape without anyone bothering about authorial intention; I suspect that these meanings come from a fusion of Grice-style natural and non-natural elements.

The purpose of these examples is to retain a place for the author's intended meaning, while admitting the legitimacy of talking about meaning in a wider sense. My position is similar to that of E. D. Hirsch in *Validity in Interpretation,* clarified in *The Aims of Interpretation,* rather than that of his successors. An author publishing an essay, poem, or novel corresponds quite well to our paradigm case of "*S* intended the utterance of *X* to produce some effect in a hearer *H* by means of the recognition of this intention," and it is therefore possible to read for the author's meaning—because it is relatively determinate and because we are interested in, and respect, others. I also share Juhl's belief that many critics are reading for the author's meaning when they imagine they are doing something else; but that doesn't mean no other meanings are available.

The editor, I suggest, has duties to intentionalist readers (and those readers who are intentionalists unawares), and the first of these is to present them with a text they can read and interpret. Current interest in the history of a work, sometimes thought of as the whole text, will be welcomed by anyone interested in textual studies, but as a guide to editorial policy it has at least two potential flaws. First, as we have seen, it may too readily assume the continuing identity of the work; it may query the authority of any one version without extending that wariness to the conception of the work as a whole. Second, it may, as Professor Gabler's *Ulysses* stripped of its reading text would, fail to provide an object for intentionalist interpretation. Authors do not mean anything at all by the history of their work, their development over the years (which is not to say that development has no meaning), but they do mean something by the text published in 1892 or 1989. And the history of the work is logically dependent on these stages, independently interpreted. To deny making access to all of them would be not to liberate the author and reader, but to render them impotent before the tyranny of the editor.

The first demand on editors, then, is that they provide a text, or selection of texts, that can be read. The second, I suggest, is that these should represent the author's intended utterance(s). The third is that the reader should be enabled to construct the relation of each intended utterance to others and to actual utterances. An utterance is a social act, and in many respects I find myself in alliance with those like Jerome McGann, who would want to call poems events: "Poetry is, from the individual's point of view, a particular type of human *experience;* from a social point of view, however, it is an *event*. Criticism studies these experiences and events in their successive and interrelated apparitions. A work of poetry is not a thing or an object, nor should criticism treat it as such; it is the result of an inter-active network of productive people and forces" (343). There is much to admire in this, but I have reservations that are best expressed before moving on to consider more traditional opposition to text as utterance. First, if all readings are events that make up the poem (or whatever is the whole), then the task of criticism is impossibly large. Second, I suspect talking of poems as events involves some idealization, as though we could somehow fuse production and consumption; if we talk of poems as actions (the name that is usual for events involving people) the two split apart again into writer and reader (as I suspect they should), and we have to ask, whose action? Finally, talking of poems as events seems to disguise the ease with which we can identify what is common to the events, what is iterated. I worry that according to this way of talking, a chair would be an event because we all have sitting experiences, each of which is a social event, and each sitting experience/event is unique. Yet I want to to on talking of chairs—and poems—as something constant in these experiences/events. And in the case of the poem the constant is what Nelson Goodman in *Languages of Art* calls a character in a notational scheme (199). The danger of the talk of poems as events is that, like the talk of the meaning of poems, it steals intentionality from where it belongs, which is in people's heads.

Where the emphasis on events is helpful to intentionalist editors is in encouraging them to pay attention to what Jack Meiland has called non-purposive intentions. Nigel intends to drive his car to the station and knows this will cause wear on the crankshaft. It isn't his intention to cause wear on the crankshaft (he would be happy to get to the station without it) but, Meiland maintains, he intends wear on the crankshaft. Similarly, Sir Keith Joseph intends to make Margaret Thatcher prime minister, knowing she is a woman; it isn't his purpose to have a woman prime minister (a man would do), but he does intend that there should be a woman prime minister. More attention should be paid to these intentions in cases where the author knows that certain consequences are entailed by the decision to utter. Dickens intended *David Copperfield* to be printed and published by Bradbury and Evans; he knew they would change his punctuation; therefore he intended changes to his punctuation.

The resistance to basing textual criticism on a theory of utterance does not come so much from those who insist on the variety of the text as from all those who seek to retain the singleness of the text. They can be divided into two camps: on the one hand the idealists, who deny that meaning has to be embodied at all; and on the other those who are committed to what I shall nickname, after Butterfield, the Whig interpretation of literary variants, and who neglect meaning when it conflicts with their presuppositions.[2] D. F. McKenzie may serve as an example of the first group. In his Panizzi lectures he advocated using intention as a speculative instrument and "creating a master-text, a kind of ideal-copy text, transcending all the versions and true to the essential intention of the 'work.' In this sense, the work may be the form traditionally imputed to an archetype; it may be a form seen as immanent in each of the versions but not fully realized in any one of them; or it may be conceived of as always potential, like that of a play" (29). This represents a valuable contribution to the current debate, but I am perturbed by the heady cocktail of otherworldliness in which it soaked; ideal, transcendent, and immanent (like God); our old friend intention (though it is not people who have intentions but works) looks very drab in comparison. These words have a distinguished history, but they usually carried with them an ontological commitment and I am not sure that Professor McKenzie believes in a spirit world where true works reside only to be spoiled by the mortals who write them down. And if there is such a world, I don't know how he has access to it. Of course, my response here is naive, because this vocabulary is being appropriated in the cause of a new editorial freedom, but I should like to see the case for liberty given a more material basis.

A more common approach to variation is based on the tacit assumption that the versions of a work are organically or telelogically related, that the work grows, or that it is always aiming at the final version. The metaphors vary—the work may mature, or be refined, or honed, or chiseled—but the pattern of the Whig historians is maintained; the early is judged by the late and is praised insofar as it conforms to, or helps create, it. This way of thinking is so enticing, seems so natural, that critics take it for granted, sometimes talking of respect for the author's final intention as though Hardy were somehow more Hardy in 1895 than he was in 1892. There is a missing argument about why the later utterances of an author are more important than his earlier ones, and T. Howard-Hill is to be congratulated on trying to supply one. He says, "If all versions are equal *historically* on account of their reception, it is nevertheless *logical*—when the necessity of choice compels—to edit the last version of a work published by its author. The assumption here is that authors aim to improve rather than debase the work by revision" (156). We are concerned, I think, not with matters of logic but with providing a general reason for editorial choice. I don't think this is a good general reason, still less a binding one. Even if we assume that an author is revising his work simply to improve it—and I suspect this happens less often than the Whigs pretend—we have here simply a value judgment by the author at time t_2; the value judgment at t_1 was different. It cannot even be argued with confidence that more information was available to the author at t_2. So even if we were willing to accept an author's value judgment of his work—and given problems of immaturity, senility, prejudice, fear of criticism, we should be wary—each value judgment is as confined to its time as its utterance and reception are.

The danger of the Whig interpretation of variants is that the critic, and the editor, who often determines which text the critic should read, construe as a simple improvement what is in fact a new stage in the author's dialogue with his public; a change in what he wants to say. I think we can find an example in Hardy's *Tess of the D'Urbervilles*. It is well known that *Tess* was censored: the famous example is for the serialization in *The Graphic*, where Angel Clare was not allowed to carry the girls over the water in the lane in his arms but had to push them across in a wheelbarrow instead. In some ways the changes made in 1892 for the "fifth edition" are more interesting because subtler. As J. T. Laird shows in his *The Shaping of "Tess of the D'Urbervilles,"* Mowbray Morris had received *Tess* in *The Quarterly* of 15 April 1892 saying, "It is indisputably open to Mr Hardy to call his heroine a pure woman; but he has no less certainly offered many inducements to his readers to refuse her the name" (174). Hardy responded to this criticism in his diary and in the preface to the "fifth edition," and I think he also changed the text of *Tess* with the particular intention of disabling Morris's reading. He modified the nature of Tess's innocence. In the "fifth edition" Hardy adds a passage in which a woman who sees Tess kissing her baby remarks, "A little more than persuading had to do wi' the coming o't I reckon. There were they that heard a sobbing one night last year in The Chase; and mid ha' gone hard wi' a certain party if folks had come along" (177). I am sure Laird is right in arguing that other changes made at this time, most importantly the removal of the suggestion that Alec drugged Tess, were made in order to bring the rest of the novel into line with this passage. Hardy is protecting his heroine by redefining her innocence; it no longer consists in a dazed unknowing but in violation, distress, and quite probably resistance. The text is being changed in response to the way it is received, just as a speaker in conversation might restate his point to make it more easily defensible. But when Laird's book is interpreted by a distinguished reviewer—and the Clarendon editors—the story becomes the familiar one: "In short, it is evident that Hardy worked away at the text of his novel over a period of nearly twenty-four years, introducing many important changes in plot, theme, characterization, imagery, and style, and meticulously revising it long after his farewell to fiction. He moved fairly steadily towards a more richly suggestive and finely-controlled work, from the 'relatively crude tale' of the earliest versions to the masterpiece we have" (208). What is missing here is a concern with meaning. The author changes his words because he wants to change his meaning, not refine it. The social life of the novel, the particularity of its utterances, are swept aside as the Whig view prevails again.

An emphasis on utterance would not have startling consequences for editors; it is, for example, perfectly compatible with Greg's view of copy-text. But the final intention that matters would become the final intention for the utterance; the choice between utterances for a reading text would be a free one, though readers would need to know the editor's reasons. The editor would try to recover the author's intended utterance, for most readers are interested in the author's meaning, not that of his nephew or compositor. Different editors might choose to present different utterances and this could vastly improve the range of texts available to a scholarly readership. Why is it, for example, that editors give so little attention to the tone of voice in which a text is uttered, so that it is not possible to buy a copy of *Henry Esmond* in its imitation eighteenth-century voice, with long *s*'s and ligatures. And why is it that so little attention is paid to the totality or fragmentation of an utterance? Dickens's novels, for example, originally consisted of a series of utterances, a month apart, in which the novelist started speaking before he knew how he was going to finish; and John Butt and Kathleen Tillotson showed some time ago that this became a principle of structure with Dickens and that he composed in this way even when he no longer needed to do so. Yet it is still not possible to buy all Dickens's novels broken into appropriate parts, repeating their covers, so that this structure can be followed with ease. It is surely an indictment of our system of publishing that so many "editions" are available with so little historical sense gone into their editing.

Intention is back in fashion, though the news hasn't circulated very far yet. Neither Derrida nor McGann, sometimes thought of as opponents of intentionalism, would have us do without it; but neither would they entertain for a moment the suggestion that it settles all our problems for us. Nor would Grice or Searle or others of the Anglo-American school of philosophy. Textual critics have to live with uncertainties, and intentionalists will respond by being as rational and consistent as they can. This means accepting that what we take to be a work may subsist in different versions with no version having particular authority (though some version might), and recognizing that it may not be possible to decide comfortably what the boundaries of a work are (which may mean settling for the status quo); there is no safe retreat from the authority of the version to the authority of the whole work. But some comfort is to be had by noticing the similarities between literary and other artifacts and the very large role that intention plays in trying to understand ordinary human affairs. The interest in authorial intention—and, therefore, the authorial text—remains legitimate and is not dependent on the claim that all meaning is authorial meaning—only that some important meanings are. As for the view that concern with authors' meanings is an improper submission to patriarchal authority and that the selection of a reading text makes this worse, I suspect it will soon be seen as the ingenious sleight of hand of a patriarchal academy up to its old trick of trying to manage without writers or readers.

Notes

A version of this paper was read at the Fifth International Interdisciplinary Conference of the Society for Textual Scholarship, 7 April 1989. I am grateful to participants in that session and to my colleague Charles Swann for his valuable suggestions and advice.

1. The chief influences on this paper, though they are indirect, and might be disowned, are John Searle, not only in his work on speech acts but in *Intentionality: An Essay in the Philosophy of Mind,* and Nelson Goodman, in the works cited. Annette Barnes makes good use of Goodman's work in *On Interpretation.*

2. I am told by Donald Reiman that I have been anticipated in this nicknaming by Stephen Parrish. His paper has now been printed as "The Whig Interpretation of Literature," *Text* 4 (1988): 343–50.

Works Cited

Austin, J. L. *How to Do Things with Words*. William James Lectures 1955. Ed. J. O. Urmson and Marina Sbisá. Oxford: Clarendon, 1975.

Barnes, Annette. *On Interpretation*. Oxford: Blackwell, 1988.

Barthes, Roland. "Le mort de l'auteur." *Manteiá* 5 (1968). Rpt. in *Image-Music-Text*. Ed. and trans. Stephen Heath. Glasgow: Collins, 1977. 142–48.

Brennan, Andrew. *Conditions of Identity: A Study in Identity and Survival*. Oxford: Clarendon, 1988.

Butt, John, and Kathleen Tillotson. *Dickens at Work*. London: Methuen, 1957.

Butterfield, Herbert. *The Whig Interpretation of History*. London: Bell, 1931.

Derrida, Jacques. "Limited Inc. abc." *Glyph* 2 (1977): 162–254.

———. "Signature Event Context." *Margins of Philosophy*. Ed. and trans. Alan Bass. Brighton: Harvester, 1982. 307–30. Also printed in different trans. in *Glyph* 1 (1977): 172–97.

Gabler, Hans Walter. "The Synchrony and Diachrony of Texts." *Text* 1 (1981): 305–26.

———, Wolfhard Steppe, and Claus Melchior, eds. *Ulysses: A Critical and Synoptic Edition*. By James Joyce. 3 vols. New York: Garland, 1984.

Gasché, Rodolphe. *The Tain of the Mirror: Derrida and the Philosophy of Reflection*. Cambridge: Harvard UP, 1986.

Goodman, Nelson. *Languages of Art: An Approach to a Theory of Symbols*. 2d ed. Indianapolis: Hackett, 1976.

———. *Of Mind and Other Matters*. Cambridge: Harvard UP, 1984.

———. *Problems and Projects*. Indianapolis: Bobbs-Merrill, 1972.

———. *Ways of World Making*. Hassocks, Sussex: Harvester, 1978.

Grice, H. P[aul]. "Meaning." *Philosophical Review* 66 (1957): 377–88.

———. "Utterer's Meaning and Intentions." *Philosophical Review* 78 (1969): 147–77.

———. "Utterer's Meaning, Sentence-Meaning, and Word-Meaning." *Foundations of Language* 4 (1968): 225–42. Rpt. in *The Philosophy of Language*. Ed. John R. Searle. Oxford: Oxford UP, 1971. 54–70.

Grindle, Juliet, and Simon Gatrell, eds. *Tess of the D'Urbervilles*. By Thomas Hardy. Oxford: Clarendon, 1983.

Hirsch, E. D. *The Aims of Interpretation*. Chicago: U of Chicago P, 1976.

———. *Validity in Interpretation*. New Haven: Yale UP, 1967.

Howard-Hill, T. H. Rev. of *Bibliography and the Sociology of Texts*, by D. F. McKenzie. *Library*, 6th ser. 10 (1988): 151–58.

James, Henry. *Letters*. Ed. Leon Edel. 4 vols. London: Macmillan, and Cambridge: Harvard UP, 1974–84.

Juhl, P. D. *Interpretation: An Essay in the Philosophy of Literary Criticism*. Princeton: Princeton UP, 1980.

Knapp, Steven, and Walter Benn Michaels. "Against Theory." *Critical Inquiry* 8 (1982): 723–42. Rpt. in *Against Theory: Literary Studies and the New Pragmatism*. Ed. W. J. T. Mitchell. Chicago: U of Chicago P, 1985. 11–30.

Laird, J. T. *The Shaping of "Tess of the D'Urbervilles."* Oxford: Clarendon, 1975.

McGann, Jerome J. *The Beauty of Inflections: Literary Investigations in Historical Method and Theory*. Oxford: Clarendon, 1988.

McKenzie, D. F. *Bibliography and the Sociology of Texts*. Panizzi Lectures. London: British Library, 1986.

Meiland, Jack W. *The Nature of Intention*. London: Methuen, 1970.

Page, Norman. Rev. of *The Shaping of "Tess of the D'Urbervilles,"* by J. T. Laird. *Victorian Studies* 20 (1976–77): 207–10.

Parfit, Derek. "On the Importance of Self-Identity." *Journal of Philosophy* 68 (1971): 683–90.

———. "Personal Identity." *Philosophical Review* 80 (1971): 3–27.

Parker, Hershel. *Flawed Texts and Verbal Icons: Literary Authority in American Fiction*. Evanston: Northwestern UP, 1984.

Searle, John R. *Expression and Meaning: Studies in the Theory of Speech Acts*. Cambridge: Cambridge UP, 1979.

———. *Intentionality: An Essay in the Philosophy of Mind*. Cambridge: Cambridge UP, 1983.

———. "Meaning, Communication, and Representation." *Philosophical Grounds of Rationality: Intention, Categories, Ends*. Ed. Richard E. Grandy and Richard Warner. Oxford: Clarendon, 1986. 209–26.

———. "Reiterating the Differences." *Glyph* 1 (1977): 198–208.

———. *Speech Acts: An Essay in the Philosophy of Language*. Cambridge: Cambridge UP, 1969.

———. "The Word Turned Upside Down." Rev. of *On Deconstruction,* by Jonathan Culler. *New York Review of Books,* 27 October 1983, 74–79.

Tanselle, G. Thomas. "The Editorial Problem of Final Authorial Intention." *Studies in Bibliography* 29 (1976): 167–211.

———. "Historicism and Critical Editing." *Studies in Bibliography* 39 (1986): 1–46.

Wheeler, Samuel C., III. "Indeterminacy of French Interpretation: Derrida and Davidson." *Truth and Interpretation: Perspectives on the Philosophy of Donald Davidson*. Ed. Ernest LePore. Oxford: Blackwell, 1986. 477–94.

Williams, B[ernard]. A. O. "Personal Identity and Individuation." *Proceedings of the Aristotelian Society* 57 (1956–57): 229–52.

Wordsworth, Jonathan, M. H. Abrams, and Stephen Gill, eds. *The Prelude, 1799, 1805, 1850*. By William Wordsworth. New York: Norton, 1979.

9

Unsought Encounters

HANS WALTER GABLER

NGLO-AMERICAN TEXTUAL CRITICISM and editing has in the 1980s been subjected to some insistent theoretical probing. This is a new and unaccustomed situation for an empirical discipline. Since securing its foundations in bibliography, it had developed with great assurance a methodology derived from the paradigm of the transmission of Shakespeare's texts. Focused on the copytext pragmatics of W. W. Greg and the establishment of eclectic critical texts under the ultimate arbitration of author's final intentions, it was the methodology available when editorial interests moved into other areas. Textual situations encountered for authors and works in the nineteenth and twentieth centuries did not prove this received methodology to be universally applicable. The widely recognized current crisis in Anglo-American textual criticism also stems from the failure of many textual critics to grapple with recent developments in literary theory. Structuralism, deconstruction, psychologism, text theory, and New Historicism have successively and together superseded the New Criticism. Anglo-American editors, however, have in general resisted employing these new approaches to question and modify the theoretical foundations and empirical procedures of modern textual criticism. While a small number of textual critics have challenged some of the tradition's basic assumptions, their work is in a curious way lagging behind the conceptualizations of "text," "authorization,"

"version," and "textual dynamics" found in German editorial scholarship and the French critical discipline of *critique génétique*. A critical reading of recent controversial books on textual criticism by Jerome J. McGann, Hershel Parker, and Peter Shillingsburg in light of such conceptualizations, while they have availed themselves of the above-mentioned theoretical developments, suggests that the Anglo-American editorial debate stands to profit from as yet unsought encounters with its continental counterpart.

The application of Greg's "Rationale of Copy-Text" to the texts of nineteenth-century American authors elicited fierce, yet on the whole unfocused, polemics. These responses and reactions gave way to the more careful competence of Jerome McGann's *Critique of Modern Textual Criticism* (1983). He analyzes the elevation of a rule of procedure, Greg's rationale, to a theory of editing. The unquestioning assumption of an editor's obligation to fulfill the author's intentions he sees as ideologically rooted, ultimately, in a concept of the autonomy of the creative artist (40–42). Against this, he assumes an alternative ideological stance in emphasizing—as James Thorpe had unideologically done before him—the social forces that contribute to shaping a literary text in production. He convincingly argues that these are important for textual criticism. Their recognition helps to define the specific historicity of literary works and texts. The consideration of such historicity, in turn, advances a discussion of the textual-critical concept of the "version" to the extent of accounting for the outward, i.e., the socio-historical, determinants of versions. In another respect, McGann's emphasis on the social, and therefore ineluctably collaborative, shaping of texts as books suggests a need to reassess the conventional editorial treatment of textual variants that result in the process of such shaping. At the same time, McGann gives little thought to their relative marginality in relation to the comprehensive range of variance characteristically encountered in the composition and production of a literary work as a whole. Conceptually, he faces the full complexity neither of "version" nor of "variance." If his *Critique* thus sidesteps, or wholly ignores, central text-critical issues, the reason would seem to be that it also neither radically questions copytext editing as a principle nor attacks the notion of "text" in relation to current theories of literature and theories of text to the length that our present-day consciousness of theory would seem to require.

In advance by some twenty years, the German-speaking countries have since the 1950s seen an indigenous discussion of theories and principles of textual criticism and critical editing. Even though there may be some truth in the self-criticism that (perhaps by a typically Teutonic failure) the intensive debate for a time prevented rather than furthered the realization of critical editions, most if its issues, if not all of its propositions, would seem relevant in the Anglo-American crisis. As it is, the Anglo-American debate has on its own terms in many cases hardly begun to discern pivotal problem areas. Of these, the most central one is that of the concept of "text" itself.

When Jerome McGann endeavors to dissociate the guiding principle of fulfilling the author's intentions from W. W. Greg's proposals for copytext editing, he attempts to revert to, but does not question the validity of, their original pragmatism. He concedes an applicability of copytext editing procedures in principle and does not submit the concept of text that implicitly underlies them to his critique, neither in general nor in relation to the textual situations for which these procedures were specifically devised. In "Struktur and Genese in der Editorik. Zur germanistischen und anglistischen Editionsforschung" (1975), Hans Zeller puts the theoretical objections to copytext editing most succinctly. The copytext editor in his avowed eclectic procedures acts in the manner of the medieval scribe, conflating, or "contaminating," textual versions of a work. Moreover, his notion of text is one unreflectedly inherited from editors of classical texts. He perceives variants only in their stemmatological relations forwards and backwards and assumes that such was also the author's perception. The critical text for him results merely from a sum of textual elements individually exchangeable and does not take their functional relationships into account. The sum of variants of the states of a work appears to him as the variants of a *single* text (114–15).

Zeller's objections are carefully aimed. They concern specifically the treatment in copytext editing of the order of variance that holds true interest for present-day German textual criticism and editing: namely, the variance of authorial composition and revision. Their unaccustomed perspective also helps to recognize the extent to which it is not authorial variance, but transmissional variance, that stands at the center of attention in the Anglo-American practice of the disciplines. Culminating in the sophistications of bibliography, the main thrust of their methodology is directed toward detecting, analyzing, and undoing transmissional corruption. Eclectic editing according to the author's final intentions, carried out as the grafting of later revisions onto the chosen copytext, is then simply patterned on the received model of emending textual error. This is how the perception of variants in their stemmatological relations and of a text in progression as an additive series of readings, a sum of variants, has come to be upheld. While McGann's main concern in his *Critique* is with variance resulting from social collaboration, his call is thus for their inclusion rather than subtraction from the critically edited text. His argument revealingly links variants of production to Greg's type of the "indifferent variant" (113– 15). Since they are capable of rescuing categorizable readings from the illegitimacy of error into the realm of legitimate text, the attitudes to text and the routines of procedure of copytext editing appear here expressly called upon to serve McGann's ulterior theoretical and critical objectives. Text-critically speaking, his frame of reference remains the text considered as the sum of its variants.

A textual error—a mistake in authorial inscription, a corruption in transmission—signals its "illegitimacy" by its apparent lack of a systematic or structural relation to the text in which it occurs. That it stands out unsystematically and as a fault in the structure are conditions upon which error-oriented textual criticism depends. To emend a textual error means to restore the system and heal the structure—and it is editors alone who confront texts to be emended. Although incidentally correcting or emending, authors, by contrast, have before them texts they are writing or wish to revise. These are not corrupt texts. If they are deemed imperfect—calling for rewriting or revision—the imperfection is not material, not on the level of the signs on paper (save for the incidental inscriptional flaw or misprint in need of emendation or correction). Rather the imperfection is conceptual and compositional, on the level of thought and imagination and their articulation in language. In shaping and reshaping language and thereby creating the total linguistic performance that constitutes a work through all its stages of composition and revision, authors bring forth texts upon texts. By way of generating and inscribing variants, they manipulate linguistic structures, be it the incipient structures of the work in composition or the temporarily stabilized structures of completed drafts and published texts. The authorial variance, consequently, is always systematic. Superseded and superseding readings each stand in a relational context, and every antecedent text, just as every succeeding text, is to be regarded as a structural system of language. If these texts are successive synchronic structures, the work as a whole appears diachronically structured as a succession of such synchronic texts. Their invariance provides the structural base, while the variance indicates the relational complexity in time of the work's texts. In total contrast to textual error, authorial variance thus provides a twofold measure to the linguistic system of a work of literature, accentuating the contextual space of their texts and sounding the temporal depth of their writing.

From such theorizing about text and variance, the objections on principle to copytext editing ultimately derive, insofar as the copytext editing method—handling authorial variance formally like textual error—reaches out to establishing a critical text of the author's final intention eclectically from a succession of discrete author's texts. (The objections do not detract from the admiration of it as a method where it operates within the confines of its error-oriented origins.) The attitude toward "text" and "variance" which I have sketched is clearly structuralist in orientation. Given our present-day state of theoretical awareness in literary studies— an awareness the Anglo-American debate over textual criticism has hitherto remained virtually untouched by—such an attitude betrays its age. The focus on authorial composition and revision in German textual criticism and editing set in with Friedrich Beissner's Hölderlin edition of the 1940s. With it arose the perspective on the context relationship of variance and, more generally, a desire to define concepts of "text." Beissner's concept centered on organic growth toward unity and superior aesthetic integrity. Since the 1960s, it has given way to the structuralist concept mainly under the influence of the work on linguistics, poetics, and aesthetics of the Prague structuralists. The first of the major collections of original essays through which the German text-critical debate has been carried forward, *Texte und Varianten* (1971), edited by Hans Zeller and Gunter Martens, therefore significantly includes a contribution by Miroslav Červenka, "Textologie und Semiotik." Followers of the Thorpe/Gaskell/McGann line of thought that attributes ontological significance for the work to the "socializing" act of publication will be gratified to find that Červenka's arguments similarly take their departure from the semiotics of the act of publication. Yet as these arguments proceed to considerations of the relationship of textual criticism (or "textology") to poetics, of diachrony and synchrony, and of the semiotics of the variant as well as of the linguistics and stylistics of variance, they reveal an attitude of exploring and questioning the fundamentals of textual criticism as yet beyond the ken of the Anglo-American debate. From its underlying concepts of "text" and "variance," the German discussion has encouraged further endeavors to situate textual criticism in relation to main critical concerns—e.g., production and reception aesthetics—and to develop principles for establishing critical texts and formats for the apparatus presentation of variance by which editions may best serve such concerns.[1]

Beissner's concept of text, under which the contextual correlations of variance were perceived in terms of an organic growth, could and did easily coexist with an orientation in editorial procedure toward authorial intention similar to that still current in Anglo-American text-critical and editorial thought. Linked with a shift of focus from author to text implied in the structuralist concept, the orientation toward intention has since been neutralized, or even abandoned, in German theorizing. With a view to the editorial realization of its system of principles, this has consequently led to an emphasis on the strict historicity of texts and their documentation. Such an emphasis follows logically, in particular, from understanding the work as a diachronic succession of discrete texts. At the same time it signals a continued adherence to the notion of textual criticism as a branch of historical scholarship despite the latent ahistoric implications of structuralism.

The Anglo-American discussion has recently seen its own turn, or return, to a mode of historicism in Hershel Parker's *Flawed Texts and Verbal Icons* (1984). From a critical point of departure, and thus by a route different from McGann's, he too perceives in the premises of received textual criticism an allegiance to a notion of autonomy, the autonomy of New Criticism's "verbal icon," by conception an ahistoric text. Against this notion he urges the historicity of the author and of the creative process. With suggestive, if on the whole unsustained, sidelights on the psychology of the creative process, he situates textual historicity biographically in the author and the conditions and circumstances of the acts of writing and revision. Assuming something like a one-to-one relationship of intention to words and of articulated language to meaning, Parker champions intention—linking it as he does not only to the words inscribed but to the meaning they embody—far beyond the observance of intention in received textual criticism. He takes intention to be unequivocally written into the words and language of the original acts of composition by the authority of the author, whence it can and must be elicited as meaning by evaluative acts of interpretation in total deference to that authority. While deploring the alleged critical affinities of the principles and practice of textual criticism he attacks, Parker appears thus at bottom not to have shed his own allegiance to the modes of interpretation and evaluation of New Criticism. He recognizes, it is true, writing as a process. Yet the acts of revision which the process involves tend to fall victim, as "flawed texts," to his evaluative grasp because he has so strongly privileged the original acts.

In the final resort, texts—the *text* itself, as it were—recede under the heavy, and at the same time curiously biography-restricted, emphasis on the author and his intentions and meanings in Parker's mode of a historicist approach to textual criticism. If an approach to textual criticism it is. Indeed, were it not for Parker's insistent and provocative engagement with current assumptions and practices in editing, one would not need to see his theses in the light of the ongoing text-critical debate. Foremost, his book is an essay in genetic criticism, a mode of criticism that, as the current French *critique génétique* demonstrates, may be profitably divorced, or kept apart, from text-critical and editorial concerns. It is clear, however, that the book is wholly unaware that the questions it empirically grapples with represent part—albeit but a fraction—of the problematics for which *critique génétique* was developing theories and a discourse during the very years that Parker's views were forming.[2] The essay nevertheless has the merit of blazoning the interdependence of textual and literary criticism.

In the present attempts to redefine the coordinates for textual criticism, it is doubtless desirable, indeed essential, to reestablish its links with literary criticism. What must be doubted, however, is that the path laid out by Parker is viable. He either rejects or ignores too much of what literary criticism and linguistics and literary theory today believe to know about the ontology and structures, as well as of the potentials of meaning and significance, of texts and the literary artifacts both in production and reception. Again, the way in which Parker's issues have been dealt with in the German text-critical discussion of longer standing may be profitably looked at.

German editorial commentary recognizes the critical activity of interpretation as relevant in two senses. Hans Zeller's position essay, "Befund und Deutung" (1971), addresses its text-critical and editorial relevance, subjecting the notion of an absolute objectivity in editing to a careful critique. Text-critical and editorial activity may begin from a given ("Be-

fund"), but the moment it engages with that given, it enters upon interpretation ("Deutung"). It is only from admitting and accepting this basic
implication of subjectivity that a critical edition can be organized and
shaped to attain a controlled objectivity. From pronouncing an apparent
home truth, Zeller penetrates to a systematic evaluation and coordination
of the premises and practices of textual criticism and editing. He analyses
the interpretative demand on the textual critic and editor arising from the
textual documents, the author's will and intention, the conditions of
textual authorization, the exigencies of transmission (e.g., how to define,
localize and deal with "textual error"), and the social determinants of
texts. The interpretative demands in every one of these areas make editorial judgment integral to a critical edition. Setting the conditions for its
controlled objectivity by signaling both "Befund" and "Deutung," a critical edition in turn calls upon the critical judgment of the reader as
counterpart to the editor's. The inevitability of interpretation renders
textual criticism and editing a hermeneutic discipline.

In the second sense, interpretation—the reader's and the user's interpretation—engages with the critical edition to unlock the text. Gunter
Martens focuses on this question in "Texterschliessung durch Edition"
(1975), emphasizing the key function that critical editions have in their
singular formating—established texts correlated to a multilevel system of
apparatus—for critical interpretative discourse. Martens's argument is
representative of the thorough revaluation that the apparatus of critical
editions has experienced in German textual criticism and editing. The
apparatus dimensions have been developed to carry the entire weight and
complexity of the editor's understanding of his object, his or her critically
subjective engagement with it, and the documentary as well as communicative function in relation to it. The transformation into apparatus in
particular of textual genesis and textual history has established the integral
apparatus—displaying variance in context—as categorically opposed to
the conventional apparatus isolating individual variants by lemmata.

Martens takes a reception-oriented approach that at the same time is
linked back to the semiotic perspective of the Prague structuralist aesthetics. It is in the apparatus, and the interrelation of text and apparatus,
that interpretation may localize the full range of material for a comprehensive critical discourse. The function of an edition is to mediate "on the one
hand, the historic determinacy of the artifact and its object representations, and on the other hand, the openness [indeterminacy] of the aes-

thetic object" (Martens 90). The potential of critical editions in particular is to lay open and render penetrable the nature of aesthetic language. The deployment of language in literary creation may be conceived as a process of desemanticization where the language tokens lose their unequivocal representational character. In the apparatus presentation of the creative process, of textual genesis, the increased self-reflexivity of language in literary texts becomes tangible.

In editions, works in their texts are laid out to be read in their diachronic depth. This may lead to the recognition that the acts of reading made editorially possible for the critical edition's user (as for no reader of straight readings texts) repeat or reenact the author's acts of reading in the writing process that shaped the text under his pen. Henning Boetius develops this notion into a model for a cybernetically dynamic simultaneity of production and reception, of writing and reading. Since the author in writing always, and near-simultaneously, is also the reader of the text in production, he may on the one hand still be regarded as the text's originator, guided by the idea of the text he wishes to produce. On the other hand, the text itself becomes the originator of its own continued production, since it will progressively guide the author's linguistic selections in writing. Not only reading acts, then, but in a sense also writing acts are acts of interpretation, and a consideration of this fact may serve to widen the appreciation of the hermeneutic implications in scholarly editions to be elicited in the critical discourse of the interpretation of literature.

From the vantage point of the theoretical considerations instanced by Zeller, Martens, and Boetius, it becomes obvious that Hershel Parker's empiric materials are amenable to a radically different understanding and critical treatment—even, and particularly, when genetically approached—from what *Flawed Texts and Verbal Icons* accords them. The strengths of the mode of historicism adumbrated in the German debate, too, become more clearly distinguishable. Its epicenter lies in the concept of the version. On the one hand, the version is defined by extrinsic historical determinants: versions are the finished draft or the published text with all the social ramifications of collaborative or contemporary reception (the German stock example is Goethe's *Die Leiden des jungen Werthers* which in its time, by the suicide it narrates, provoked a wave of suicides) or the radical postpublication revision (e.g., Wordsworth's second *Prelude*). The extrinsic definitional criteria are echoed both by McGann in his *Critique* (101) and Peter Shillingsburg in *Scholarly Editing in the Computer Age* (1986). The latter gives these criteria an extra twist by linking them to intention and ideality (47 ff., 51 ff.). On the other hand, the version is intrinsically definable in relation to textual variance. This is the criterion that orders the successive synchronic textual states within the diachrony of the work. Shillingsburg marginally touches upon the intrinsic differentiation of versions, yet neither McGann nor he seriously pursues the concept of the version much beyond the question of which version to select as the reading text of an edition. This is a question purely of editorial pragmatics. It may become problematic when the editing rationale is both dominantly single-text-centered and intention-oriented. Without such orientation, the issue is text-critically moot and may be settled at the editor's critical discretion and in consideration of the general interest in the edited work the edition expects to be catering to.

The specific text-critical relevance of the concept of the version lies in its intrinsic determinants. From a strict structuralist understanding of "text," Hans Zeller, as is well known, has gone in "A New Approach to the Critical Constitution of Literary Texts" (1975) to the extreme of declaring a single variant sufficient to differentiate versions, since by a single variant a text attains a new system of structural interrelationship of its elements (241). For all its editorial impracticability, this is a sound enough theoretical proposition. From Anglo-American respondents, it has sensibly encountered empirical objections.[3] In German editorial theory, one may say that it has been balanced from within the system. It is tempting to recognize in the one-variant determination of the version a last foothold of a notion of the static, or stable, text. By logical application of the definition, the diachrony of the work is divided into a virtually endless series of discrete texts, each of them stable as a synchronic structure. The integral apparatus then in a sense cuts across this unwiedly abstraction, functionalized as it is to transform editorially a virtual series of stabilities into a presentation of the dynamics of a genetic process as textual progress. By force of the close interrelation of text and apparatus, the basic concept of the version is not jeopardized. While dynamically correlated in the apparatus presentation, the intrinsic criteria that mark the versions remain transparent as the variance representing the acts of writing whose history resides in the documents of composition and revision. Moreover, the version selected as a given edition's reading text additionally accentuates that history.

Such a concept of the version is distinctively text-related. Its historicity resides less in the author than in the text. With a view to Parker's contentions, such a concept does not view the text as a function of the author's biography. Rather the author and his biography are regarded as functions of the text. The basis for such a reversal of the commonsense perspective lies in the structuralist concept of the text. From it, a notion of the autonomy of the text may be freshly entertained as residing not in the realm of meaning and significance, or even of language positivistically conceived as a sum of readings and variants, but as arising from the dynamic reciprocity of writing and reading and hence to be defined as a semiotic autonomy of indeterminate potential.[4]

At this point in our survey, we can see that the notions in the German text-critical debate of text, interpretation, apparatus, and version interrelate and contribute to what may be called a "textual orientation in editing." We form the phrase by analogy to Peter Shillingsburg's key statement for the organization of his argument in *Scholarly Editing in the Computer Age:* "The authorial orientation in editing has been for thirty or more years the dominant one in American scholarly editing" (31). Alone among the recent contributors to the Anglo-American controversies, Shillingsburg endeavors to systematize the terms and concepts relevant to textual criticism and editing. Unsurprisingly, in view of the approach he rethinks, the book's "Theory" section mainly sets out the conditions for arriving at an author-oriented *text*. Reflections on the apparatus, by contrast, remain a matter of "Practice." Predictably, too, the problem areas of "Authority" and "Intention" loom large as problem areas in his discussion. At their logical intersection we may observe intriguing ripples in the argument. It shows in the introduction of the notion of the "authenticated text" as the editorial result of observing authorial authority and intention and in a sense of the insufficiency of the "authenticated text" as an exclusive editorial goal in view of compositional and revisional variance (40–43). With an awareness of the German text-critical discussion, one recognizes that Shillingsburg is here on the brink of a consideration not only of the practical but also of the logical status of the apparatus in an edition. He also seems ready to consider the text-critical and editorial implications of an exploration of the genetic process in the specificity of the acts of writing.

A particular strength of Shillingsburg's book lies in the theory sections "Forms" and "Expectation." Options of editorial orientation are identified in the one, and their consequences outlined in the other. Together, these chapters show how theories and principles of textual criticism as well as rationales and procedures of editing both derive from and influence the editor's medial position between authors and texts, on the one hand, and users and readers of editions, on the other. In light of our present endeavor to sketch out the contrast between the Anglo-American and the German text-critical approaches, we may take a step further and say that, given a shift in the dominant orientation—the authorial orientation here, the textual orientation there—distinct differences follow, for the definition, weighting, and correlation of what, by name, appears to be a largely identical series of theoretical and practical terms and issues.

This applies with some force to the notions of intention and authority. Problematical under the authorial orientation, they become marginalized under the textual one. Early in the German discussion, intention was discredited by its association with what was called *Intuitionsphilologie*, the type of subjective, even divinatory, editorial approach that in Germany, owing to the absence of a methodological control movement like that of harnessing bibliography to text-critical ends, persisted far longer than in England and America. In "Befund und Deutung," Zeller rejects the intuitional approach, and its authorial orientation and invocation of intention. Zeller's subsequent encounter in "A New Approach to the Critical Constitution of Literary Texts" with the principles of copytext editing in general, and a close reading of the controversies around the CEAA Hawthorne and Crane editions in particular, reinforces that rejection. The complexities of definition that characterize the Anglo-American intention debate, as well as the contradictory editorial results under the auspices of authorial intention, lead him to the conclusion that "intention" is unsuitable as a text-critical and editorial guiding principle.

Taking pride of place instead as the editorial guiding principle in the German conceptual system is the notion of "authorization." By its nature it is a concept from which the author cannot be eliminated; yet by the way it is defined it does not admit to the full his authority over the text. (Hence it implicitly allows from the outset for the collaborative and social factors in text production that have been so bothersome in the intention debate). Under the overall historical and textual orientation of the German approach, "authorization" is peculiarly document-related. Its definition is a purely formal one, which is considered an advantage. A manuscript or typescript is regarded as authorized if the author has written it, has participated in its production or has demonstrably ordered it to be produced. A printing is regarded as authorized if the author has requested or sanctioned it and if, moreover, he has provided copy, taken influence on its production, contributed his own revisions, or has requested it to be revised. By deliberate extension of the definition, as Zeller argues in "Struktur and Genese in der Editorik," the authorized document furnishes the editor with an authorized text version (118).

The authorized text version, then, is what the editor under the system must present with historical faithfulness and with emendation only of indubitable textual errors. This begs the question of the textual error. The attempts to define it have been deliberately narrow. A textual critic trained in bibliography and empirically aware of the vagaries of textual transmission will balk, in particular, at Zeller's restricted conception of textual error in "Struktur und Genese in der Editorik": in a linear series of authorized documents/texts, errors definable as such in one document/text but untouched by correction in a subsequent act of document/text authorization must no longer be regarded as errors (120–21). If this is logical, it is nevertheless insistently contradicted by common sense and experience.[5] The logical fault appears to lie in the premise of equating document and text under the notion of authorization, and a concept of the authority of the text as distinct from that of the authorization of the document would seem to be called for.

To develop a broader definition of textual error, German theory would stand to profit from closer encounters with Anglo-American text-critical thinking. Initial steps in this direction have been taken. For its part, Anglo-American editors would gain an added orientation by confronting continental editorial scholarship. Such contact might, for example, modify the school of Greg's hitherto almost exclusive focus on the empiric and theoretical problems surrounding the text. For the discipline of textual criticism and editing, it is no less important to reflect on the nature and potential of conceptions and designs of the apparatus. In certain respects, apparatus and apparatus forms may, in editing, claim functional precedence over text. The encounters of Anglo-American textual criticism with theories and methodologies outside its school, however, have as yet remained unsought.

Notes

1. The focal essay is Gunter Martens, "Texterschliessung durch Edition."
2. A comprehensive survey of the aims and methods of *critique génétique* is

P. M. de Biasi's "Vers une science de la littérature. L'analyse des manuscrits et la genèse de l'oeuvre."

3. See, e.g., G. Thomas Tanselle's "The Editorial Problem of Final Authorial Intention," esp. 197.

4. Jerome McGann has perceptively explored the critical potential of an edition which, as it happens, represents an attempt to wed Anglo-American and German text-critical thought and editorial procedure. In "'Ulysses' as a Post-Modern Text," he recognizes that the notional indeterminacy of texts according to deconstructionist theory is yet determinate within the textual materiality of scholarly editions.

cf 82 r 45

5. Hans Zeller has recently reviewed the state of the art in German text-critical theory and editorial methodology in "Fünfzig Jahre neugermanistischer Edition." Among future requirements he mentions the need for further reflection on the concept of textual error.

Works Cited

Biasi, P. M., de. "Vers une science de la littérature. L'analyse des manuscrits et la genèse de l'oeuvre." *Encyclopaedia universalis*. Paris: Encyclopaedia Universalis France, 1988. 466–76.

Boetius, Henning. "Vorüberlegungen zu einer generativen Editionstheorie." In *Lili. Zeitschrift für Literaturwissenschaft und Linguistik* 5 (1975). Heft 19/20: *Edition und Wirkung*. 147–59.

Červenka, Miroslav. "Textologie and Semiotik." In *Texte und Varianten. Probleme ihrer Edition und Interpretation*. Ed. Hans Zeller and Gunter Martens. München: C. H. Beck, 1971. 143–63.

Greg, W. W. "The Rationale of Copy-Text." *Studies in Bibliography* 3 (1950–51): 19–36. Rpt. in *Collected Papers*. Ed. J. C. Maxwell. Oxford: Clarendon, 1966. 374–391.

Hölderlin, Friedrich. *Sämtliche Werke*. Ed. Friedrich Beissner and Adolph Beck. 7 vols. Stuttgart: W. Kohlhammer, 1946–1977.

Martens, Gunter. "Texterschliessung durch Edition." *Lili. Zeitschrift für Literaturwissenschaft und Linguistik* 5 (1975). Heft 19/20: *Edition und Wirkung*. 82–104.

McGann, Jerome J. *A Critique of Modern Textual Criticism*. Chicago: U of Chicago P, 1983.

———. "'Ulysses' as a Post-Modern Text: The Gabler Edition." *Criticism* 27 (1985): 283–306.

Parker, Hershel. *Flawed Texts and Verbal Icons: Literary Authority in American Fiction*. Evanston: Northwestern UP, 1984.

Shillingsburg, Peter. *Scholarly Editing in the Computer Age: Theory and Practice*. Athens: U of Georgia P, 1986.

Tanselle, G. Thomas. "The Editorial Problem of Final Authorial Intention." *Studies in Bibliography* 29 (1976): 167–211.

Thorpe, James. *Principles of Textual Criticism*. San Marino: The Huntington Library, 1972.

Zeller, Hans. "Befund und Deutung." In *Texte und Varianten. Probleme ihrer Edition und Interpretation*. Ed. Hans Zeller and Gunter Martens. München: C. H. Beck, 1971. 45–89.

————. "Fünfzig Jahre neugermanistischer Edition. Zur Geschichte und künftigen Aufgaben der Textologie." *Editio* 3 (1989): 1–17.

————. "A New Approach to the Critical Constitution of Literary Texts." *Studies in Bibliography* 28 (1975): 231–64.

————. "Struktur und Genese in der Editorik. Zur germanistischen und anglistischen Editionsforschung." *Lili. Zeitschrift für Literaturwissenschaft und Linguistik* 5 (1975). Heft 19/20: *Edition und Wirkung*. 105–26.

———— and Gunter Martens, eds. *Texte und Varianten. Probleme ihrer Edition und Interpretation*. München: C. H. Beck, 1971.

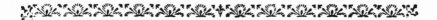

IO

The Textual Event

Event - cf Mclenity (x)?

JOSEPH GRIGELY

The self-relation that forms identity is necessarily mediated by opposition to otherness. —Mark Taylor, *Altarity*

NE OF THE MOST USED, ABUSED, and powerful words in our critical vocabularies is the word *text*. As a critical term it is enormously convenient and often seems to do when nothing else will do. If one doesn't know whether to call something a book, a word, a work, or the world, then one calls it a text because it simply sounds right, supplanting a vague uncertainty with a certain vagueness. Yet it is a word with a history (or rather histories), and by unpacking some of this history I want to examine the textual-critical tradition of seeing the text as an object, and redefine the text in an interdisciplinary format utilizing semiotics, deconstruction theory, and philosophy; that is, I want to relocate the tradition of textual studies within the larger nexus of critical theory and the philosophy of art.

The Textual-Critical Tradition

Implicit in this effort is a more general intention of encouraging a theoretical (perhaps even metatheoretical) approach to textual philosophy—a kind of interdisciplinary philosophy of textuality. Until the last decade, textual "theory"—even in the work of Sir Walter Greg and Fredson Bowers—was in effect no more than a defense of textual practices; it was essentially anterior to textual study and the experience gained through what was considered the "success" and "failure" of those practices. James Thorpe, for example, describes his *Principles of Textual Criticism* as being "an effort to present . . . a discussion of the basic principles which underlie the practice of textual criticism" (vii), and this experiential approach is typical of the cautious reserve that characterizes the discipline. Traditionally, textual studies has involved an objective of stability, a way of organizing, stabilizing, or "framing" a work of literature as an ordered set of texts. This is both useful and understandable, perhaps because criticism itself has instituted its own kind of ordering of literature in various sets and subsets that are variously classified by genre, period, author, and so on. Order, in short, seems to make things easier: it allows us to move beyond the act of ordering to other issues that build upon the distinctions we make. This is both tempting and beguiling, since it promises a certain good: it promises to deliver us from the chaos of reality—textual entrammelment—and answer our desire for such deliverance.

The ordered and organized literary signifier has thus been the desideratum of textual criticism and bibliography, but actual textual practices have not always acknowledged the implications of semiotic "order"—an order that threatens to deceive us and return to disorder. Such "order" is substantiated by the presence of a physical text, which in turn is a reflection of the Anglo-American textual tradition of seeing the text as a physical object, as a book, manuscript, a holograph, a galley proof.[1] This is partly because bibliography is acknowledged as the study of books as physical objects, but it is also because such texts are what Jerome McGann, in "*Ulysses* as a Postmodern Text," calls "determinate" representations of a work's overall instability; they provide us with specific, concrete, historical, and institutional evidence which in turn guides us toward understanding that instability (291). There is a tendency here not toward the humanistic and psychical, but towards the *physicalis* of objectivity. McGann's point is also suggested by Peter Shillingsburg, when he emphasizes that "a text is contained and stabilized by the physical form [of a document]" (49–50).[2] But it is even more emphatically stressed by William Proctor Williams and Craig S. Abbott, who explain in their *Introduction to Bibliographical and Textual Studies* that "the basic commodity for a literary scholar is the text, which is physically embodied in letters written, impressed, or transferred onto a surface" (3). This emphasis on objects, commodities even, like soybeans and pork bellies, is not unusual, particularly if we consider the etymological force of the word *literature: littera,* a letter. In another sense, however, if the business of texts and the business of literature is defined by that which gets written and printed, we are also saying—by default—that "oral literature" (which is itself a contradiction in terms) is not literature, nor can it be literature until it has written texts. Even the postmodern oral poetry is, as Jerome Rothenberg observed, mediated by print by appearing in print (*Pre-Faces* 10–11, 36)—a fact undoubtedly true for David Antin's "talk poetry" and Allen Ginsberg's tape-recorder poems. This may seem a priggish matter, but it is also a serious matter in cultures with linguistic systems that do not get written down—sign language poetry or Native American literature being good examples of what can be lost or disparaged by being different.

The idea of the text-as-an-object is, I would like to suggest, the legacy of the boundaries of the Anglo-American and German textual tradition. Both Sir Walter Greg and Ronald McKerrow, as well as Fredson Bowers and G. Thomas Tanselle, have all worked within a somewhat narrow range of literature—Anglo-American works between (roughly) 1560 and 1960—and this exposed them to a certain set of writing and publishing conventions. Within this set of conventions they produced an admirable program of admirable approaches to the vicissitudes of textual transmission. Just as Saussure changed linguistic theory by emphasizing the synchronic study of language, the early textual scholars emphasized the synchronic activity of book production, which in turn made diachronic and typological studies more viable. In essence, textual criticism is a metachronic activity, both in time and out of time; its activity retrospective, and in many ways, canonical. We do not, for example, have a postmodern textual theory to deal with postmodern texts and genres—sound poetry, video poetry, and performance art, to cite a few—simply because textual theory is for the most part dependent on an institutional view of that canonical authority (usually for practical reasons that are also, unfortunately, economic reasons: it's easier to get a grant to edit Hawthorne than it is to get a grant to edit Johnny Rotten). The idea of the text-as-an-object is thus bound to the idea of the text-as-a-*literary*-object, and only insofar as textual theories consider texts outside canonical traditions will we arrive at a less medium-governed idea of textuality.

Such interdisciplinarity might be expanded even beyond the socio-economic conception of text production that characterizes Jerome McGann's work. For McGann a poem is not itself an object, but "a unique order of unique appearances," a network of human actions and human forces that can best be characterized as a historical event (*Beauty of Inflections* 343). Like that of his spiritual mentor, Mikhail Bakhtin, McGann's work calls for a closer look at the human element in poetry, the manner in which poetry (and literature in general) is shaped by the human condition, and the extent to which literature is a part of larger, socio-economic systems. What I have to say in the following pages might be regarded as an attempt to take this notion further by considering how human languages and the modalities of those languages (written? spoken? signed?) affect textual structures in the domain of the creative arts—poetry, painting, or performance, to name but a few.

When we theorize about "textuality" in this broader sense, we begin to realize that although texts manifest themselves as objects, they are also more than objects, and particularly more than literary objects; they are also (to take one position) signifiers, in which case we are confronted with additional questions that are less germane to textual criticism and bibliography than to semiotics and philosophy: What are the semiotic boundaries of a text? Where does a text "begin" or "end"? How is a text of a poem different from—or like—a text of a painting? Do performances have texts, or *are* they texts? Traditionally, semiotics has been understood as a kind of mediating discourse on the relationship between language and art—it informs many of the interartistic comparisons in Wendy Steiner's *Colors of Rhetoric*, for example—but in our case the arguments and answers offered by semiotics or the more nominalistic philosophy of Nelson Goodman lead us toward further questions that are not only germane to "texts" but to the very idea of literature as literature or art as art. This is the point where textual criticism becomes textual philosophy.

Given these considerations, my approach, and my critical sources, are fairly eclectic; were this essay a dinner party, one would find sitting around the table Fredson Bowers, Jerome McGann, Jacques Derrida, Nelson Goodman, and Arthur Danto—not exactly the sort of gathering that makes happy company. At times it may seem that I am unduly harsh in my criticism of textual studies (as a critical school), and at times I am. It is not that I disparage the achievements of the Anglo-American and German textual tradition; rather, I lament what seems to me the ideological closure of that tradition—a closure that is based on the consequence of decades of editing institutionally qualified, canonized works of literature. The questions I bring up are intentionally provocative; for years textual critics lamented that readers of literature take their texts for granted, and my position now is that those same textual critics might perhaps be taking their conception of textuality for granted.

Iterability

In textual studies, the notion of iterability (from the Latin *iterum,* again) is present at levels that include the iterative function of language and the implied iterability of texts. We might think of "repeatability" as being a universal quality in textual studies, where efforts are made to produce or reproduce a particular text that lends itself toward a kind of scholarly utilitarianism. Even our critical discourse includes the terms *reprint* and *reissue,* although neither can be taken literally: reprints do not always re-print, inasmuch as they may include intentional or unintentional intrinsic changes, or reflect the extrinsic influence of political and economic conditions. What this suggests is that the philosophical foundations that underlie the concept of iterability in textual studies are vulnerable and open to question. Language is iterative to the extent that it is a socially shared code; but are utterances of language or units of utterances (such as texts) iterative also? In the section that follows I shall investigate (briefly) the iterability of language in literary discourse, and what I believe to be the noniterability of texts. The resources for my argument are somewhat diverse and not in a strict sense "textual" or "theoretical," if only because iterability is—at its barest—an interdisciplinary issue.

The iterability of language is presupposed by being a condition of language: it is a symbolic system comprising learnable and repeatable symbols. This is a typical feature of many semiotic systems and not in itself surprising. Repeatability allows us to formulate utterances that, as part of a shared social code, are understood within the realm of that code's usage and (if one follows Derrida on the matter in "Signature Event Context") even beyond the limits of code itself (317). It is important to remember that language is composed of units that signify in an interactive and (both) linear and nonlinear manner: the phoneme, the morpheme, the word, the phrase, the sentence: these are units that do not necessarily signify exclusively at their own level but at recombinant levels as well. Hence, we might say that the iterability of these units is essentially paradigmatic; yet it is paradigmatic only in theory, only in an ideal vacuum that is free from the actual conditions of articulation (either spoken or signed) and writing. Derrida's position—a controversial position—is that, as he says in "Signature Event Context," "A writing that was not structurally legible—iterable—beyond the death of the addressee would not be writing" (315). We can "read" an utterance beyond the death (i.e., presence) of the addressee, but what are we reading? Or, as Robert Scholes frames the question: "We would have made a sense *for* the marks, but would we have made sense *of* them?" (280).

What Derrida is suggesting is that although language is conceived as being paradigmatic—like a kind of semantic lego kit—in actual practice, our utterances (constructions, buildings) are more properly syntagmatic. They may survive the death of the addressee, but in a special way: they become desyntagmatized, lifted from the context of articulation, but do not cease to function. What happens is that the utterance—whether written or otherwise recorded—is recontextualized, or, as Derrida says, "grafted" (317), and such grafting is omnipresent: language deceives us as to how its iterable presence (written words, marks, inscriptions) do not translate to an iterable intention, or meaning. The original boundary of an utterance—the moment of its inscription—becomes null, but not void. We merely graft it, decontextualize it, and recontextualize it so that the utterance gives way to its new location: it becomes, so to speak, the resident of a particular (and new) discourse community. And so on.

What Derrida doesn't do in "Signature Event Context" is give us a satisfactory definition of "the moment of inscription" (317); nor, for that matter, does anyone else. "Inscription" can be taken to mean a moment of writing by the author, the moment of publishing, or the moment of reading—or any point in between. A moment like this defines itself rather loosely and metaphorically as a moment of stasis. Such a moment is not the singular representation of a work of literature (or art even), which is instead more of a series of moments of inscription, some authorial, some not, some authorized, some not; yet all of them are realities to the extent that are scripted, (a)scribed, and more particularly, read. Moments like these are best characterized not by what they say but what they do not say: they leave us with a disembodied, decontextualized text that does not mean anything unless bound to an agent of meaning—an interpreter.

Yet in an odd sense Derrida seems to me to be on to something quite germane to the tradition of textual criticism. Historically, textual criticism has tried to qualify moments of inscription according to their relative authority, and establish a hierarchy of inscriptions according to authorial intent. It does not (from my point of view) matter whether these efforts succeed or not; indeed, there's no way to know. Nor does it matter whether the editions produced are judiciously emended texts, eclectic texts, or facsimile texts, for they constitute (and continue to constitute, as in Gabler's edition of *Ulysses*) further moments of inscription. This is where Derrida's point strikes home: a moment of inscription is no more than a moment of inscription. It may be a significantly reformulated moment, like Bowdler's 1808 edition of Shakespeare, in which case even Bowdler's moment of inscribing Shakespeare is a moment of contextualized presence; in essence, unique, and in its uniqueness, telling. It's "wrongness" is a historical argument about truth values, and such an argument cannot exist except by comparison with other moments of inscription. A play by Shakespeare (or by anyone else) cannot claim final authority because it cannot claim to be finished at any point: just as there is no consensus in editorial theory as to what constitutes the "final intentions" of a work, there is no consensus (as far as I know) in philosophical theory as to what constitutes a "finished" work of literature.[3] At one point Nelson Goodman asserts in *Languages of Art* that "the composer's work is done when he has written the score" (114)—but the corollary to this statement—"the poet's work is done when he has written the poem"— will not do because a work at this point is unrealized as a social commodity. Even if we take publication as a moment of completion, then we must also consider the fact that further publication—or even withdrawal from publication—controverts this moment but certainly does not negate it. Here I concur with the general thrust of McGann's work: instead of viewing literature—or artworks—as finished productions, we might instead view them as works of fluxion that experience stasis, as in, say, a particular edition, or a particular exhibition space. This stasis is not so much strictly temporal as it is contextual; that is, "spatial" within a historical context. In other words, we can say there are no final or finished works, but only final or finished texts; no final work of *Hamlet* or Keats's ode "To Autumn," but final (and particular) texts of *Hamlet* and Keats's ode. These texts redefine Derrida's original moment of inscription as a series of moments of inscription: they are utterances, "writings acts," and by the time they reach us—no matter how generous an editor is in explaining those texts—they have already, in varying degrees, broken free from those moments: they drift. A work of literature thus cannot be stabilized any more than a sculpture or a building can be stabilized: the re-location that threatened (and subsequently retextualized) Richard Serra's sculpture *Tilted Arc,* or the additions that threaten Marcel Breuer's Whitney Museum or Frank Lloyd Wright's Guggenheim Museum are not in this sense any more threatening than the next editor to face *Ulysses* or *Hamlet.* Timelessness is an illusion to the extent that there is no timeless text: *a* text is of *a* time.

The value of Derrida's argument is that it reminds us although language (*language*) is iterable, this iterability begins to rupture when applied to utterances (*parole*), even when those utterances are written. We move further and further from the moment of inscription and are attached to that moment by a small thread of words that are at once both the residue of that moment and our bond to it. Textual criticism and editorial theory do not help us here; editions imply that texts are not only repeatable but that they can be reconstructed along the lines of authorial intentions, and such reconstruction draws attention to itself as being re:construction. They are texts that are a part of the social institution of professionalized literature (again: a moment of inscription), and these texts serve all kinds of social, economic, and political purposes as much as Galignani's pirated texts ever did. This may seem a harsh thing to say, but I am not trying here to apply value judgments to particular texts. I only wish to say that if two texts are different, they are essentially equal in their differences, if only because those differences—and the interpretations we bring to bear upon them—are individual in their context: one text cannot be more "individual" than another.

One possible objection to this is to say that a facsimile edition is one way to repeat a text. My response is that this too will not do, for a facsimile is at best an illusion of iterability: it draws attention to itself as something *factum simile,* as something *much like* an "original," where $X_1 \rightarrow X_2$ but $X_1 \neq X_2$. However much two texts are like each other physically or perceptually (whether real or apparent), they are not the same. What stands out particularly are the circumstances that illustrate a need or purpose for the facsimile (such as Black Letter texts), for such circumstances are a part of the event that frames the facsimile's moment of inscription. The letters and words of the facsimile may look exactly like that of its parent, but the metatextual distance between the two would be remote. Again the message is that the repeatability of language is not synonymous with the (ir)repeatability of texts.

A more nominalistic approach to literature might suggest otherwise, and Nelson Goodman is one person who might not be swayed by this argument. Goodman is one of our most important philosophers in dealing with interartistic issues, and he has a knack of asking particularly difficult questions that we otherwise might (and often do) take for granted. One of his questions that bears upon our argument goes like this: Why is it possible to make a forgery of, say, Rembrandt's *Lucretia,* but not Haydn's *London Symphony* or Gray's "Elegy?" Goodman's response is that certain fundamental differences underlie the notion of a literal, or representative iterability in the arts. He explains: "Let us speak of a work as *autographic* if and only if the distinction between original and forgery of it is significant; or better, if and only if even the most exact duplication of it thereby does not count as genuine. If a work of art is autographic, we may also call that that art autographic. Thus painting is autographic, music nonautographic, or *allographic*" (*Languages* 113). Like music, literature is described as allographic because it is "amenable to notation" (121, 207–11).[4] "Notation" in this sense suggests the presence of some kind of semiotic system, whether that system is primarily symbolic (as language), or symbolic and indexical (as music), or symbolic, indexical, and iconic (as dance notation). With the presence of a notation system, each "forgery" is not a forgery but merely another instance of that work. As Goodman puts it, we need only verify the spelling of a work to produce "an instance" of the work (115–16). He emphasizes the business of spelling and punctuation because, I think, he sees the printed or inscribed texts as symbolic representations of oral utterances, and in the process glosses over the gross distinctions that "literature" involves—particularly uninscribed oral genres.[5]

One response to Goodman would be to offer a clarification of the terms *work* and *text* and use the foundation of such clarification to reorient his argument. At times Goodman uses the two terms interchangeably—a habit unnerving, but not in any way unusual, for many of us are inclined to do likewise. As I discussed earlier, texts can be described along the lines of Derrida's "moment of inscription"—and such texts do not always "comply," in a strictly authorial sense, to a conception of correctness or finality. Such moments are singular, and this singularity (over time) becomes sequential. With this in mind Jerome McGann's work again offers us a clarifying perspective. I shall have rather more to say about McGann in a moment, but I would like to address here the temporal organization that McGann's work brings to textual theory. McGann's thesis in *The Beauty of Inflections* is that literature, and the act of producing literature, is a dynamic process in which the literary work is represented by a series of successive texts, each with its own historical, semantic, and aesthetic value—values that explain literature as "a dynamic event in the human experience" (108), and not, as the formalists made it, a mere aesthetic object. As McGann explained in his *Critique of Modern Textual Criticism*, this series of texts can be generically described as "a series of specific acts of production" (52). In this sense a literary work—be it a poem, a play, or a letter to Auntie Em—is an assemblage of texts, a polytext.[6] This formulation can be expressed by the equation

$$W \rightarrow T_1, T_2, T_3, \ldots T_N$$

where W = work and T = text. It is important to note that the work is not equivalent to the *sum* of its texts (which would create some kind of hybridized eclectic text), but instead is an ongoing—and infinite—manifestation of textual appearances, *whether those texts are authorized or not.* Such infinity reinforces my earlier view that a work of literature cannot be "finished," just as a building is never finished: it evolves into textual states of being, in which case even ruins are an additional text along this line of time. It is thus impossible to say that the work of, say, Shakespeare's *Tempest,* exists as anything more than a Platonic form or idea; and it is ideal in its implicit acknowledgment of the impossibility of the ideal. It is a concept, but not a concept limit; a class, but not a compliance class, for its boundaries are not prescribed. It is defined by the manifestation of texts, in which case we can say there is no "text" of *The Tempest,* but only a series of texts that comprise *The Tempest's* polytext. *The Tempest* is a work, and a copy of the First Folio represents one text of that work. Nor is it necessary to exclude performances from this formulation. Where a series of performances is based on a specific text (what Goodman might call a score), and given

$$W \rightarrow T_1, T_2, T_3, \ldots T_N$$

then we might say that

$$T_x \rightarrow P_1, P_2, P_3, \ldots P_N$$

What is important about such formulas is that they remind us we do not normally conceive a book in terms of itself as a work, but in terms of its texts, or in any case the specific texts with which we have had encounters. We might perhaps speak of a work in terms of its extratextual myth, for works do indeed reach a stage where they are discussed as realities that we have not experienced in a more literal sense; that is, we speak *about* them, but not *of* them. Yet it seems to me that much of our critical discourse (and our "creative" discourse as well) depends upon our encounters with specific texts.

If then we consider a work as a nontangible idea represented by a sequential series of texts—whether these texts are inscribed or performed, whether they are authorized or not—then we might be able to make more out of Goodman's original question. Is it possible to make a forgery of Gray's "Elegy," or any other work of literature? The question is important because it asks us if the iterability of language is an explanation for (as Goodman sees it) the iterability of texts. Given the above discussion, my response to Goodman is two-tiered: it is not possible to make a forgery of Gray's "Elegy," but it is possible to make a forgery of a particular text of Gray's "Elegy." In this sense "literature" in the broad sense is an allographic art, but literary texts are more properly autographic in their autonomy.[7]

Suppose, for example, I wanted to forge Keats's ode "To a Nightingale" and wrote out the poem, with a pencil, on a piece of greenish paper (as I am doing now). In itself the poem I have inscribed does not purport to be any other text of the poem other than what I have written: it is simply another instance of the work, another text amongst the hundreds or thousands of such texts. In this respect Goodman is right: I cannot forge Keats's "Nightingale" ode.

Suppose, however, I wanted to make a forgery of the fair copy of Keats's poem that is in the Fitzwilliam Museum in Cambridge. Using early nineteenth-century paper and ink that were found locked in a vault beneath St. James Place, I manage to replicate Keats's admirable scrawl and (we will assume my luck is really with me) surreptitiously replace Keats's holograph with my forged transcript. Bingo. Some years later a young D.Phil. candidate at Oxford visits Cambridge and notices one of the *t*'s doesn't look quite right, and, after careful paleographic inspection using infrared photography, earlier photostats, and Robert Gittings's *The Odes of John Keats and Their Earliest Known Manuscripts,* concludes that the manuscript is a forgery. Troubled Fitzwilliam officials review their records and find that another Keats scholar had "consulted" the holograph some years back. They send out a legal posse which of course catches me, and, in court, I stammer the truth: "N-N-Nelson Goodman made me do it."

What we learn from this is that the uniqueness of texts passes for Goodman's condition of something that can be forged (he admits in *Languages of Art* that performances can be forged [113]), which more emphatically says that texts are not iterable. Such a conclusion requires us to maintain our sharp distinction between a work and a text, and this is a distinction that Goodman's otherwise thoughtful analysis overlooks. Even if we grant Goodman this distinction, his argument is caught up in what exactly he means by a "correct copy" of a poem: he would have to impose a standard of correctness, in which case a "deviant" copy—one with, say, a misplaced comma—would not be another instance of that work, but a completely new work.

Another way of looking at the question of iterability is to examine Jorge Luis Borges's story entitled "Pierre Menard, Author of the *Quixote*," which runs like this: A friend of Menard, enumerating his publications and manuscripts, notes the inclusion of the ninth and thirty-eighth chapters of the first part of *Don Quixote*, and a fragment of chapter twenty-two. Not Cervantes's *Quixote* (which was written in the seventeenth century), but Menard's (which was written in the twentieth). Menard, says his friend, "did not want to compose another *Quixote*—which is easy—but *the Quixote itself*. Needless to say, he never contemplated a mechanical transcription of the original; he did not propose to copy it. His admirable intention was to produce a few pages which would coincide—word for word and line for line—with those of Miguel de Cervantes" (39). This indeed is exactly what Menard did, and did successfully. The story proceeds:

> It is a revelation to compare Menard's *Don Quixote* with Cervantes'. The latter, for example, wrote (part one, chapter nine):
> . . . truth, whose mother is history, rival of time, depository of deeds, witness of the past, exemplar and advisor to the present, and the future's counselor.
> Written in the seventeenth century, written by the "lay genius" Cervantes, this enumeration is a mere rhetorical praise of history. Menard, on the other hand, writes:
> . . . truth, whose mother is history, rival of time, depository of deeds, witness of the past, exemplar and advisor to the present, and the future's counselor.

History, the *mother* of truth: the idea is astounding. Menard, a contemporary of William James, does not define history as an inquiry into reality but as its origin. Historical truth, for him, is not what has happened; it is what we have judged to have happened. The final phrases—*exemplar and advisor to the present, and the future's counselor*—are brazenly pragmatic.

The contrast in style is also vivid. The archaic style of Menard—quite foreign, after all—suffers from a certain affectation. Not so that of his forerunner, who handles with ease the current Spanish of his time. (43).

The two *Quixotes* are thus, notwithstanding their identical spelling and punctuation, quite different works—or are they? Pressed to respond to the question by his colleague Richard Wollheim, Goodman is reluctant to concede that two identically spelled inscriptions ought to be considered instances of different works (*Of Mind and Other Matters*, 140–41). It is a difficult position: for Goodman to say that they are different works, he would also be saying that two iterable inscriptions are ontologically different—and this is as he admits either untenable or an aporia. What is possible here is that the inscription is iterable, but the inscription-as-an-utterance is not. If literature (or in a broad sense human communication) boiled down to mere spellings, we would have to concede agreement with Goodman. But we can't do this because literature is not mere spellings, and Borges's story makes this its central point. The two *Quixotes* are overtly different: Cervantes's is quite at home in its enunciation of the vernacular; Menard's, in contrast, seems strangely archaic. Cervantes's *Quixote* is rhetorically straightforward, while Menard—contemporary of Bertrand Russell and William James—writes with a certain kind of philosophical and pragmatic reserve. Their differences arise not from the moments of our reading (though this may be so), but from the moments of their respective inscriptions, and only later from our investigation of those moments. The works are ontologized—that is to say, contextualized semantically—by the temporal history that surrounds their composition. In an excellent discussion of the story, Arthur Danto adds:

It is not just that the books are written at different times by different authors of different nationalities and literary intentions: these facts are not external ones; they serve to characterize the work(s) and of course to individuate them for all their graphic indiscernibility. That is to say, the works are in part constituted by their location in the history of literature as well as by their relationships to their authors, and as these are often dismissed by critics who urge us to pay attention to the work itself, Borges' contribution

to the ontology of art is stupendous: you cannot isolate these factors from
the work since they penetrate, so to speak, the *essence* of the work. (35–36)

From the discipline of philosophy, Danto's point of view seems to me
informed and right; from the angle of literary criticism he is perhaps more
naive, but certainly no less right. The critics he implicates for extolling us
to "pay attention to the work itself" are no small lot: they constitute a
tradition that began (in its most concerted form) with the New Critics (in
America) and the Prague structuralists (in Europe), and gained momen-
tum, as well as an inimical presence, with Euro-American structuralism
and poststructuralism. Yet in urging us (as either literary critics or art
critics) to locate the ontological "essence" of a work with that work's
history, Danto is implicitly (and I suspect unconsciously) guiding us
toward New Historicism and the work of one of structuralism's most
important antagonists, Mikhail M. Bakhtin.

Bakhtin's name is hardly new to the field of textual criticism; McGann,
particularly, has found it purposeful to cite from Bakhtin's work, and
behind those citations is a much larger theoretical framework. The insights
Bakhtin adds to textual philosophy are not only germane, but germinal as
well: they constitute—in their professedly antiformalist stance—one of
our first discussions on the text as a discrete social and historical utterance.
A collection of Bakhtin's unfinished essays, published in English under the
title *Speech Genres and Other Late Essays,* is particularly useful in that it
directly confronts two of the issues I have been dragging along through
this essay: the iterability of language and the illusion of iterability of texts.
Bakhtin writes: "Behind each text stands a language system. Everything in
the text that is repeated and reproduced, everything repeatable and re-
producible, everything that can be given outside a given text (the given)
conforms to this language system. But at the same time each text (as an
utterance) is individual, unique, and unrepeatable, and herein lies its entire
significance (its plan, the purpose for which it was created). This is the
aspect of it that pertains to honesty, truth, goodness, beauty, history"
(105). It seems to me that the two profound truths of this statement (that
the language of a text can be repeated, but that the text as an utterance
cannot) are marred by Bakhtin's attempt to claim a third truth: that the
"entire significance" of a text lies within its uniqueness as a social utterance, as an act of communication. This position is illustrative of Bakhtin's
inflexibility towards formalism and structuralism, and the absolutism of

his historical hermeneutics also infects McGann's work (I shall have more to say about this in my conclusion). This problem is disconcerting, but not in a manner that turns one away from Bakhtin; it instead pulls us closer to the ideological edge on which his ideas move. A bit further into his essay he takes up (unknowingly) a hypothetical position vis-à-vis Nelson Goodman and the two *Quixotes*:

> Two or more sentences can be absolutely identical (when they are superimposed on one another, like two geometrical figures, they coincide); moreover, we must allow that any sentence, even a complex one, in the unlimited speech flow can be repeated an unlimited number of times in completely identical form. But as an utterance (or part of an utterance) no one sentence, even if it has only one word, can ever be repeated: it is always a new utterance (even if it is a quotation). . . . The utterance as a whole is shaped as such by extralinguistic (dialogic) aspects, and it is also related to other utterances. These extralinguistic (and dialogic) aspects also pervade the utterance from within. (108–9).

Given Cervantes's and Menard's *Quixotes*, Bakhtin would, on the basis of this position, unhesitatingly pronounce them different works, and he would do so for similar reasons Danto does: they are separate utterances, tied by "dialogic relations" to their historical circumstances, and different in their relation to those circumstances. The emphasis on the extralinguistic nature of these dialogical relations also serves, to an extent, to delimit the range of those relations: Bakhtin seems perfectly willing to grant that that relationship cannot be closed ("A context," he wrote, "is potentially unfinalized; a code must be finalized" [147]). Bakhtin's inclination here brings him as close to Derrida and Barthes as he can possible come. Why? Because the deconstructionist conception of the text as a text(ile) composed of weavings is in its own way "dialogic," but not in a manner solely exterior to language: it rather works *in* language, and between language and the world. Derrida's position is that the interweaving (*Verwebung*) of language combines both the discursive and the nondiscursive, both language and "other threads of experience" into a cloth, into a text(ile), that is inextricable and for the most part unweavable.[8] Such a text is related to social history, but it is not related to social history alone: it is related to other texts as well, and their chaotic system of interrelationships (warp, woof) undergoes (in theory) a kind of semantic fusioning and fraying. A text is thus intertextual, "caught up," as Foucault says, "in a system of references to other books, other texts, other sentences: it is a node within a network" (*The Archaeology of Knowledge* 23). In practice the textile is more controlled (Robert Scholes, for example, points out a kind of hermeneutic centering in Derrida's writing); but this does not seem to matter much here. Bakhtin's position is one that suggests that the utterance's singularity is protected by the utterance's volatility: we can never go back to that utterance with complete assurance, can never, literally or conceptually, conceive it in totality. Thus we face a necessity, perhaps a rule, in proclaiming a text (as a textile) is never complete. Bakhtin seems to lean in this direction when he asserts that "dialogic boundaries intersect the entire field of living human thought" (120), and as boundaries go those are pretty big. If the natural boundaries of a text can never be located (as the moment of inscription can never be recalled), by what rule or rubric do we create artificial boundaries for texts in the creative arts?

One answer is that textual boundaries are projections of our social and political identities; that they are in a sense mental conceptualizations of historical spaces. For McGann, for example, there is no such thing as a text without a context, and it is only by a combination of historical evidence and our interpretation of that evidence that this context is circumscribed. In other words, textual boundaries are not the product of reality, but of our "reading" of reality. In summarizing the work of McGann and David McKenzie, John Sutherland has written: "The force of McKenzie's critique, like McGann's is that it specifically controverts the faith of modern bibliography in the reproducibility of the 'essential' text, if only institutionally approved procedures are followed. There is, for McKenzie and McGann, no ahistorically essential text to reproduce. The task of McKenzie's 'sociology,' as he sees it, is in any case not reproduction but the reinsertion of the text into the critical moments of its historical and political existence" (586). This is a good basic overview of the situation, but I think it can be taken further. I would venture to say that not only can we not "reproduce" an "essential" text, but we cannot reproduce *any* text. To be able to reproduce a text would suggest, in Goodman's allographic terms, that a text is composed of an ahistorical, "neutral" language: it suggests that language alone constitutes a text. And it further suggests that speech events or writing events can be replicated in a manner in which a photographic negative can produce several photographs. But this won't do, either for texts or for photographs as texts, because we would in this case have to say that photographs likewise have no historical contexts, which is obviously false: as for literature, it matters how they are printed, where they are printed, how they are mounted, where they are exhibited, and where they are published.

Sutherland's use of the term *reproduce* is perhaps unavoidable; yet it is misleading. Each time we "reproduce" a text—whether we do so in an edition or in an apparatus of an edition—we do not reproduce that text at all, but rather print it in another new and different context. By changing the extralinguistic component—e.g., the publication—we change the extratextual community, and hence the interpretative strategies that are brought to bear upon that text. The audience changes; assumptions about it change. Furthermore, this applies to art and photographs as much as it applies to literature, for which reason an Anselm Kiefer painting on the wall of Marian Goodman's gallery is not the same as the identical painting on the wall of the Podunk town library. The textual-bibliographical dilemma that arises from such situations is a question—posed earlier—of what constitutes the semiotic boundary of a text; i.e., if the text is seen as a signifier, what constitutes the boundary (or boundaries) of this signifier? By arguing that the text extends beyond its physical presence in language to the context of itself as an utterance, we are saying that a text includes what is extralinguistic, even what is supposedly extratextual. In short, we are proposing a model of a text that is as radically unstable as our interpretations for that text. The free (or floating) signifieds that characterize some models of deconstruction are now matched by equally free (or floating) signifiers; and in concurrence, we find ourselves agreeing with Derrida that the "presence" of a text-as-an-object belies the absence of the text-as-an-utterance-of-another-time-and-place. That is to say, the fixedness of a text is as illusory as the fixedness of an interpretation; neither is "final," neither is "authorial." Such a proposition threatens to upset the very foundations upon which the textual-bibliographical tradition is based.

Perhaps it is just as well that this happens. Textual criticism has placed a considerable amount of (undue) faith in the idea of a definitive edition, particularly as much of this faith is placed in the textual apparatus, which is often said to allow us to "reconstruct" authoritative and collaborative versions of a work. What it doesn't do, of course, is give us the supposedly nonauthoritative, nor does it give us oral texts, nor does it give us the extralinguistic contexts of those very texts it purports to be giving. What it does give us, then, are surrogate texts that appeal to the iterability of language, but not of texts as historical events. My position here might come across to editors as unusually hard, in which case I can only say that we need to be more realistic about what an apparatus can and cannot do. Perhaps its greatest benefit is that the apparatus is indexical in its reference to, and summary of, texts; we still have the onus of chasing after them on our own. But an apparatus, or for that matter an edition, that purports to "reproduce" a text is an apparatus that lies. To reproduce is to reenact. And this won't work because the word *reenact* is an oxymoron: we can no more print the same text twice than we can step in the same stream twice. To reprint—even in facsimile—Shelley's *Adonais* merely adds another pearl onto the string of textual enactments. Bowers's Hawthorne does not reproduce or reenact Hawthorne any more than Menard's *Quixote* reenacts Cervantes's. Nor does it matter (as it seems to matter to Goodman) if two texts are alike in all physical respects, whether perceptual or inherent: their difference is instead one that is ontological.

cf Cohen & Jackson

Let me illustrate for a moment how this might be. Suppose that one should stumble upon a press operation locked away in a forgotten warehouse. Still set up in type, with original inks, paper, and binding equipment, is Ernest Hemingway's *Torrents of Spring*. Suppose now that one were to follow through on this discovery and print and bind several volumes of the book: physically they would be absolutely identical to those distributed from the initial imprint. Are they identical texts, however? My answer is that they are not. The volumes are transposed ontologically by their historical context: they are *extensions* of their discovery as texts-in-progress. That is, their stasis (or hibernation) as texts-in-progress is unbound (awakened) by their discovery. They become texts only inasmuch as they are discovered and printed. Where this historical truth is hidden, we cannot decide whether the texts are identical or not, in which case one may just as well make a killing selling them at book fairs. To borrow from (and adapt) Arthur Danto's argument in his *Transfiguration of the Commonplace,* we cannot vouch that holy water is holy water except by our belief as such (18). Whether the water is actually tap water or Evian water does not seem to matter so much as our belief that the water, having been blessed, is "transfigured" from a substance of quotidian consumption to a substance of religious signification. Chemically it is still the same stuff, just as the Hemingway printed in 1926 is materially the same as the Hemingway printed in 1989. Hence, we cannot reproduce, reprint, or reenact a text: each act of textual production is an act of sequential (even homeostatic) production.

This brings us vis-à-vis an important—perhaps the most important—

aspect of a philosophy of textuality: we can say, quite emphatically, that *a work of literature is ontologized by its texts;* it is identified as literature, or as being of a particular genre, by its particular textual manifestations. Literature does not define itself as literature; it is rather we who undertake this task of defining what we come to know as the highbrow and the lowbrow, the good and the bad, the canonical and the noncanonical. One particularly good example of this surfaced quite recently in the *New Yorker.* In an extended essay on the Great Plains, Ian Frazier tells how, after a night's sleep at a truck stop, he awoke in the morning to find (as he describes it) a stock truck parked beside his car, and "on the truck's door, in big letters, a poem":

> Buck Hummer
> Hog Hauler (68)

Buck Hummer certainly seems real, and the poem certainly is real, but what surely isn't real is Buck's consciousness of having a poem on the door of his truck. On that door, Buck's statement is both illocutionary and perlocutionary: it advertises and solicits, and, one supposes, the stock truck's text of this poem contained an address of sorts, and perhaps even a phone number. Frazier's text of "Buck Hummer" doesn't do this, however, because it doesn't have to: it rather announces itself as a poem. If the hog hauling business picks up for Buck as a result of his truck door being reontologized in the *New Yorker,* then he's in luck. Offers to publish his future truck doors might be slow in coming, and understandably so because Buck Hummer is not the author of "Buck Hummer/Hog Hauler"; rather, Frazier is. Buck merely wrote the door; Frazier wrote the poem. What is important here is that the poem stands in relation to literature as Marcel Duchamp's "Fountain" stands in relation to art. As a readymade (or more precisely, a readywrit), the poem becomes a poem only by virtue of Frazier's transcription and his offering of it as such. We accept it as a poem just as we accept the fact that Duchamp has transfigured (to use Danto's phrase again) a urinal into an artwork. For all we know Buck Hummer might not even exist—a point that explicitly contradicts the first sentence of this paragraph. The Buck Hummer of the truck door, the Buck Hummer of *New Yorker* fame, and (presumably) the Buck Hummer of the *Yellow Pages* present different texts that are also defined by our perception of their contexts. If this is an extreme example, it has the benefit of showing us how much semantic and historical information is couched within the individual texts of a work of literature; and it emphasizes (as the two *Quixotes* emphasize) that these differences do not necessarily have something (if anything) to do with the spelling or punctuation of texts: they extend themselves to the extralinguistic, extratextual context of that text, in which case the *New Yorker* and the door of Buck's stock truck are two very different vehicles for literature—and hogs.

Objects, Events, Outcomes

Earlier I mentioned that the tradition of textual criticism and bibliography has historically sought to provide an "organizing principle" in literary studies, and this principle is normally reflected by the ideas of authority and reliability in texts and editions. Much of this authority has been found in, or contrived from, the representation of authorial intent, whether these intentions are "final" or "original" or compounded in some way. Distinguishing authority is no doubt important; and from this point on it seems to me beneficial to our interests that we qualify (but not quantify, or stratify) this authority along the notion of alterity—as differences—and seek to explain what those differences mean, and why they are there. Freed of the burden of intentionality, texts become, as we saw, radically unstable, tenuously tied to a historical context that is at best ephemeral and in many ways irrecoverable. And this is to some a problem because it controverts the faith we have invested in modern textual criticism and bibliography, particularly in editions we use and have come to rely upon. Perhaps, however, this departure, or this shaking of our faith, is precisely what we need: something that will replace textual security with textual cynicism. The idea of a physically objectified text offers a false sense of security by being advertised as "objective," and since we can hold it in our hands (say, a book or a manuscript), we find additional comfort in its tangibility. This is understandable to the extent that our Western canonical traditions treat literature as a commodity for mass consumption. Problems, however, become apparent when we realize that language (langue) is not an object, nor for that matter is speech (parole). Speech may become objectified in a recording or (in a more limited way) in a printed text, but it is not in itself a physical entity. C. S. Peirce's semiotics is grounded in the basic tenet that "a sign, or *representamen,* is something which stands to somebody in some respect or capacity" (2:135). There is no indication of physical fixedness here, nor is it present in Saussure's semiology. The sign (or signifier, as I have been calling it in accord with more widely accepted European usage), is structurally free and may or may not take any kind of permanent embodiment. It need only be, in the words of the Prague structuralist Jan Mukařovský, "a reality perceivable by sense experience" in order to have life as a signifier (5). Hence, the evanescence of speech, of gestures, or of performances poses no problems for semiotics. Logic would tell us that no art form—no poem, no painting, no dance—can exist without a "text" comprising a semiotically endowed signifier, even if the boundaries of that signifier are indeterminate. One could even argue that silence—as in John Cage's 4'33"—is itself a text, or in any case textual, and give further validity to his statement "silence is sound" (*Poetry in Motion*). Though Cage's work is tangential and not the norm of the canons of textual traditions, it is just the kind of thing textual critics need to begin thinking about. When Williams and Abbot argue that textual embodiment consists of "letters written, impressed, or transferred onto a surface" (3), one wants to add that not only does the surface itself matter (as in Blake), but—to take Cage's reversal seriously—so too does the white space between the letters and words, particularly when that white space has a paralinguistic function. This is a sensitive matter when typographical boundaries are subject to manipulation, as in the decollage poetry of Tom Phillips and Ronald Johnson. Thus, our expansion of the description of textual "boundaries" is one that must go inward (to the tangible) as much as it must go outward (to the intangible): we need to have a description that bears signification in whatever form it appears.

Since literature by its definition (but not its etymology) includes the idea of verbal constructs (whether aesthetic or nonaesthetic, whether conceived, contrived, or appropriated), then it seems imperative that a definition for a text be able to include various modes of the literary experience: oral performances, particularly, and sign language poetry, as well as dramatic performances and the genre of performance art. Even though performance art like Karen Finley's "Yams Up My Granny's Ass" is a good long way from the Shakespearean experience, the interdisciplinary context of performance art is particularly suited to textual studies since performances by their very nature exist in different "states." As Goodman admitted, individual performances can be forged, and this establishes their autographic mode. Because performances are overtly detached from the apparent (but not real) fixedness of books, they force us quite directly to confront their ephemerality and describe it in a way that is part of the scheme of textual semiotics.

One way to do this is to describe a text in terms of the speech act, or perhaps more usefully, as an event. Bakhtin's idea of the text as an utterance, McGann's idea of the text as a dynamic event, and Derrida's abandoning (and reformulation) of the moment of inscription, all move in this direction, and much can be said for their positions. Paul Ricoeur, in an essay on literary ontology published in 1974, perceptively suggested that because literature consists of discourse, and since discourse occurs as an event, then literature is by consequence a "language event" (94). Such language events—like Bakhtin's theory of the utterance—retain their singularity in their (arguably) irrecoverable history, whether that history is spoken or written. In this respect the speech act is not structured in any way that is fundamentally different from the writing act: both emphasize the unboundaried "space" of the act, as well as the act's location in time—what Bakhtin calls "chronotopicity" (134).

Because such events are articulatory, their phenomenology is oriented toward the production, not the reception, of signifiers. This small point needs to be stressed. Traditional schemas for phenomenology, whether in philosophy (such as Husserl's and Merleau-Ponty's) or in literature (such as Fish's and Wolfgang Iser's) stress the perceptual aspect of the phenomenological experience: it constitutes *the moment of recognition* of the signifier/signified, a process of relational discourse in the reader's mind. Discussing Stanley Fish, for example, Stephen Mailloux wrote that a sentence is not "an object, a thing-in-itself, but an *event,* something that *happens* to, and with the participation of, the reader" (20). The event is a moment of encounter: the text meets the reader, and the reader in turn decides (or as Husserl puts it, "reduces") the text's essence. In a way the text is absolved of its textuality; it becomes absorbed by (and by default possessed by) the reader, which in turn gives rise to Fish's lemma: "The reader's response is not *to* the meaning; it *is* the meaning" (*Is There a Text in This Class?* 3). It is arguable that the realities of production and "reading" entail a more composite structure of interaction where production entails reading and reading entails production. However, such an argument is outside the scope of the present essay. The point traditional phenomenology offers us is one of contrast: it reminds us that the phenomenology of perception is paralleled by the phenomenology of text production (in a literal sense), even if reading reduces the production model to a single text.

In all of the quotations I have just cited—Ricoeur's, Searle's, and McGann's—the word *event* is pivotal. But just what is an event? This is a crucial term, and it is difficult too. Are events objects? Clearly they are not, although they can be described as objectlike, or paraobjects. We tend to objectify events (such as Christmas, the Fourth of July, or Shakespeare's birthday) giving them the religious or cultural status of objects; yet they are not physical entities. At this point we again realize that a definition of a text as an object is not going to do in the long run, however well it has served us in the past. Considered empirically, events do not consist of matter, nor are they in a conventional sense entities. Since an object suggests a kind of "retainable" entity, an event is more of what the linguist George Lakoff describes as a "conceptual" entity (542). A conceptual entity is not, as it seems to imply, an oxymoron: the space it displaces is a *mental* space, and texts—all texts, whether spoken or written—occupy such space. Although this mental space is central to critical ideology, whether that ideology belongs to Derrida or Fish, it does not normally concern textual critics and bibliographers. But perhaps it should, if only in a subconscious manner. A physical text, say, the holograph of Keats's "Nightingale" ode, occupies, simultaneously, different dimensions of space: literal space, mental space, and (as we discussed earlier) historical space—and none of these locations is entirely discrete. This helps us understand how the concept of an oral text (like oral literature) fits into this paradigm; and even if the acoustic signal of the speech act is not literally an entity (how many dimensions do displaced molecules occupy?) this does not matter. What does matter is that Homer reciting the *Iliad* or Johnny Rotten ranting at Wembley are both creating and producing texts that are also events—not objects. Because events are temporarily discrete, they are finite in a useful way. Yet because events take place in space, they are in another sense infinite, since, for example, we can never know the full setting in which Homer and Rotten might have been performing, even if we ourselves are (or were) a member of the audience. The beauty of such texts is that their literal space and their historical space are largely concomitant by being an extension of the present; and as we witness them, we become a part of this extension, a part of the text itself. If such texts have a problem (some might call it an advantage) it is that they cannot be replicated; there is no "going back" to an event that, gone once, is gone forever. Since textual studies is by its nature a retrospective activity, this partly explains why oral texts and oral recordings do not find their way into editions. Occasionally they squeak into bibliographies, particularly when the recordings themselves are canonized (as in the case of Dylan Thomas). But these cases are rather exceptional. Exceptional too are critical discussions of oral textual events, perhaps because—as the artist Julian Schnabel once uttered in a rare insight—it is difficult to examine and talk about a text one cannot go back to for a second look.

Events, however, can be recorded, if only to a degree, using any of the various technologies available. Recordings are necessarily imperfect; they cannot record the speech act. Yet if the process is flawed, it is flawed only as much as *all* processes of textual transmission are inherently flawed. What is important, I think, is the denominator that links together recordings with books and manuscripts: they are objects. I would like to suggest that these objects can be more properly and usefully described as *outcomes* of events. If speech is an event, the recording of it is an outcome. If writing is an event, the recording of it (i.e., the MS, the TS, the floppy disc) is an outcome. While some events have outcomes by their very nature (writing for example), others may have deliberate outcomes (a performance that is recorded), while others do not specifically have outcomes (an unrecorded performance). The text-as-an-outcome is not necessarily better than the text-as-an-event; they are different, both physically and ontologically, and furnish their own kinds of critical playgrounds. The outcome is particularly unusual (and from the hermeneutic point of view, desirable) because it tends to recall the event that produced it, whether that event is historical (McGann), sociological (Bakhtin), or "compositional" (as in Gabler's edition of *Ulysses*). Such theories constitute a nostalgia for the moment of inscription: they want to go back. Whether we can actually arrive at that point of recall, or trace it through what Barthes calls "the myth of filiation" (77) is a big question. Here, however, we move outside the critical text into critical theory—at which point the disinterested textual critic can go no further.

No further, precisely because textual theory that pretends to be critical theory betrays itself. It is an ironic way to size up the situation: is there such a thing as a disinterested critic? The notion of textuality is recessive against a foreground of critical theory: Jerome McGann stands out not as a textual theorist but as a political historicist; Hershel Parker not as a textual theorist but as a hermeneut. They may claim they are textual theorists, but only inasmuch as their textual theory serves their critical program—and it is, consequently, their critical programs that assert an institutionally political shadow over their textual work. Earlier I suggested that Bakhtin marred the persuasiveness of his argument of the text-as-an-utterance by saying that the *entire* significance of a text lay in the "dialogic relations" with its individual history. This strikes me as being unnecessarily coercive. Along nearly identical lines McGann has written in *The Beauty of Inflections:* "If we are to understand how poems mean—if we are going to gain knowledge of literary productions—we must pay attention to a variety of concrete historical particulars, and not merely to 'the poem itself' or its linguistic determination" (96). Textual studies helps one do just that: it helps reveal the complex compositional and production aspects of literature, and how these aspects are part of larger historical, political, and economic structures. But textual studies cannot necessarily tell us how language works per se, in which case McGann's light treatment of the "linguistic determination" of a poem seems to overlook abstract semantic issues as much as it is generous to concrete historical issues. If, as McGann says, we are to understand *how* poems mean, then perhaps we first need to understand how language itself means—and this is precisely where Derrida has chosen to locate himself. Linguistic determination wouldn't be such a difficult thing were we not so overwhelmed by linguistic indetermination. We can hardly be expected to make sense out of a poem if we can't make sense out of the most basic relationship between a signifier and its signified—a questionable relationship that gave Derrida the basis for grammatology, the gram as *différance* replacing the sign. It seems to me that whatever assumptions we make about texts and textual histories, our assumptions are guided by the kinds of "literary" (or even linguistic) questions we are asking. Literature after all is an art; its medium is language; language is both cognitive and social; and there is, simply, no way any one critical theory is going to tell us how all these things coalesce. Like literature itself, criticism thrives on a kind of discursiveness engendered by alterity, and explorations like McGann's, Bakhtin's, and Derrida's—explorations that have something new to say—constitute the critical discourse of the perpetual present. Literature is not a study of truths, not a study of falsities, but a study of disguises. If it were a study of truths and such like operations, we would imply that literature is also a study of closure; and this, clearly, is not the case.

We should also remember that the noniterability of texts means that textual displacement is a temporal (and hence spatial) issue: it presents the literary critic (confronted with numerous authorial and nonauthorial versions of a single work) or the art critic (with numerous re-presentations of a single work) or the performance critic (with numerous instances of a work's performance texts) with an overwhelming sense of the burden of textual history. This is daunting, and at the same time it is good: as our awareness of the numbers (and kinds) of textual states and modalities increases, so too do our interpretative possibilities. There is in fact something fundamental to how textual literacy—an awareness of the textual histories of the poems, plays, and novels we are discussing—informs literary criticism, perhaps because it makes real the endless diversity of historical spaces in which literature occurs, just as it makes real the different modalities in which language occurs. Yet these possibilities can only be the product of our own initiative. Texts do not come to us; we must go to them. The differences which texts reveal amongst themselves, and which distinguish themselves from each other, are the product of an uncentered alterity: there is no "correct" text, no "final" text, no "original" text, but only texts that are different, drifting in their like differences. By exploring, but not stratifying, these differences, we begin to understand how textual dynamics can be broken down into a phenomenology of text production, and such recognition is, I think, the beginning of a philosophy of textuality.

Notes

1. In contrast to the textual-critical tradition, the deconstructionist use of the term *text,* rather than closing itself on a material state of language, opens itself up to the intertextual, even metatextual, loci of language. See Roland Barthes in *Image-Music-Text:* "The text is not a line of words releasing a single 'theological' meaning (the 'message' of an Author-God), but a multi-dimensional space in which a variety of writings, none of them original, blend and clash" (9).

2. For Shillingsburg a text is more particularly an immaterial representation of words and punctuation inasmuch as that order has some kind of physical representation.

3. Shillingsburg discusses four different conceptions, or "orientations," of completion: the historical ("the work of art is finished when it becomes a material artifact"); the sociological (a work is finished when it is ready to be distributed); the aesthetic (a work of art is never really complete); and the authorial (a work is finished when the author says so) (75–78). Although there are some holes in these orientations (particularly where they overlap), Shillingsburg's distinctions are very useful outlines.

4. See also Goodman's *Of Mind and Other Matters,* 139.

5. For an illuminating reply to Goodman on this topic, see Barbara Herrnstein Smith's *On the Margins of Discourse*, 3–13.

6. A similar, but more finely honed point of view is shared by Shillingsburg (46–7).

7. I leave aside for now the theoretical implications of sound poetry, as well as some *Zaum* and L=A=N=G=U=A=G=E poetry (which for the most part is intranscribable, but recordable), and some concrete poems (which are not speakable, or in some cases transcribable, but are reproducable by other means). As an oral language, the implications offered by sign language poetry would fall under the rubric posited for sound poetry, i.e., intranscribable, but recordable.

8. Derrida, "Form and Meaning: A Note on the Phenomenology of Language," in *Margins of Philosophy* 160–61; see also *Positions* 26–7.

Works Cited

Bakhtin, Mikhail M. *Speech Genres and Other Late Essays*. Trans. Vern W. McGee. Ed. Caryl Emerson and Michael Holquist. Austin: U of Texas P, 1986.

Barthes, Roland. *Image-Music-Text*. 1977. Trans. Stephen Heath. New York: Hill & Wang, 1977.

Borges, Jorge Luis, "Pierre Menard, Author of the *Quixote*." In *Labyrinths*. Ed. Donald A. Yates and James E. Erby. New York: New Directions, 1964. 36–44.

Danto, Arthur. *The Transfiguration of the Commonplace*. Cambridge: Harvard UP, 1981.

Derrida, Jacques. "Signature Event Context." 1976. In *Margins of Philosophy*. Trans. Alan Bass. Chicago: U of Chicago P, 1982. 309–30.

———. *Positions*. Trans. Alan Bass. Chicago: U of Chicago P, 1981.

Fish, Stanley. *Is There A Text in This Class?* Cambridge: Harvard UP, 1980.

Foucault, Michel. *The Archaeology of Knowledge*. 1969. Trans. A. M. Sheridan Smith. New York: Pantheon, 1972.

Frazier, Ian. "A Reporter at Large: Great Plains III." *The New Yorker*, March 6, 1989, 41–68.

Goodman, Nelson. *Of Mind and Other Matters*. Cambridge: Harvard UP, 1984.

———. *Languages of Art*. 2d ed. Indianapolis: Hackett, 1976.

Lakoff, George. *Women, Fire, and Dangerous Things: What Categories Reveal about the Mind*. Chicago: U of Chicago P, 1987.

Mailloux, Stephen. *Interpretive Conventions: The Reader in the Study of American Fiction*. Ithaca: Cornell UP, 1982.

McGann, Jerome. "*Ulysses* as a Postmodern Text: The Gabler Edition." *Criticism* 27 (1985): 283–306.

———. *The Beauty of Inflections*. Oxford: Clarendon, 1985.

———. *A Critique of Modern Textual Criticism*. Chicago: U of Chicago P, 1983.

Mukařovský, Jan. "Art as a Semiotic Fact." 1936. *Semiotics of Art: Prague School*

Contributions. Ed. Ladislav Matejka and Irwin R. Titunik. Cambridge: MIT P, 1976. 3–9.

Parker, Hershel. *Flawed Texts and Verbal Icons: Literary Authority in American Fiction*. Evanston: Northwestern UP, 1984.

Peirce, Charles Sanders. *Collected Papers of Charles Sanders Peirce*. Ed. Charles Hartshorne and Paul Weiss. 1931. 6 vols. Rpt. Cambridge: Harvard UP, Belknap, 1960.

Poetry in Motion. Film. Dir. Ron Mann. 1985.

Ricoeur, Paul. "The Model of the Text: Meaningful Action Considered as Text." *New Literary History* 6 (1974): 95–110.

Rothenberg, Jerome. *Pre-Faces and Other Writings*. New York: New Directions, 1981.

Scholes, Robert. "Deconstruction and Communication." *Critical Inquiry* 14 (1988): 278–95.

Shillingsburg, Peter L. *Scholarly Editing in the Computer Age: Theory and Practice*. Athens: U of Georgia P, 1986.

Smith, Barbara Herrnstein. *On the Margins of Discourse: The Relation of Literature to Language*. Chicago: U of Chicago P, 1978.

Steiner, Wendy. *The Colors of Rhetoric*. Chicago: U of Chicago P, 1982.

Sutherland, John. "Publishing History: A Hole at the Centre of Literary Sociology." *Critical Inquiry* 14 (1988): 574–89.

Taylor, Mark C. *Altarity*. Chicago: U of Chicago P, 1987.

Thorpe, James. *Principles of Textual Criticism*. San Marino: The Huntington Library, 1972.

Williams, William Proctor, and Craig S. Abbott. *An Introduction to Bibliographical and Textual Studies*. 2d ed. New York: Modern Language Association, 1989.

II

Making Texts New: A Response to Gabler, McLaverty, and Grigely

WILLIAM E. CAIN

HE ESSAYS BY HANS WALTER GABLER, James McLaverty, and Joseph Grigely all reflect the new spirit of openness and interdisciplinary debate that has enlivened textual studies and bibliography. Gabler admirably, if somewhat polemically, contrasts developments in German and Anglo-American scholarship, taking note in particular of the impact of literary theory on German approaches; in his "intentionalist response" to textual instability, McLaverty employs insights that he gleans from Nelson Goodman and the speech-act theorist John Searle; and Grigely, in his account of a "philosophy of textuality," draws upon a range of sources that includes Goodman as well as Jacques Derrida and Arthur Danto. As these essays testify, the conversations in textual studies have become wider and richer, more attentive to ideas—even radical ideas—about the nature of language and textuality that were formerly neglected or scorned.

Literary critics and textual scholars have usually remained fairly distant from one another. The scholars have prepared the texts, and the critics have proceeded to teach and write analytical essays about these texts. Both parties have accepted, though not always happily, a division of labor, and have not intruded upon one another's activity.

The reasons for this state of affairs are complicated. When the New Criticism emerged as the dominant force in literary criticism in the 1940s and 1950s, it undercut the authority of philological, historical, and textual scholarship. Slowly but steadily, the nature of graduate training changed, with work in bibliography coming to occupy only a small part of the student's progress toward his or her doctoral degree. As Hershel Parker has demonstrated, the reign of the New Criticism enabled critics to speak very sensitively about "meaning" in texts even as it encouraged them not to care about or query the status of the text that they so subtly interpreted. This trend away from knowledge about and interest in textual and biblio-graphical matters accelerated during the late 1960s and 1970s when struc-turalism, deconstruction, feminist theory, and reader-response criticism moved to the fore. The capacious field of literary theory prompted many critics to challenge (and some to defend) the New Criticism, and it also turned critics and their students in the graduate schools toward a host of dense, demanding texts in philosophy, anthropology, and other disci-plines. Texts were interpreted from many different vantage points, and the work that resulted was often stimulating, but critics persisted in being, for all their deep theorizing, revealingly unsuspicious about the authority of the copy of "the text" that they held in their hands. They took it for granted.

The critics may have simply been careless and irresponsible, as textual scholars sometimes have charged. But in large measure their behavior followed from the understanding of professionalism that the New Criti-cism had introduced. Allen Tate, John Crowe Ransom, Robert Penn Warren, and Cleanth Brooks sought to legitimate criticism as a discipline in the academy and make it "professionally" respectable. They judged that the only valid way to achieve this goal was to focus attention on the text itself, and to cultivate precise discussion about it. In their view, philology and related forms of textual/historical scholarship were valuable, but specialized, endeavors. These were not equivalent to literary criticism, and hence could not furnish critics and teachers in departments of literature with a rationale for their enterprise. It was not that textual scholars were unprofessional as much as that they were *too* professional—too narrowly keyed to technical and scientific-sounding languages that were ill-suited to a group of men and women intent upon retaining humanistic values while managing at long last to acquire credibility as professionals with a product to sell. (Ransom titled his essay about the professionalization of literary studies "Criticism, Inc.") The New Critics and their followers perceived themselves as professionals—men and women who practiced and taught rigorous interpretative techniques—but not as specialists tied to private, ungainly discourse about variants and accidentals.

The scholars retreated, unable to show the bearing of their labor upon criticism and interpretation. Perhaps their key failure was not articulating the manner in which "editing" might be a cogent topic for undergraduate teaching. The New Criticism triumphed, after all, because it was closely connected to the day-to-day problems of the classroom teacher and his or her students; indeed, Brooks and Warren's tremendously influential 1939 book, *Understanding Poetry,* first took shape as a mimeographed booklet that the authors put together to aid their students at Louisiana State University. The scholars need not have made students into fledgling editors, but they could have presented a case for the literary and historical gains that result when textual and bibliographical studies enter into the business of the classroom. Perhaps the New Critics should have been quick to seize upon editorial problems and choices in their teaching of texts, showing students the excitingly complex (and often fiercely debated) "object" that is the play by Shakespeare or lyric by John Donne. But the scholars were as much, and maybe more, to blame, because they were unwilling to describe for critics how the work of editing might affect classroom teaching in productive ways.

The essays by Gabler, McLaverty, and Grigely do not take up the relationship between textual studies and pedagogy, and this marks a limitation in the field in general that still needs to be addressed. But they do at least, as noted earlier, grapple with important arguments about meaning and intention that contemporary theorists and philosophers have advanced, and in this respect indicate a boundary-breaking attitude that eventually could prompt textual scholars to ponder the kinds of innovations they might bring to teaching. But while Gabler, McLaverty, and Grigely have supplied informative contributions to this volume, they share an overconfidence about their ability to control editing and text-making through theory. To be sure, theory is essential; scholars need to explain and justify, as best they can, the grounds for their activity in presenting a text for readers and assembling an apparatus for fellow scholars. But theory is also doomed to failure: no theory will ever succeed in taking the measure of the elusive, dynamic textuality of texts, nor will any single theory, however comprehensive, lead to the end of further theorizing about and making of new texts.

Along these lines, possibly the most conspicuous phrase in the three essays I have read appears in Gabler's summary of Hans Zeller's position. When Gabler refers approvingly to "controlled objectivity," he reveals an inevitable, if ultimately indefensible, strategy of containment that textual scholars have always invoked to describe their labor. Gabler's essay is quite radical in what it concedes about the multimeaningfulness of texts. But it is not theoretical—or maybe one should say, not historical—enough, in that it fails to acknowledge the central, abiding lesson of textual scholarship: the job will always have to be done again. No text or theory about text-making will ever be able to stand free from rival versions of that text and theories propounded about it. "Control" is something scholars aim for but can never acquire.

In this respect, the essays by Gabler, McLaverty, and Grigely (though he less than the others) are also revealing for their embrace of radical positions about language that would seem to undercut the editorial/textual programs they aim to promote. In his account of Zeller's work, Gabler states that "Zeller penetrates to a systematic evaluation and coordination of the premises and practices of textual criticism and editing." But this stress on system and, earlier, on objectivity sits awkwardly, in my view, with the claims about language that Gabler identifies in the articles he summarizes by Gunter Martens and Henning Boetius. These scholars, says Gabler, foreground the multilayeredness of literary language, the nature of reading as an act of interpretation, and, more radically still, the fact that writing, too, is an interpretive act. Gabler seems to assume that systematization, like "controlled objectivity," will open up an awareness of language's self-reflexive properties, but these properties of language *come first* and hence are always cutting against and mocking efforts at objectivity and control.

Something similar happens in McLaverty's essay. Following Derrida, McLaverty notes at the outset that "authors produce different versions of their works, and even when they don't, any attempt to repeat a text is likely to produce variation and will certainly project the text into a new context, inducing different reader responses." "The attempt," he continues, "to get at an authorial version would, according to one version of the doctrine, be not only vain but wrong-headed: any text is so thoroughly shaped by the demands of the readership, the publisher, and the market in general that any attempt to purge it of the resulting characteristics would be a mistake. At its extreme this approach obliterates iterability in favor of alteration; poems become events, and each reading is a new event." These are powerful arguments, McLaverty admits, and he proceeds to "sidestep them here." One is inclined to say that he *has* to sidestep them, because if he faced them directly he would be obliged to postpone or recast his desire to discriminate between degrees of importance among meaning. He can only pursue this project if he does not quite absorb the troublesome arguments that Derrida and his kin have circulated about the ceaseless alteration of texts that transpires whenever they are read. For Derrida, the act of assigning importance to meanings is interminable, because no text is stable enough for us to name one meaning as more important than another. If we want to do this, we need to remember that it can only be done in quotation marks, ironically. Meaning is relational, and so any "important" meaning will be important only alongside other meanings that call its priority into serious question. Texts are self-reflexive, but they are not closed. They are always open to more interpretations, and to unending debates about the relative importance of the meanings that they generate.

Grigely's essay is enlightening in that he criticizes the "closure" that editors and textual scholars have typically favored. "Textual critics," Grigely suggests, "might perhaps be taking their conception of textuality for granted." "A play by Shakespeare (or by anyone else)," he goes on to explain, "cannot claim final authority because it cannot claim to be finished at any point: just as there is no consensus in editorial theory as to what constitutes the 'final intentions' of a work, there is no consensus (as far as I know) in philosophical theory as to what constitutes a 'finished' work of literature.'" Grigely advances a key insight here, though he then diminishes its impact by averring, in line with Jerome McGann, that while "there are no final or finished works," there are "final or finished texts." This distinction serves Grigely only momentarily, however, for by the end of his essay, he concludes that "there is no 'correct' text, no 'final' text, no 'original' text, but only texts that are different, drifting in their like differences."

All texts are interim reports, and all authoritative editions will one day be replaced. Consider the imposing new editions of Stephen Crane, Shakespeare, William James, James Joyce, John Donne, and so many other authors that have appeared during the past two decades. No sooner does a text materialize than scholars, and sometimes critics, declare their dissatisfaction with it; they either prefer the earlier editions, or else insist that the new one is so flawed and improves so little upon its predecessor that the editorial task will have to be done from scratch. It is perfectly appropriate to devise a principle of controlled objectivity, as Gabler does, as it is also eminently sensible to construct, with Grigely, an "interdisciplinary format" for textual studies, or sketch, following McLaverty, a reasonable "guide to editorial policy." But these schemes can at best offer only some rough tips and pointers for textual and editorial practice. No theory, set of guidelines, or new foundation can check the partiality and incompleteness of all acts of text-making.

It is surprising that this fact has not been more widely acknowledged. Of course many scholars do recognize that editorial work is extremely controversial and that no edition is likely to please all who examine it. But they have not sought fully to incorporate the temporality of texts into their scrutiny of their craft. A number of scholars, Gabler included, have observed that different versions of "the same text" can legitimately coexist. But this is not the same as saying that no version will ever remain unscathed, immune from the inevitable assault on its sufficiency and integrity. Texts are always in process, always being made, and possess no more stability or finality than the interpretations that critics furnish for them. In his essay, McLaverty contends that the "problems surrounding 'textual instability'" can be discussed in "quite ordinary ways," and, in part, he is correct. But the capacity to express these problems in ordinary language does not mean that ordinary language resolves them: it just states them clearly.

"Different versions," then, is misleading, though it does seem an attractive path out of the flux of textuality. This phrase implies that while the versions are different, each one of them is discrete, as though it could be isolated (seen in freeze-frame) and inspected before the scholar moves to the next one. But that version, too, is subject to time, and hence subject to change. And it is unclear whether it can be detached from the other versions of itself and of "the same text" that saturate it. Scholars will go on producing texts, and laying out versions of texts, and will continue, like the essayists here, to build theoretical foundations for their work, a theory that will defend what they have undertaken to provide. But no theory will ever be able to control or limit the unending productivity of textual practices, and the only true theory may therefore be the one that admits the falsification that textual scholars produce.

Of the three essayists, I feel closest to Grigely, in that he stresses, as I have done, that "*a* text is of *a* time," interrogates scholarly dependence on notions of "textual security," and urges that we abandon our attachment to the "correct," "final," and "original text." But again it is striking that his argument falters and seeks distance from its radical implications at the conclusion, where Grigely seeks somehow to envelop his insights in a "philosophy of textuality." This is not so much a theory as it is a name for a practice. It describes a kind of work that some textual scholars might deem that they perform, but it does not make that work more theoretically controlled. "Theory" is the form taken by the self-defending explanations that critics and scholars hope will corral the insights about language that they glimpse in the midst of their activity. It enables them to believe that they have directed and limited the nonstop process of textual refashioning. Theory cannot do so, however much all of us who work with texts would prefer to think otherwise.

But perhaps theory is something more. It may additionally be the form that editors employ to deny or avoid confronting the fact that editorial work is a sheer contest of wills between author and editor. The blunt truth of the matter is that editors are always tempted, and frequently succumb to the temptation, to smooth out what they deem to be the author's mistakes. The editorial and textual theory proves little more than a device to mask the act of self-assertion that the editor undertakes when he or she presumes to know better than the author what this author intended or really meant. Editorial practice is thus a difficult pursuit both because of its commerce with language, which is so eager to break any boundaries assigned to it, and because it involves very audacious moral and ethical maneuvers that are hard to justify.

Take, for example, Robert Frost's poem "Stopping by Woods on a Snowy Evening." The first line of the final stanza, as Frost wrote it, is: "The woods are lovely, dark and deep." When Edward Connery Lathem edited *The Poetry of Robert Frost,* he changed the punctuation of the line so that it reads: "The woods are lovely, dark, and deep." This alteration, one of hundreds that Lathem made, is unwarranted and modifies (and simplifies) the meaning. Frost suggests that the woods are lovely because they are dark and deep, whereas Lathem's rendering crudely arranges the terms into a list, with the woods having lovely, dark, and deep as attributes. Lathem's procedures here testifies to the editor's *impulse to reject.* He or she cannot bear the text as it stands; the human labor that the author did ought to have been done better. And so the editor intervenes—often in the guise of an honorable, theoretically based desire for "regularization"—and willfully skews the text.

From this angle, editorial practice seems uncomfortably close to the

Miltonic/Emersonian vision of "reading" that Harold Bloom has described. Editors are readers engaged in combative relationship with authors, and the strongest editors might thus be those who survive the forceful presence of authors, and who become authors in their own right. We are likely inclined to rebuke Lathem for his self-serving corrections of Frost, but another, more Bloomian way to interpret his act would be to regard it as his effort to stand up to Frost's authority. The changes that Lathem makes are outrageous and indefensible, yet intriguing or precisely their lack of textual (or ethical) grounds. He had no right to do what he did but he did it anyway.

Conceivably one could argue that Lathem has actually done Frost a service: changing the punctuation *away* from what Frost wrote enables readers to understand more readily and richly why Frost wanted it his own way. Lathem provides the evidence of his wrongful deed, listing the variants for his text in the back of his edition. Before he changed the text, readers might not have noticed the purposeful punctuation of the line that Frost wrote, but now, thanks to Lathem, they do. Lathem's willful conduct is, in a sense, rather admirable and even self-sacrificing: he imposes himself on the text, and apparently mars and distorts it, yet in doing so he illuminates meaning in the text. He enables readers to see "Stopping by Woods on a Snowy Evening" anew by a Bloomian swerve away from the text that Frost wrote. Lathem's edition is maddening but extremely valuable, and perverse as this may sound, it may be more useful than the edition which Frost authorized and with which Lathem tampered. It is an instructive "critical edition" of Frost's poetry, for its hundreds of changes continually point to features in the verse that Frost shrewdly designed but that, without Lathem, might not have been visible or audible.

This is not really a new insight on my part, but once again it is one that receives less attention than it merits. When William Empson, in *Some Versions of Pastoral*, used eighteenth-century editions of Milton to interpret *Paradise Lost*, he showed a savvy recognition of the immense utility of badly edited texts. The same holds true for Helen Vendler's resourceful analysis of editorial revisions in George Herbert's poems, and for Stephen Booth's curiosity about editorial interferences in Shakespeare's sonnets. Often it is not possible to see what is in the text until a disruptive editor comes along to dramatize it—dramatize it by correcting it for a new, regularized, rationalized edition. The absolute unreasonableness that we observe in such changes often allows the text to seem all the more reasonable, complex, coherent, wonderful. Bad editors can make authors look very good. Every author should be blessed with one.

We can indeed teach, talk, and write about different texts, contrasting, for instance, Lathem's edition of a poem with the poem as Frost wrote it, but must realize as we do so that these texts cannot be easily separated from one another. They merge, shadow, and compete with one another, and each apparently distinct text has lots of texts behind and underneath it. On one level, we can compare Lathem's and Frost's texts with clarity and point, but on another level, we cannot, since the "text as Frost wrote it" itself carries so many problems and unanswerable questions. When Henry James revised his novels and stories for the New York edition of his works, he insisted that he was not rewriting the texts that he wrote but, rather, was rereading them—and was, therefore, bringing to light words that his texts already contained, or at least should have contained. Who can say for certain what Frost's full intentions were when he wrote "Stopping By Woods on a Snowy Evening?" No one *can* say, and the question itself may be misleading, in that it implies that we could spotlight when Frost's intentions were clear and unmistakable, as though these were outside the movement of time and change. Who knows how much or how little was in the text that Frost wrote? There could have been as much in it when he wrote it, or when he reread it, as James discovered when he reread his texts and proceeded to make explicit the words he found there.

Gabler, McLaverty, and Grigely demonstrate well the benefits to editorial study and textual scholarship that result from close attention to recent literary and philosophical theories. All three essayists recognize the flaws in the kinds of textual criticism undertaken in the past, and all aim adroitly to move beyond them. But the more that they and like-minded others delve into these theories, the more that they will radically unsettle their own programs and practices. They will be steadily building barriers against the implications of their fresh (and disturbing) insights into language, looking to preserve forms of control that their perceptions of language's destabilizing power will inevitably undermine.

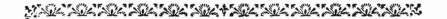

Contributors

WILLIAM E. CAIN is a Professor of English at Wellesley College. He is the author of *The Crisis in Criticism: Theory, Literature, and Reform in English Studies* (1984) and *F. O. Matthiessen and the Politics of Criticism* (1988). He is now at work on a study of W. E. B. Du Bois.

PHILIP COHEN is an Assistant Professor of English at the University of Texas at Arlington. His articles on American literature have appeared in *American Literature, The Faulkner Journal, Mississippi Quarterly, Southern Literary Journal, Studies in American Fiction,* and other journals. He is currently working on a study of the composition, revision, publication, and reception of Faulkner's *Sanctuary.*

PAUL EGGERT is a Senior Lecturer in the English Department, University College ADFA, Canberra. He edited *The Boy in the Bush* (1990) as part of Cambridge University Press's D. H. Lawrence Works series and *Editing in Australia* (1990), the proceedings volume of a conference he convened in 1989.

HANS WALTER GABLER is a Professor of English at Munich University. He has edited *Ulysses: A Critical and Synoptic Edition* (1984) and John Fletcher's *Monsieur Thomas* (1979), *Women Pleased* (1982), and *Wit without Money* (1985). His work on bibliographical and editorial matters has appeared in *Studies in Bibliography* and *Text.*

D.C. GREETHAM is a Professor of English at the City University of New York Graduate Center. He is the Executive Director of the Society for Textual Scholarship, and his essays on textual theory have appeared in *Studies in Bibliography, Modern Philology,* and *Papers of the Bibliographical Society of America.* He is the author of *An Introduction to Textual Scholarship* (forthcoming) and is currently editing an MLA book on scholarly editing from biblical and classical literature to modern times and writing a book on the interrelations of literary and textual theory.

JOSEPH GRIGELY is an Assistant Professor of English at Gallaudet University. He has taught at Stanford University, where he was a Mellon Postdoctoral Fellow. His essays have appeared in *The Keats-Shelley Journal* and *The Keats-Shelley Memorial Bulletin,* and he is currently writing a book on textuality.

T. H. HOWARD-HILL is E. Wallace Martin Professor of English Literature and Chair of the Department of English, University of South Carolina. He has compiled the *Oxford Shakespeare Concordance* (1969–73) and *The Index to British Literary Bibliography* (1969–). More recently, he has published on the text of *King Lear,* Fletcher and Massinger's *Barnavelt,* and Middleton's *A Game of Chess* of which he has completed editions for the Malone Society and Revels Plays. He has also published papers on the theory of editing drama and is now engaged on a book on *The Editorial Tradition of Early English Drama.*

DAVID H. JACKSON is a senior consultant with Alexander & Alexander Consulting Group. Formerly he was an Associate Professor of English at Centenary College. His publications on textual scholarship have appeared in *American Literature, Studies in Bibliography,* and *Review.* He is at work on an edition of Robert Louis Stevenson's novella *The Ebb-Tide.*

STEVEN MAILLOUX is a Professor of English at Syracuse University. He is the author of *Interpretive Conventions: The Reader in the Study of American Fiction* (1982) and *Rhetorical Power* (1989) and coeditor with Sanford Levinson of *Interpreting Law and Literature: A Hermeneutic Reader* (1988). His articles have appeared in *Critical Inquiry, Genre, Studies in the Novel,* and *New Literary History.*

JEROME J. MCGANN is Commonwealth Professor of English at the University of Virginia. The last two volumes of his Oxford University Press edition of *Byron: The Complete Poetical Works*, vols. 6 and 7, will appear in 1990.

JAMES MCLAVERTY is a Lecturer in English at the University of Keele. His articles on the bibliography of Pope and on textual criticism have appeared in such journals as *Modern Philology, Review, The Library*, and *Studies in Bibliography*. He has recently revised and edited David Foxon's lectures on *Pope and the Early Eighteenth-Century Book Trade*.

PETER SHILLINGSBURG is a Professor of English at Mississippi State University and the general editor of the William Makepeace Thackeray Edition being published by Garland. He is a former chairman of the Committee on Scholarly Editions and author of *Scholarly Editing in the Computer Age* (1986) and articles on editorial theory and practice in *Studies in Bibliography, Analytical and Enumerative Bibliography*, and *Papers of the Bibliographical Society of America*.

Index

Analytical bibliography: and psychoanalysis, 89

Apparatus: in Cambridge UP Lawrence, 73–74; of Gabler's *Ulysses*, 113–14; in German editorial theory, 159–61, 161–62

Authorial intention, x–xi, 96, 105; and New Criticism, x; and New Historicism, 66–67; and Anglo-American editing, 79; and literary ontology, 104–6; structuralist critique of, 107; reader-response critique of, 107–8; Zeller and Gabler on, 116; Shillingsburg on, 116–17; and German editorial theory, 156–57, 162–63; Parker on, 157–58

Bakhtin, Mikhail M., 180–82

Barthes, Roland: "The Death of the Author," 107

Beissner, Friedrich: Hölderlin edition, 156

Binder, Henry: and *The Red Badge of Courage*, xii–xiii, xvii n. 2

Boetius, Henning, 160

Bowers, Fredson, 3, 54, 168, 169; and eclectic editing, xi; "Textual Criticism," 104–5; on authorial intention and literary ontology, 105; "The Editor and the Question of

Value," 105; on final authorial intention, 120 n. 3

Byron, George Gordon, 6th Baron: McGann's edition of, 111–12, 120 n. 6

Center for Editions of American Authors, xi, 26, 61–62, 73

Center for Scholarly Editions, xi, 26

Červenka, Miroslav: "Textologie und Semiotik," 156

Committee for Scholarly Editions, 42 n. 3, 106

Crane, Stephen: publication history of *The Red Badge of Courage*, xii

Crane, Elaine Forman, 80

Critique génétique, 121 n. 7, 158, 164 n. 2

Culler, Jonathan: *Structuralist Poetics*, 107

Danto, Arthur: *The Transfiguration of the Commonplace*, 179–80

Dearing, Vinton, 84

Derrida, Jacques: and authorial intention, x–xi, 107–8; and editing, 85–86; "Signature Event Context," 107–8, 134, 171–73, 174; "Limited Inc. abc," 134–35; and language, 181–82